Herman Beavers

Geography and the Political Imaginary in the Novels of Toni Morrison

palgrave
macmillan

Herman Beavers
Department of English
University of Pennsylvania
Philadelphia, PA, USA

Geocriticism and Spatial Literary Studies
ISBN 978-3-319-88148-5 ISBN 978-3-319-65999-2 (eBook)
https://doi.org/10.1007/978-3-319-65999-2

Printed on acid-free paper

This Palgrave Macmillan imprint is published by Springer Nature
The registered company is Springer International Publishing AG
The registered company address is: Gewerbestrasse 11, 6330 Cham, Switzerland

Geocriticism and Spatial Literary Studies

Series Editor
Robert T. Tally Jr.
Texas State University
San Marcos
TX, USA

Geocriticism and Spatial Literary Studies is a new book series focusing on the dynamic relations among space, place, and literature. The spatial turn in the humanities and social sciences has occasioned an explosion of innovative, multidisciplinary scholarship in recent years, and geocriticism, broadly conceived, has been among the more promising developments in spatially oriented literary studies. Whether focused on literary geography, cartography, geopoetics, or the spatial humanities more generally, geocritical approaches enable readers to reflect upon the representation of space and place, both in imaginary universes and in those zones where fiction meets reality. Titles in the series include both monographs and collections of essays devoted to literary criticism, theory, and history, often in association with other arts and sciences. Drawing on diverse critical and theoretical traditions, books in the Geocriticism and Spatial Literary Studies series disclose, analyze, and explore the significance of space, place, and mapping in literature and in the world.

More information about this series at
http://www.palgrave.com/gp/series/15002

For Lisa, Michael, and Corinne
My sky, my moon, and my stars

For Rudolph and James
Double-conscious brothers in the Veil

Series Editor's Preface

The spatial turn in the humanities and social sciences has occasioned an explosion of innovative, multidisciplinary scholarship. Spatially oriented literary studies, whether operating under the banner of literary geography, literary cartography, geophilosophy, geopoetics, geocriticism, or the spatial humanities more generally, have helped to reframe or to transform contemporary criticism by focusing attention, in various ways, on the dynamic relations among space, place, and literature. Reflecting upon the representation of space and place, whether in the real world, in imaginary universes, or in those hybrid zones where fiction meets reality, scholars, and critics working in spatial literary studies are helping to reorient literary criticism, history, and theory. *Geocriticism and Spatial Literary Studies* is a book series presenting new research in this burgeoning field of inquiry.

In exploring such matters as the representation of place in literary works, the relations between literature and geography, the historical transformation of literary and cartographic practices, and the role of space in critical theory, among many others, geocriticism and spatial literary studies have also developed interdisciplinary or transdisciplinary methods and practices, frequently making productive connections to architecture, art history, geography, history, philosophy, politics, social theory, and urban studies, to name but a few. Spatial criticism is not limited to the spaces of the so-called real world, and it sometimes calls into question any too facile distinction between real and imaginary places, as it frequently investigates what Edward Soja has referred to as the "real-and-imagined" places we experience in literature as in life. Indeed, although a great deal of important research has been devoted to the literary representation of certain identifiable and well-known places (e.g., Dickens's London, Baudelaire's Paris, or Joyce's Dublin), spatial critics have also explored the otherworldly spaces of literature, such as those to be found in myth, fantasy, science fiction, video games, and cyberspace. Similarly, such criticism is interested in the relationship between spatiality and such different media or genres as film or television, music, comics, computer programs, and other forms that may supplement, compete with, and potentially problematize literary representation. Titles in the *Geocriticism and Spatial Literary Studies* series include both monographs and collections of essays devoted to literary criticism, theory, and history, often in association with other arts and sciences. Drawing on diverse critical and theoretical traditions, books in the series reveal, analyze, and explore the significance of space, place, and mapping in literature and in the world.

The concepts, practices, or theories implied by the title of this series are to be understood expansively. Although geocriticism and spatial literary studies represent a relatively new area of critical and scholarly investigation, the historical roots of spatial criticism extend well beyond the recent past, informing present and future work. Thanks to a growing critical awareness of spatiality, innovative research into the literary geography of real and imaginary places has helped to shape historical and cultural studies in ancient, medieval, early modern, and modernist literature, while a discourse of spatiality undergirds much of what is still understood as the postmodern condition. The suppression of distance by modern technology, transportation, and telecommunications has only enhanced the sense of place, and of displacement, in the age of globalization. Spatial criticism examines literary representations not only of places themselves, but of the experience of place and of displacement, while exploring the interrelations between lived experience and a more abstract or unrepresentable spatial network that subtly or directly shapes it. In sum, the work being done in geocriticism and spatial literary studies, broadly conceived, is diverse and far reaching. Each volume in this series takes seriously the mutually impressive effects of space or place and artistic representation, particularly as these effects manifest themselves in works of literature. By bringing the spatial and geographical concerns to bear on their scholarship, books in the *Geocriticism and Spatial Literary Studies* series seek to make possible different ways of seeing literary and cultural texts, to pose novel questions for criticism and theory, and to offer alternative approaches to literary and cultural studies. In short, the series aims to open up new spaces for critical inquiry.

San Marcos, USA Robert T. Tally Jr.

Acknowledgements

Scholarly monographs are notoriously entangled with indebtedness. Whether it be the scholarship we use to formulate a thesis and substantiate an argument or the personal and professional affiliations we draw upon to guide us past intellectual and emotional obstacles of all sorts, no scholarly undertaking can succeed without recognizing one's limitations and turning to those able to render aid. I thereby wish to acknowledge the various forms of support that have made this project possible. I would first like to thank Dr. Rebecca Bushnell, the former Dean of the University of Pennsylvania School of Arts and Sciences, Associate Dean for the Humanities, Jeffrey Kallberg, and Dr. Suvir Kaul, past Chair of the Department of English, for supporting my application for a Dean's Leave that allowed me to have a year-long sabbatical during the 2009–2010 academic year. I also want to thank Dr. Valerie Swain Cade McColloum, Vice Provost for University Life, for providing me with a research funding to bring this project to completion. Thanks go, as well to Dr. Noliwe Rooks and Dr. Eddie S. Glaude at the Center for (now, the Department of) African American Studies at Princeton University for arranging appointments for me on two different occasions as a Visiting Fellow in African American Studies during the 2009–10 and 2016–17 academic years.

Sincerest thanks go to April Miller in the Access Office in Princeton's Firestone Library for providing me with scholarly privileges in the main collection as well as the Toni Morrison Papers, which are held in Special Collections in the Firestone Library. I would also like to thank the

Toni Morrison Society, in particular Dr. Carolyn Denard, the President of the Society's Advisory Board, and current and former Board members Dr. Adrienne Seward, Marc Connor, Maryemma Graham, and Marilyn Sanders Mobley for their work in organizing the numerous biennial conferences where I first developed the ideas constituting the foundation for this book as well as welcoming me into an international community of Toni Morrison scholars. I was honored by the Society's invitation to deliver the inaugural Toni Morrison Society Lecture at my alma mater, Oberlin College, in 2014. I'm equally grateful to Adrienne Seward, Justine Tally, Maryemma Graham, Andree-Anne Kekeh Dika, Janis A.Mayes, and Lucille Fultz for inviting me to submit essays in their respective edited volumes that provided the skeletal framework for this book. I would also like to thank audiences at Ohio and Villanova Universities and of the Society for the Study of Narrative, as well as the American Literature Study Group in the Penn English Department for the opportunity to present sections of the manuscript. In each of these instances, the feedback I received was indispensable. I would like to extend special thanks to Brigitte Shull, who read a draft of the manuscript and suggested that I submit it to the Geocritical Studies and Spatial Criticism series at Palgrave Macmillan, edited by Robert Tally. Thanks as well to my Palgrave editors, Ryan Jenkins, Allie Bachicchio, and Emily Janakiriam for their diligence and patience. And I'm grateful for the careful and nuanced comments from the peer reviewer that helped me to bring this project into its final form.

My colleagues in the Departments of Africana Studies and English provided stimulating conversation and camaraderie: Barbara Savage, Mary Frances Berry, Camille Zubrinsky Charles, Tukufu Zuberi, Heather Williams, Anthea Butler, Michael Hanchard, Eve Troutt-Powell, Grace Sanders Johnson, John Jackson, Dorothy Roberts, and Tim Rommen have each been tremendous sources of intellectual acuity and good will. Among my English Department colleagues, none are more dear to me than Salamishah Tillet, Alan Filreis, Nancy Bentley, Toni Bowers, and Josephine Park. Michael Gamer, Paul Hendrickson, Lorene Cary, Heather Love, J.C. Cloutier, Paul Saint-Amour, David Wallace, Marybeth Gasman, Vivian Gadsden, and Zack Lesser have each been steadfast colleagues who have modeled a brand of integrity, open-mindedness, and scholarly rigor that makes me optimistic about the future of literary and cultural studies and reassure me that scholars working in different periods and subfields can not only coexist, but engage in mutual gestures of nurturing I am also delighted to welcome my new colleagues, Margo Crawford and Dagmawi Woubshet, both of whom have joined us from Cornell this past Fall. And thanks go as well to Andy Binns, Beth A. Winkelstein, William Gipson, Charles Howard, Brian Peterson, Valerie DeCruz, Harriet Joseph, Ira Harkavy, Carol Muller, Peter Conn, Rogers Smith, Alan Lee, and Janice Curington, whose steadfast presence as collaborators and sustainers underscore the importance of creating learning communities committed to inclusiveness and social justice.

I need to acknowledge those individuals whose lights have shone brightest and longest as they illuminate my tiny corner of the universe: Douglas A. Banks, Johnny T. Jones, Robert Doward Williamson, Bryan Huddleston, Frank Flonnoy, Lester L. Barclay, George O. Barnwell, Daphne Brooks, Valerie Smith, Sandra and Basil Pacquet, Kristin Brinkley, Millicent E. Brown, Lisa B. Thompson, Rafia Zafar, Angelyn Mitchell, Tanji Gilliam, Mary Helen Washington, Danille Taylor, David Ikard, Mark Sanders, John Edgar Tidwell, Robert G. O'Meally, Frances Smith Foster, Richard Yarborough, Vincent Peterson, Carolyn Beard Whitlow, Crystal J. Lucky, Anthony Foy, Adrienne Dale Davis, Farah Jasmine Griffin, Dwight D. Andrews, Robert B. Stepto, Kimberly Wallace Sanders, Vera Kutzinski, Pamela Robinson, Elaine Freedgood, Gwendolyn DuBois Shaw, Elizabeth Alexander, Karen Mapp, Paula Krebs, Lillie Edwards, Donna Akiba Sullivan Harper, Regina Wilson, Mencer Donahue Edwards, David A. Thomas, Bill Lowe, Cheryl A. Wall, Kali Tal, Meta DuEwa Jones, Adrian C. Hernandez, Peter Schmidt, Chuck James, Rafael Perez-Torres, Peter Vaughan, Kenneth Shropshire, Andre Hughlett Bugg, Clemmie Harris, Allen Green, Maghan Kieta, Ayo Fapohunda, Robin B. Means-Coleman, Nell Painter, Gloria Watkins, Guthrie Ramsey, James Braxton Peterson, Kerry Haynie, John Lowe, and Tim Powell have provided me with safe harbor in the harshest of storms and model daily what it means to live a real and honest life. Though Nellie McKay, Joseph Skerrett, Gay Wilentz, Oni Faida Lampley, Jim Miller, Rudolph P. Byrd, James Richardson, Todd Middleton, Clyde Woods, Sylvia Wilson, Terry Adkins, Claudia Tate, and Vincent Woodard had all transitioned by the time this project came to fruition, the lives they led and what they stood for continues to edify and inspire me.

It is also necessary to send thanks to two people who took time away from their own work to read an early draft of this manuscript at a moment when, overcome with despair, I frantically reached out in need of their assistance. Without the benefit of their intense attention and the confidence that attention engendered, this book would never have gotten past the conceptual stage. For that, I want to express my deepest gratitude to Dr. Deborah Barnes and Dr. Theodore Mason, who looked past the obvious flaws in my initial conception and helped my ideas to come into flower. They are the embodiment of a quality of friendship that values truth-telling and encouragement over dissembling and discouragement.

And to this number, I would add my beloved colleague, Thadious Davis. During our time as colleagues at the University of Pennsylvania, she has been my mentor, sounding board, collaborator, co-consipirator, role model, and guardian angel all in one. It was Thadious who insisted that the best way to launch a project was to begin by writing one's unruliest thoughts out longhand on a legal pad and then proceed to boil it down to a single paragraph. This latest piece of advice was part of our extended history dating back to my time as a graduate student. To say that she has been with me every step of the way doesn't come close to expressing the magnitude of her influence and support in my life and career. She embodies the very best aspects of the academic profession and does so with such incredible grace and dedication that I feel that even in the wake of the most devastating failure, opportunity is at hand.

Many thanks to the students in my graduate seminar on the works of Ralph Ellison and Toni Morrison (most notably, Anusha Alles, Aundeah Kearney, Julius Fleming, and Omari Weekes) and the various students in classes that featured Morrison's work for helping me to hone my thinking on Morrison's novels (with a special shout out to Michael King!). Over the years, I've been blessed with wonderful research assistants: Janet Chow, Kassidi Jones, Nikki Spigner, Leslie Collins Overton, Yolande Tomlinson, Maya Martin Bugg, Marcia Henry, Courtney Patterson, Ann Desrosiers, and Rachelle Skerritt, who combined labor with devotion and good humor. Thanks go as well to my Alpha Baptist Church family, especially our pastor the Reverend Doctor Danny Scotton, for "laying hands" on the manuscript, reminding me that "It's not your clock!," and pointing me to Isaiah 55:11 (words that should accompany any attempt at writing or speaking. And of course, a special and extended shout-out to my family: My mother, Gloria Beavers Strickland, and my sisters, Daryl Edwards, Dibri Beavers, and Dionna Beavers, who have circled me with an abundance of love, laughter, and patience.

My wife, the Honorable Lisa James-Beavers, and my children Michael and Corinne, have loved me without reservation and kept me grounded, while reminding me that writing is important because putting good into the world far outstrips seeking the rewards it brings.

Gratitude for all the assistance notwithstanding, responsibility for the mistakes and shortcomings of this book rests with me, and me alone.

Contents

CHAPTER 1

Introduction

Early in Toni Morrison's *Paradise*, one of the Fleetwood twins takes a moment to reflect upon life in the all-black town of Ruby and how its inhabitants feel "free and protected."[1] He thinks about how a

> sleeping woman could always rise from her bed, wrap her shawl around her shoulders and sit on the steps in the moonlight. And if she felt like it she could walk out the yard and on down the road. No lamp and no fear. A hiss-crackle from the side of the road would never scare her because whatever it was made the sound, it wasn't something creeping up on her. Nothing for ninety miles around thought she was prey. (9)

It is hard not to find this passage compelling. What black person living in the U.S. wouldn't want to experience this kind of geographical security in their place of residence? However, when viewed in the context of the plot, we find that the passage is meant to be ironic, especially since the thought occurs in the midst of murderous violence wrought by a group of men from Ruby, who have taken it upon themselves to hunt down and kill the nine women living at the Convent located a few miles outside of the town. Understood in this context, the passage carries an air of menace, control. A woman living in Ruby might not consider herself to be "prey," but such a feeling is contingent upon whether she recognizes that her sense of well-being is underwritten by the violence sanctioned by a select few among its residents.

H. Beavers, *Geography and the Political Imaginary in the Novels of Toni Morrison*, Geocriticism and Spatial Literary Studies,
https://doi.org/10.1007/978-3-319-65999-2_1

I selected this passage from *Paradise* because it provides a useful demonstration of the overarching power of place. More specifically, it indicates the importance of what geographers have come to describe as *place-making*. Reading *Paradise*, we come to understand that the town of Ruby is sustained by an assertion of will. As far as the men attacking the Convent are concerned, residing in Ruby is akin to living "in paradise." But as we will discover, occupying paradise always has its costs; place-making happens inside history and is always fraught with politics. *Paradise* acquires greater legibility with regard to place-making if we view it through the disciplinary lens of geography, which situates place as a fundamental aspect of its practice.[2] Marco Antonsich, for example, discusses place in terms of an expanding notion of scale (ranging from the local to the continental). He argues that "place identity" is the product of "experiences, feelings, attitudes, and values, which are not only unconscious, but also conscious" (122).[3] And as Kevin R. Cox observes, any discussion of the politics of place must reflect territorial politics. "It is about including and excluding," he writes, "establishing and defending boundaries, and laying claims to particular spaces and to inclusion in them on equal terms" (12). According to Cox, cities are not just a concentration of large numbers of bodies, structures, and systems, but also a system of "nodes that gather, flow, and juxtapose diversity, as places of overlapping—but not necessarily locally connected—relational networks, as perforated entities with connections that stretch far back in time and space," leading to "spatial formations of continuously changing composition" (34).[4]

Here, it is important to juxtapose the definitions of place from male geographers cited above with the work of feminist geographers. It is not my intent to insinuate feminist geographers are necessarily at odds with established definitions of place, but thinking about Toni Morrison's novels in relation to the practices that underwrite acts of place-making, it becomes important to understand how feminist approaches to geography feminist geographers complicate the disciplinary assertion that "places are contested, fluid, and uncertain," in which we find "multiple and changing boundaries, constituted and maintained by social relations of power and exclusion" (Massey, qtd. in McDowell, p. 4). As Linda McDowell argues in her book *Place and Gender*, the work of geographers like Neil Smith aptly describes place-making as a process that "implies the production of [geographical] scale in so far as places are made different from each other" (4). Like Smith, McDowell believes that it is "geographical scale that defines the boundaries and bounds the identities around which control is exerted and contested" (4). But geography's attention to notions of locality are equally important and thus McDowell acknowledges the work of Doreen Massey, who argues, "localities are produced by the intersection of global and local processes—social relations that operate at a range of spatial scales" (4). And as Mona Domosh and Joni Seager point out, moving through space involves overcoming what they call the "friction of distance." "Insisting that individual forms of mobility differ as one moves along the socioeconomic continuum," Domosh and Seager propose that attention to the concept of mobility needs to assume the body to be a logical starting point (110). They argue further, "Social norms, and the spaces constructed to hold those norms, shape what we think a body can and cannot do…In all societies there is an intertwined reciprocity between space, bodies, and the social construction of both—neither 'space' nor 'bodies' exist independently of a social imprint" (112).

Feminist geographers' attempts to problematize the concept of place, is incomplete without also figuring in the importance of mapping as a function of place-making. In her book, *Shuttles Rocking in the Loom*, Jennifer Terry relates how mapping constitutes a form of spatial politics which in turn evokes the political imaginary of the European colonial-project because of

> Its loaded associations with colonial incursions, codification, and control; its rendition of geography as experienced from a particular vantage point, whether it claims otherwise or not; and more straightforwardly, its spatial emphasis. (1)[5]

But Terry insists that writing in the African Diaspora proffers "a more diverse set of counter-geographies that speak to the African American and Caribbean experiences, each somehow affirming or reorienting in the face of oppression" (1). Through her effort to "counter scholarly atomization (sic) in terms of nation and language," Terry ascertains the extent to which the histories of people of the diaspora must take into account the forms of displacement, disembodiment, and disenfranchisement synonymous with New World slavery and oppression. However, she also seeks to understand how writers in the U.S. and other points across the diaspora seek to reimagine the relationship between acts of mapping and identity formation. For example, she looks at Morrison's *Jazz* with an eye toward how acts of displacement and eviction inhibit her characters' ability to fashion coherent versions of themselves and the ways they must re-orient themselves to the spatial realities of the North in order to achieve it (18).

As I see it, the point of contact between the work I do in this study and Terry's emerges around the notion of place-making and the creation of "counter-geographies" involves the act of reimagining how maps function. Then, the act of place-making has to do with creating an alternative poetics of mapmaking. Here, Siobhan McEvoy-Levy's arguments regarding issues of place are persuasive, in particular McEvoy-Levy's observation that, a place "is more than a physical space, a place is space plus meaning" (1). Seen in this regard, maps are meaning-laden enterprises whose interpretation is influenced by those who control the production of spatial meaning. Thus, place-making is

> a process with an indefinable end. While places have a material reality, their meanings evolve over time and not in wholly predictable or controllable ways. Places are constantly reinterpreted and reconstituted, and entail ongoing power struggles and negotiations. Place-making, therefore, has a potentially intimate connection with the social, cultural, and political processes of peacebuilding. (2)

While the violence and discontent to be found in Morrison's fiction would make it odd to equate place-making and peacebuilding, her fiction is replete with examples of agential place-making. In *Sula*, an example of place-making is the story of how an act of subterfuge that lets whites retain the best, most arable land and blacks come to occupy what is known as the Bottom. Another occurs in *Song of Solomon* when Mains Avenue becomes known, first, as Doctor Street and subsequently as Not Doctor Street, despite its designation on the town's maps. The house Sula grows up in is described as "a house of many rooms," and built to suit the specifications of Eva Peace "who kept on adding things: more stairways—there were three sets to the second floor—more rooms, doors and stoops. There were rooms that had three doors, others that opened out on the porch only were inaccessible from any other part of the house; others you could get to only by going through somebody's bedroom" (30). Eva's unruly approach to making a home leads her to take in Tar Baby as a tenant and burn her son, Plum, to prevent him from crawling back into her womb. Yet another instance can be found in *Jazz* when a parade of "silent black women and men marching down Fifth Avenue to advertise their anger over two hundred dead in East St. Louis" constitutes a moment when place-making, disaffection, and commemoration intersect. Finally, the two months in which Frank Money's ailing sister, Cee, is ministered to by "country women who loved mean" as they gather at Ethel Fordham's house to make quilts and where Cee finds herself "[s]urrounded by their comings and goings, listening to their talk, their songs" and paying "them the attention she had never given them before" (122).

Thinking of these examples and many others, *Geography and the Political Imaginary in the Fiction of Toni Morrison* seeks to determine whether Morrison's publication of *Beloved* in 1987 constitutes a departure from previously established iterations of place-making. Did the novel elaborate upon previously established notions of place or does it serve as a bellwether for what comes after in which the idea of place is troubled in new ways? Should we read the transition from *Tar Baby*, with its setting on a fictional island in the Caribbean in relation to *Beloved* with its marked return to the geographically and historically recognizable location of Cincinnati as an iterative gesture?

For answers, I turn to the closing pages of *Beloved* in order to bring these questions into focus. When Paul D hears Sethe claim that her murdered baby was her "best thing." Paul D's thoughts about Sethe makes him realize he

> is staring at the quilt but he is thinking about her wrought-iron back; the delicious mouth still puffy at the corner from Ella's fist. The mean black eyes. The wet dress steaming before the fire. Her tenderness about his neck jewelry—its three wands, like attentive baby rattlers, curving two feet into the air. How she never mentioned or looked at it, so he did not have to feel the shame of being collared like a beast. Only this woman Sethe could have left him his manhood like that. *He wants to put his story next to hers.* (322, my italics)

Paul D's decision is indicative of what I am calling *horizontal place-making*. His desire to situate his own history *alongside* Sethe's is a radical gesture since it eschews hierarchy in favor of a more paratactical approach to cohabiting with her, as if one story cannot be considered without taking heed of the other, as if a grammar of equivalence has emerged and taken root. Paul D's realization that he wants to "put his story next to" Sethe's, likewise rests on the assumption that she is her "best thing." When Paul D tells Sethe, "me and you, we got more yesterday than anybody. We need some kind of tomorrow" (320), it is a gesture that dismantles the implicit connection between memory and injury in favor of imagination and aspiration by committing to overcoming the friction of distance that has undermined their efforts to cohabit in a space safe for them both.

I refer to the individual and collective forms of trauma Morrison's characters experience as *tight space*. As I conceptualize it, tight space signals a character's spiritual and emotional estrangement from community and the way it inhibits their ability to sustain a meaningful relationship to place. Tight space induces strategies that result in vertical forms of place-making which emphasizes individualism, materialism, violence, and abjection as key components of their estrangement. Only by eschewing verticality and opting for horizontal systems of collaboration and reconciliation that lead to more egalitarian and open forms of place-making can Morrison's characters loose themselves from the tight space that immobilizes them.

She dramatizes this struggle by employing the recurring trope of the *two-story house*, where the spatial and domestic geographies we find in Morrison's fiction are revealed to be sites of narrative contestation, where the occlusion of history and the wholesale erasure of black subjects can only be countermanded by the establishment of counter-publics that privilege collaborative forms of narration that penetrate silence and counteract the effects of tight space. Paul D's and Sethe's location in, and subsequent escape from, *tight space* means that if "place is space plus meaning," the works that follow *Beloved* instantiate place-making as a phenomenon that occurs across multiple registers and thus creates the possibility of political imaginaries in which her protagonists and the communities they inhabit can thrive. Hence, the eradication of tight space within the context of the two-story house means that the vertical arrangement of narrative gives way to a more horizontal circumstance.[6]

Because the characters often become aware that they are caught in tight space through the near-exhaustion of personal resources, their only recourse is to loose themselves from previously held assumptions in order to reimagine their possibilities. This often means that they must understand how their circumstances are informed by the politics of scale. As one of geography's core concepts, scale allows us to identify and then "negotiate the boundaries between difference and similarity" (82). An awareness of the challenges of scale empowers individuals and groups to "delimit inclusion or exclusion in such social constructions as home, class, nation, rural, urban, core, and periphery" (82).[7] The recurrence of tight space in Morrison's fiction has much to do with her propensity to represent local circumstances in which power relations are managed at varying scales of influence. Scarcity in the village may be the by-product of surplus in the city. The abuse a man inflicts on his wife may be a by-product of a decision to close a factory at the company headquarters hundreds of miles away. A child is orphaned because the men who dominate county politics decide they want her father's land. A man wearing a military uniform barely survives the wrath of a mob because the black warrior is an incongruent metonym for the U.S. body politic.

Our ability to have a meaningful attachment to place has much to do, then, with the ways scale often pivots on the symbiosis that inheres between systems of exclusion and systems of evaluation. This study highlight issues of scale in her novels by considering scale as an outward progression. Which means that I move outward from how the individual engenders a sense of place, to the ways place is manifest on a neighborhood scale, to how place signifies on the scale of the town, and finally to how place reflects social relations on a global scale. Organizing the discussion in this manner is key to a conceptual mapping of how acts of place-making figures directly and indirectly into black life. Because place-making for Morrison's characters often emerges amidst turmoil, they often face the difficulty of ascertaining the exact source of the turbulence that enshrouds them. They are required in turn to cast their figurative gaze backward to think about trauma which is located within the form of power relations growing out of systems of scale.

The sites of contestation in which these systems become discernible requires an understanding of what Guitar, in *Song of Solomon*, refers to as "the condition our condition is in," a "meta-awareness" that invites us to think beyond acts of exclusion in order to consider the structural imperatives underwriting a politics of exclusion. Morrison's characters often discover that they cannot elucidate what an alternative imaginary founded on principles of inclusion and equity might look like by themselves, hence, they find that horizontal place-making is a collaborative gesture that hinges on the characters' realization that interdependence is a key element. In trying to understand community as the result of conscious acts of place-making, I seek to investigate the spatial nature of communal politics and history. How are boundaries established and policed? What sort of thinking informs how the inhabitants establish what forms of place-making (vertical or horizontal) they seek to effect?

How are attachments formed or broken, sustained or abandoned? What this means is that the acts of voice occurring in Morrison's novels are contingent on her characters' ability to understand that the effects of tight space cannot be overcome without a radical rethinking of how space is transformed into place.

Thinking about the title of this study, I mean for "Geography" to function as an interpolation of the phrase "Political Imaginary." Wolfgang Iser describes how an imaginary functions by stating that "imagination manifests itself only as an impact on relationships brought about by forces external to it, and therefore to a large extent conditioned by them" (180, 637). The imaginary exists, he asserts, "not only in ideas, dreams and daydreams, but also in memory and to a smaller degree in perception itself." According to Cornelius Castoriadis, the imaginary is distinguished by the fact that it is not indeterminate. Rather, for him, "the very fabric of social life consists of imaginary significations" (639). Imaginaries, Castoriadis argues, "are the product of significations that acquire meaning in a social context in which power is unequally distributed, where acts of defective decision-making are rationalized through the use of mystified information" (639).

The issue of power is especially relevant to political imaginaries. As Allan Tullos relates, a political imaginary consists of the "public shape of power, representation, and possibility." Moreover, a political imaginary is an

> affective terrain rather than a sovereign polity, a political imaginary configures possibilities and outlines limits, suggests the boundaries of the legitimate and the outrageous, limns the contours of power. Political imaginaries take shape through popular narratives as much as by legislative acts; in the words and deeds of public figures of speech; through rumor, jokes, statistics, journalistic ascriptions, blog entries, art, and music. (5)

Tullos observes further that political imaginaries are a by-product of statistical inference, stereotypes, popular narratives, and mythic figurations. In view of such an observation, a central tenet of this study is that Morrison's fictional characters provide the means through which to illustrate how the quest to fashion a political imaginary informs everyday behaviors. How do her characters and the communities in which they reside go about conceptualizing what a prosperous future would look like? What values cement the community into a viable whole where everyone's presence is cherished? What are the negative energies working to tear the community asunder? Are the vertical forces at play in a community countered by horizontal forces that result in the discovery of new ways to define belonging, where the transformation of social relations leads to a more grounded sense of place?

Here, I reprise Paul D's insistence that he and Sethe are in "need of some kind of tomorrow," as way to underscore how Morrison's characters driven to direct their gaze forward, toward what is approaching, rather than always contending with what lies behind them till the past becomes perpetually present. But achieving a state of mind open to what is to come requires a break with the past. Iser, Castoriadis, and Tullos in their respective fashions intimate that the affective nature of political imaginaries is made legible in the everyday interactions that help us to ascertain boundaries, limits, and potentialities. The structures of feeling that flourish in the wake of these learned behaviors and responses are, once again, meaningful only in the context of our relationships with others. Traversing affecting terrain often signals a need to domesticate experience in the form of habits and preferences. As such, communities can be understood as sites of interdependencies that are only partially realized, and we thus need to be mindful of how the political imaginary is reliant on what Tullos refers to as habits of judgment that "sustain the everyday conventions, patrol the borderlands of expectation, shepherd the trails of personal satisfaction and disdain," and "animate the political in the personal" (27). Furthermore, habits of judgment "animate the political in the personal" and "grow from location, historical practices, institutional affirmation, and cultural repetition" (27, 9). Achieving a state of mutuality sufficient for communities to set about challenging the status quo is contingent on the individuals' ability to reassess their feelings, monitor their responses to social stimuli, and hold themselves accountable for their adherence to social conventions that demean them.

This points to what I see as one of the main achievements of the civil rights movement. Black communities all over the South opted to resist the covenant of Jim Crow by placing their bodies in harm's way at lunch counters, in department stores, and on public transportation. In so doing, they opted out of the racial skirmishing that involved the recognition on the part of blacks that making their displeasure and discomfort visible in the form of heavy sighs, frowns, hesitations, covert sabotage, and isolated acts of physical retaliation would no longer suffice. What had long been accepted as a way to register discontent, had a political dimension that the community had elected not to bring to full flower.

The movement constituted the abandonment of habits of judgment based on the premise that acts of individual assertion would bring large-scale forms of violent retribution down on the community. Non-violent resistance, with its silent assertion that black bodies were occupying space but with a difference, marked a radical departure from convention. All of a sudden, black people were no longer content to "stay in their place," nullifying badges and jail cells, physical and verbal assault, police dogs and hoses as methods of enforcing boundaries.[8]

However, changes in habits of judgment can just as easily be the product of collective forms of misinterpretation. Readers of *Sula* will remember that moment when the inhabitants of Medallion, Ohio, take it upon themselves to wreak havoc on the construction site of the tunnel being built near the river. Morrison's point is that if a community's habits of judgment reflect interpretive consensus, then changes of order often result when communities elect to abandon the interpretive protocols that created it. In the case of Medallion, though, their acts of destructive protest can be traced to the death of Sula Peace, whose return to Medallion many years earlier "changed them in accountable yet mysterious ways" so that they "cherish their husbands and wives, protect their children, repair their homes and in general band together against the devil in their midst" (117–118). But Sula's death leads them to relinquish their nurturing posture.

And when the new year brings unseasonably warm weather that sweeps away Winter's bitter cold and ice, the resulting exultant mood leads first to infectious laughter and subsequently to a "parade" that induces their neighbors to join them, "as though the sunshine would last, as though there really was hope" (160). Hope informs their previous habits of judgment such that it

> kept them picking beans for other farmers; kept them from finally leaving as they talked of doing; kept them knee-deep in other people's dirt; kept them excited about other people's wars; kept them solicitous of white people's children; kept them convinced that some magic "government" was going to lift them up, out and away from that dirt, those beans, those wars. (160).

The narrator continues: "Old and young, women and children, lame and hearty, they killed, as best they could, the tunnel they were forbidden to build," in a fit of massed rage (161). But in their exuberance, "their need to kill it all, all of it," they go too far inside the tunnel, at which point the earth loosens and the poles holding back the water fall away: Water rushes in and kills a large number of Medallion residents (161).

Sula asserts that a change in habits of judgment cannot be contingent upon anomalous circumstance that creates the illusion of altered conditions. An alternative political imaginary is not a product of the carnivalesque, where celebratory and ceremonial acts signal the temporary suspension of established habits of judgment. In *Sula*, what appears to be a reversal of the power dynamic actually demonstrates how the seeming nullification of the existing system of scale is momentary. The onrushing water symbolizes the status quo reasserting itself with greater force. Acts of resistance are opportunities for new beginnings only if defiance gives way to tactical behaviors that seek to reimagine the future. News of Sula Peace's demise and the celebration it occasions intimates that what seemed to be a reversal of fortune, a nullification of the existing system of scale, was at best momentary. Though Sula's return did lead to an attitude of caretaking and protectiveness in the Bottom, the tunnel tragedy suggests that the political imaginary that grew up in response to her presence was purely reactionary. Black communities, both in actuality and in Morrison's fiction, engage in political discourse in a variety of settings and in ways that are not often acknowledged as being political.[9] Hence, it is by no means a far-fetched notion that the novel is Morrison's approach to engaging the question of the political imagination since her work regularly depicts characters who wrestle with habits of judgment that directly impact on how they conceptualize acts of place-making and empowerment.

Another way to ascertain what it means for Morrison's characters to imagine the point where place-making and the political imaginary intersect is through geographer Yi-Fu Tuan's concept of topophilia. Tuan describes topophilia as "the affective bond between people and place" (4). As such, topophilia is how we measure the extent to which space is transformed into place. Tuan's judicious definition of place increases in resonance when read alongside George Lipsitz's provocative notion that the "persistence of unequal racial-outcomes" in the U.S. forces us to "come to grips with the fatal couplings of place and race in our society" (5). Although Tuan's description of topophilia is couched in humanistic terms that are sufficiently capacious to allow the idea of place-making to operate across a variety of registers, we nonetheless need to be mindful of the political machinations inherent in Tuan's formulation.[10] Tuan's concept of topophilia allows us to see Morrison's novels as an investigative circumstance through which to highlight the inherent difficulty that accompanies acts of generating and sustaining community in the face of hostility and disenfranchisement. In short, she invites us to think about how we come to *love* where we are and how, in occupying space, we elect to *face up to* its challenges rather than hiding from them.

But the relationship between affect and belonging can just as easily assume negative characteristics. For example, in *Paradise*, when Reverend Pulliam presides over the wedding ceremony of Arnette and K.D., he offers remarks on the nature of love. "Love is divine only and difficult always," he declares, "If you think it is easy you are a fool. If you think it is natural you are blind. It is a learned application without reason or motive except that it is God" (141). The reverend's thoughts veer sharply away from conventional understandings of love, which is in part the reason for his jeremiad. For him, love exists outside of both human intentionality and human physiology. Further, he insists that love should not be considered a basic human right, an expectation with no prior requirements. Pulliam asserts that as individuals, we do not deserve love simply because "of the suffering [we] have endured," because "somebody did [us] wrong," or even "because [we] want it." By his judgment, "Love is not a gift. It is a diploma. A diploma conferring privileges: the privilege of expressing love and the privilege of receiving it" (141).

Reverend Pulliam's assessment of love is not intended, as one might expect, for the bride and groom, especially when he declares, "God is not interested in you." Rather, Pulliam sees love as the possession of a God "who is interested only in Himself," because "he is interested only in love." Hearing Reverend Pulliam's troublesome characterization of love, Anna Flood concludes that his views are not for the benefit of the couple. They are directed at Reverend Misner, who pastors the Baptist church in Ruby, who has been deeply involved in the civil rights and Black Power movements, and who ministers through what might be termed liberation theology. Anna concludes that Pulliam's diatribe is meant to discredit Misner's overall approach to ministry, to reject the "namby-pamby sermons of a man who thought teaching was letting children talk as if they had something important to say that the world had not heard and dealt with already" (143). But we also need to regard Pulliam's observations regarding love as assertions of scale. His version of God is so consumed by an ontology of self-interestedness, any concern he might display toward human frailty, need, or longing ultimately fall outside his gaze. Within Pulliam's spiritual geography, individuals seeking to cleave one to another commit sin which, in its capriciousness, makes love akin to blasphemy.

What makes Pulliam's observations about love intriguing in the present context is that by directing them at Misner, he is rejecting any thought of a political imaginary not organized from the top downward, an arrangement in which men like Deek and Steward Fleetwood preside and everyone else conforms to their will. By asserting that human beings are of little interest to God, Pulliam is likewise insisting that the effort to exercise agency in the face of injustice is beside the point. The model of leadership he values most is one in which the individual submits to God's externalized will; it involves setting aside the question of unconditional acceptance to embrace an ethic that is wholly conditional, leaving the individual scarcely able to ascertain whether a spiritual walk is motion at all.

Reverend Misner's response to Pulliam's diatribe is not a verbal rebuttal. Misner is angered by Pulliam's attack, angry at the wound inflicted upon him for reasons he does not fully understand. But rather than voicing his dissent, he walks to the rear of the church and unhooks the cross hanging on the wall and walks back up to the pulpit, where he holds it "before him for all to see—if only they would. See what was certainly the first sign of any human anywhere had made: the vertical line, the horizontal one" (145). By holding the cross aloft, Misner seeks to communicate that in its simplicity lies its power as a symbol of human agency, a symbol that is integral to a meaningful life:

> Without this sign, the believer's life was confined to praising God and taking the hits. The praise was credit; the hits were interest due on the debt that could never be paid. Or, as Pulliam put it, no one knew when he had "graduated." But with it, in the religion which this sign was paramount and foundational, well, life was a whole other matter. (146)

Once again, the theological debate between Pulliam and Misner is less a concern than the ways that their respective approaches to religious practice articulate approaches to place-making and the ways it contributes to building and sustaining a political imaginary. In the former, Pulliam describes a power relationship that mirrors the white supremacist imaginary: it is arbitrary and punitive, indifferent and self-centered. In the latter, the cross asserts that the relationship reflects egalitarian principles, a symbol that poses the question to the entire gathering, "See how this official murder out of hundreds marked the difference, moved the relationship between God and man from CEO and supplicant to one on one?" (146).

What seems on the surface to be a disagreement over religious dogma can likewise be understood as Morrison's dramatization of a political exchange, the assertion of opposing political imaginaries. In this instance, she makes it possible for the reader to glean a sense of how past trauma can either restrain us or provide the terms of our liberation. The debate between Pulliam and Misner—the intensity of feeling it invokes as well as the numerous interpretations it occasions—constitutes once more the effort to work through the meaning of a traumatic circumstance shared by both ministers: how is the place slavery holds in the collective memory contested? *Paradise* is Toni Morrison's seventh novel, and the exchange between Reverends Pulliam and Misner once more suggests that they are cohabitants of the "two-story house." As I noted above, a conventional description of a built structure that has more than a single floor is relevant to the ways that *Paradise* dramatizes a circumstance in which opposing narratives compete for position in the foreground and at the top of Ruby's social hierarchy.

We can locate both Reverend Misner's church and the Convent from *Paradise* alongside the Breedloves' house in *The Bluest Eye*, Eva Peace's house in *Sula*, Macon Dead's house in *Song of Solomon*, Valerian Street's L'Arbe de le Croix in *Tar Baby*, 124 Bluestone Road in *Beloved*, and Bill Cosey's Resort in *Love*. What links these domiciles across the entirety of Morrison's fiction is that they all feature narratives in which the characters struggle—and often fail—to build a healthy attachment to place. We should be equally cognizant, then, of how Harlem and Virginia, the Southside and Shalimar, Paris and Eloe, Lorain and Kentucky, Philadelphia and Isle des Chevaliers, Cincinnati and Kentucky, or more recently Lotus, Georgia, and Korea function as spatial binaries in Morrison's fiction. And this is the case not simply because they are necessarily binary opposites, but rather because one location is often illegible without a facile grasp of what (and how) distant locations can wield an impact on local experience. The political affect in Morrison's fictional settings are in many instances distinguished by their location above or below the Mason-Dixon Line. Her fiction has dramatized the power relations fundamental to the workings of the southern political imaginary, which is fraught with the foreclosures and limits on black political agency that only a white-supremacist imaginary can impose.

As Isabel Wilkerson's *The Warmth of Other Suns* helps us to understand, writing about the South that existed prior to 1965 involves a thick description of the volatility of the southern political imaginary. This volatility hindered efforts by both individuals and coalitions in black communities to project a sense of the future that they could materialize through their actions in the physical world. A political imaginary can be thought of as a way for communities to begin the difficult work of determining their collective fate. Hence, efforts to improve the conditions in which this discussion occurs constitute a political project that seeks, as Keally D. McBride argues, to balance the imperatives of particularity and universality (44). McBride states further that communities in a liberal democracy are cleaved into public and private spheres, which means that while the latter space might offer a space of nurturance and affirmation, the former might be a site of nullification. However, because Morrison understands the private space of the family as "one realm where inequality persists," her work is in accord with McBride's assertion that those "who are perceived as less than equal in private cannot check their identities at the invisible barrier between public and private to achieve equal citizenship" (44). I reiterate the notion of a counter-public in order to suggest that Morrison's characters are often in search of spaces in which the particularities of a community can be juxtaposed against the myth of inclusiveness and equity advanced by the body politic.

A character embodying such counter-public thinking is Baby Suggs. In the years between her arrival at 124 Bluestone Road and the arrivals of her three grandchildren and subsequently, her daughter-in-law, Sethe, and her newborn baby, Denver, Baby Suggs fashions a counter-public through the preaching she undertakes in the place designated as the Clearing. Surrounded by her fellow ex-slaves, many of whom relive on a daily basis the traumas suffered under the indignities of bondage, Baby Suggs endeavors to guide them back to a state of emotional wholeness by asking the men, women, and children alternately to cry, dance, or laugh. Baby Suggs insists that before freed slaves can endeavor to nurture the spirit, they must first recover the ability to experience a full range of emotional and sensory stimuli. Knowing slave bodies *matter*, Baby Suggs invokes the material substance of the black body in order to rescue it from the precarious system of meaning created by the pseudoscientific, philosophical, and biblical discourse that slaveholders insist deems the black body to be inferior. Her efforts seek to countermand the ideological entrapment of the freed person in a symbolic economy whose main tenet is the assumption that commodified bodies are in a constant state of [d]evaluation. Schoolteacher's desire to quantify black bodies is indicative of such thinking.

Hence, Morrison's decision to use the name "the Clearing" for the space where Baby Suggs finds her voice as an "unchurched" preacher ministering to a flock is suggestive of her effort to dramatize the process by which freed persons sought to reclaim their bodies from bondage through acts of intentional purgation. Though it would likely be difficult to locate the Clearing on a map as anything more than a gap in a stand of trees, the presence of black freed persons seeking to reclaim their bodies asserts that cathartic acts do not occur in random space; they can only have meaning in a space in which the negative social valences attached to black bodies are reversed. Baby Suggs's arrival at 124 Bluestone Road leads to her realization that the body that labored in the fields of the Garner farm is not the same body that has come to rest across the Ohio River in a free state. And yet she understands that even as a "freed person," a process of reclamation is required before she can embrace the idea of self-ownership.

A major aspect of what happens in the Clearing takes the form of nonverbal behaviors: "It started that way: laughing children, dancing men, crying women and then it got mixed up. Women stopped crying and danced; men sat down and cried; children danced, women laughed, children cried until, exhausted and riven, all and each lay about the Clearing damp and gasping for breath" (193). I am most interested in Baby Suggs's "sermon," when she states,

> Here… *in this place*, we flesh; flesh that weeps, laughs; flesh that dances on bare feet in grass. Love it. Love it hard. *Yonder* they do not love your flesh. They despise it. They don't love your eyes; they'd just as soon pick em out. No more do they love the skin on your back. *Yonder* they flay it. (88)

And she continues:

> And O my people they do not love your hands. Those they only use, tie, bind, chop off and leave empty. Love your hands! Love them. Raise them up and kiss them. Touch others with them, pat them together, stroke them on your face 'cause they don't love that either. You got to love it, you! And no, they ain't in love with your mouth. *Yonder* out there, they will see it broken and break it again. (88; emphasis)

Baby Suggs's call demonstrates the political imaginary at work. Note how she imagines the Clearing apart from those other spaces in which black bodies are devalued and mutilated through her juxtaposition of "this place" and "yonder." In doing so, her observations are suggestive of how political imaginaries take place at the boundaries of the "legitimate and the outrageous". But perhaps most important is the manner in which Baby Suggs sutures a conscious regard for the black body, as flesh, to the imperatives of place-making.[11] It is important to consider, further, the ways that the Clearing is correctly viewed as the site of a *local* form of corporeal and spiritual healing. Though one can certainly understand the desire to extrapolate on her assertions in order to apply them on a global scale, Baby Suggs's notion that "knowing when to stop" is ultimately a statement, attuned to the individuals living in Cincinnati's black community. With that notion in mind, this study draws examples from the entirety of the Morrison canon, including novels published prior to 1987. But my ultimate aim is to trace Morrison's turn from settings in the North toward spatial and domestic geographies in the Southern United States.[12]

Ranging across the four novels published both before or shortly after *Beloved*, Chap. 2, titled "Held in the Thrall: Morrison's Southern Men and the Arrested Motion of Tight Space," focuses on three of what I am calling Morrison's "southern men": Macon Dead, Joe Trace, and Son Green. Each of these characters are distinguished by the arrested motion that results when they elect to remain fixed on an object or person lost in the distant or recent past. The acts of place-making they endeavor to perform are fraught with the desire to recover things they have deemed to be precious. But as we will discover, these characters' respective enterprises prove dangerous, not only to themselves, but to other inhabitants of the community, no matter if it be family members or neighbors.

Chapter 3, "From Zero to Nowhere: Tight Space and the Topophilia of Violence" picks up where Chap. 2 left off by turning its attention to a second group of Morrison's "southern men": Guitar Bains, Cholly Breedlove, and the 8-Rock Men from *Paradise*. I argue in Chap. 3 that the aforementioned characters are as caught up in tight space as the men in the previous chapter, but with a difference. For them, the solution to negotiating through tight spaces is to use violence as a way to determine a coherent notion of selfhood. For these men, space and place might begin as referents of physical and material reality, but violence soon enables them to privilege symbolic approaches to place-making that place family and community into a precarious state.

Chapter 4, "The Housing of Hurt: The Optic of Tight Space in *Jazz*," fashions a reading of Morrison's 1992 novel that interrogates the consequences that arise when communal relations are governed by a visual politics that privileges surface over depth. Though *Jazz is* set in the 1920s, when southern migrants arriving in the city are becoming acclimatized to the demands of urban life, the novel's concern with stimulation, titillation, and satiation is meant to reflect the era in which it was published. The struggle of the main characters, Joe and Violet Trace, to restore their damaged marriage, happens at the same time that they seek to loose themselves from past traumas that inhibits their ability to lay claim to authentic notions of self. Amidst shifting definitions of respectability and responsibility, along with the concomitant rise of new forms of expressive culture, like jazz, the city itself invites the individual to transgress boundaries and indulge in a single-minded quest for stimulation.

Chapter 5, "A Measure of Last Resort: Limerence and the Geometrical Shape of Community in *Love*" takes up the recurring trope of the two-story house as it assumes the form of Cosey's Resort. The resort's motto, "The best good time," obscures the betrayal and despair in a family laboring under the legacy of a patriarch who places individual pursuits of pleasure and distraction above compassion and devotion. Chapter 5's main argument is that habits of judgment based on greed and denial must be challenged in order to create an alternative imaginary that de-emphasizes *Eros* and privileges *Agape*. *Love* features communities whose geometric configurations serve either to discredit or enable horizontal forms of place-making.

Chapter 6, "A Pox on All Your Houses: Susceptibility, Immunity, and the Dilemma of Allegory in *A Mercy*," focuses on Morrison's use of an outbreak of smallpox on a Virginia farm as an allegory for how the economic and ontological tenets of slavery come to infect other parts of the South. Though the characters begin as residents of the colony of Virginia, by the novel's end they come to be distinguished from one another on various scales of difference. For example, the spread of smallpox gives readers a variety of ways to distinguish the characters: between those with acquired immunity and those with natural immunity, between black and white, indentured and slave labor, and ultimately the ways that the transformation of indentured labor into paid labor ultimately reifies slave labor's relationship to social death.

Chapter 7, "Clothed in the Most Absurd Garment Space-Time Can Imagine: *Home*'s Precarious Counter-topography," discusses the intriguing question of whether it is is possible to feel a sense of topophilia in a place where social boundaries are tightly enforced and possibilities limited. *Home* begins with an image of horses that "rose up like men." At the end of the novel, then, Frank and Cee's newfound sense of place signals that Du Bois's "problem of the color line," did not turn, as some would have it, simply on a contest between victim and victimizer." Rather, greater emphasis should be placed on trying to determine who has the deeper commitment to seeing what *is* as opposed to what *might be*. In such a circumstance, what is required is a sensibility prepared to improvise on that knowledge and move toward more liberatory forms of place-making. Morrison's symbol for this posture is a man wearing a zoot suit, which signals the manner in which the outrageous is an emotional passageway to being whole.

As I hope to argue across the length and breadth of this study, one of the most important functions of Morrison's fiction is that it is committed to the de-centering of black men's experience as the dominant aspect of African American narrative.[13] Providing readers with an up-close perspective on African American political thought, Morrison's fiction seeks to reimagine the normative configurations of power in black communities. Hence, I am likewise suggesting that she is foregrounding, both through the act of writing, and through the characters and plots she creates, what Patricia Hill Collins refers to as a "black feminist standpoint epistemology." A character like Pecola Breedlove, who is ensnared in a web of racial self-hatred and desires what she deems to be one of the most attractive attributes of whiteness (i.e., blue eyes), cannot be understood simply as a victim of racism. Nor can Cholly Breedlove's violent rape of his own daughter be attributed solely to the ways racism has distorted his approach to fatherhood. As Collins insists, black feminist standpoint epistemology can "provide new angles of vision not only on the African American experience, but on the basic concepts used to describe that experience" (43). Hence, *The Bluest Eye* is not only a rumination on racism but as well an effort to reflect on the dialectical nature of inter-sectionality, where the reader is made aware of how race, gender, and class combine to foreground the central role white supremacy and patriarchy play in Pecola's victimization and how they buttress Cholly's decision to participate in that victimization. To talk about Morrison's fiction and its deployment of tight spaces, then, is not only to speak about how the work fashions new understandings of how black men find themselves alienated from a sense of place, handicapped in their effort to embrace horizontal forms of place-making, but also to ascertain how a truly transformative political imaginary *prioritizes* black women's negotiations of space and place. As Collins suggests, "Pivoting the center and theorizing from multiple angles of vision … new themes, approaches, and questions become visible" (44). Ultimately, the houses, neighborhoods, and towns Morrison creates and the tight spaces to be found there can be understood as the author's constant engagement with a strategic mode of representation whose ultimate aim is not to say something different about what it means be black in the twenty-first century, but to say a different thing altogether about what it means to be human.

Notes

1. Toni Morrison, *Paradise* (New York: Plume Books, 1997, rpt. 1999), p. 9. All further references to this work are from this volume.
2. The late 1990s saw an explosion of scholarship in the field, led by Doreen Massey and her colleagues at the Open University, who sought to develop "a relational sense of place and space, supported by a rich vein of philosophical enquiry (sic) into why we must take space also to mean dwelling, affinity, immanence, relationality, multiplicity, and performativity" (34) Ash Amin, "Regions Unbound: Towards a New Politics of Place," *Geografiska Annaler: Series B. Human Geography* 86, no. 1 (2004): 33–44.
3. Marco Antonsich, "Meanings of Place and Aspects of the Self: An Interdisciplinary and Empirical Account," *GeoJournal* 75, no. 10 (2010): 119–32.
4. As Tuan makes clear, distinguishing between space and place is a highly fraught process, one that clarifies (partially at least) why some communities thrive and others falter.
5. Jennifer Terry, *Shuttles in the Rocking Loom: Mapping the Black Diaspora in African American and Caribbean Fiction* (Liverpool: Liverpool UP, 2013).
6. Toni Morrison's arrival on the literary scene happened at a time when critics were tremendously concerned with black writing's relationship to the achievement and assertion of voice. Though she was among the first writers to insist upon the importance of place in her work, it was nonetheless an impulse among critics to consider the authenticity of her characters' voices, as if for the first time a writer had captured a way to *sound* black in way that eschewed caricature in favor of substance. By shifting our attention away from voice to consider and place-making in Morrison's fiction, I hope to re-conceptualize voice as a feature of place.
7. Andrew Herod, "The Production of Scale in United States Labor Relations," *Area* 23, no. 1 (1991): 82–8. Cf. also Julie Cidell, "The Place of Individuals in the Politics of scale," *Area* 38, no. 2 (June 2006): 196–203. And Niel Brenner, "The Urban Question as a scale Question: Reflections on Henri Lefebvre, Urban Theory, and the Politics of scale," *International Journal of Urban and Regional Research* 24 (June 2000): 361–78. More

recent scholarship suggests that the idea of scale is highly contested, but the alternative methods of describing its effects are nonetheless resonant in Herod's assessment.

8. I have become increasingly aware of and informed by Erica Edwards' excellent inquiry into the relationship between charisma and political agencyagency, *Charisma and the Fictions of Black Leadership* (Erica Edwards). In her Introduction to the volume, Edwards states, "African American literature has registered the fault lines in black politics since Reconstruction, contesting how the charismatic scenario has often structured black political desire, the social life of black politics, and black political history as a field of knowledge itself. Broadly conceived as the means by which blacks articulate their desires for solidarity, wholeness, nationhood, access to public facilities and distribution of public resources, reparation for collective injury, and/or sovereignty, the term *black politics* encompasses, for my purposes here, a range of informal and formal movements and gestures that have defined black public culture since Reconstruction within black social and religious movements, black nationalist movements, black electoral politics, and black intellectual culture." Edwards' notion that African American expressive culture is a site at which notions of leadership, strategy, and affiliations are contested and managed has impacted my approach to reading Morrison's fiction as political discourse (Kindle version, loc. 107 of 3543).
9. In her book *Barbershops, Bibles, and BET: Everyday Talk and Black Political Thought*, Melissa Harris Perry (nee Harris-Lacewell as her name appeared when the book was published) seeks to demonstrate that there, "are spaces where African Americans jointly develop understandings of their collective interests and create strategies to navigate the complex political world. These strategies are best understood as ideologies, tied to a black intellectual tradition and alive in contemporary African American public opinion. The study of everyday talk in spaces of ordinary black life provides a framework for understanding what African Americans think and the mechanisms of how black people develop political attitudes" (p. xxii).
10. As Lipsitz observes, "When I say that racism 'takes place' I mean it figuratively in the way that historians do, to describe things that happen in history. But I also us the term as cultural geographers do, to describe how social relations take on their full force and meaning they are enacted physically in actually places" (5).
11. I would be remiss if I did not acknowledge the importance of Hortense Spillers landmark essay, "Mama's Baby, Papa's Maybe: An American Grammar Book" to this assertion. Spillers' essay, read as a corrective to what she terms as "Moynihan's fiction," which argued that "black males should reign because that is the way the majority culture carries things out…" She notes further:

> But I would make the distinction in this case between "body" and "flesh" and I impose that distinction as the central one between captive and liberated subject-positions. In that sense, before the "body" there is the "flesh," that zero-degree of social conceptualization that does not escape concealment under the brush of discourse, or the reflexes of iconography."

And she concludes:

> Even though the European hegemonies stole bodies—some of them female—out of West African communities in concert with African "middlemen," we regard this human and social irreparability as high crimes against the flesh, as the person of African females and African males registered this wounding. If we think of the "flesh" as the primary narrative, then we mean its seared, divided, ripped-apartness, riveted to the ship's hole, fallen, or escaped overboard.

Cf. Hortense Spillers, "Mama's Baby, Papa's Maybe: An American Grammar Book," in *African American Literary Theory: A Reader*, ed. Winston Napier (New York: NYU Press, 2000), 257–79. In thinking about Baby Suggs' assertion, "Here…, in this here place, we flesh…," then, I see her as returning the idea of black flesh back to its original starting point; the Clearing is distinguished by its devotion to facilitating acts of self-recovery that are not only spiritual but corporeal as well.

12. I am mindful, of course, that Morrison's fourth novel, Tar Baby is set for the most part on an island in the Caribbean, but even there, life in some version of the North, be it in the U.S. or Europe, weighs heavily upon what unfolds in the book.
13. In an earlier version of this manuscript, I stated "Though African American womenmen, women writers like Morrison have been credited with modeling a feminist identity politics which seeks to contravene forms of oppression that occur at the intersection of race, gender, and class, such characterizations rarely insist that works by African American women writers are assertions of political imagination concerned with how black communities as a whole seek to strategize about the exercise of power and how it resonates across public and private registers." Though I meant to invoke the practice of cordoning off black women's intellectual practice from mainstream (e.g. masculinist, patriarchal) black political thought, what I failed to consider was how such a statement obfuscated the ways a black feminist analytic is *by definition* an assertion of political imagination that should be understood as transforming our understanding of how communities work (or don't work) by collapsing the centrality of black male experience as the signification of powerlessness and oppression and placing female experience squarely in the center of the critical gaze.

PART I

North

CHAPTER 2

Held in the Thrall: Morrison's Southern Men and the Arrested Motion of Tight Space

Well, how do colored people get where they want to go?
—Toni Morrison, *Song of Solomon*

Macon Dead, Joe Trace, and Son Green can each be understood as figures held in the thrall of aspiration, consternation, and rage, the by-products of an overriding sense of estrangement. As such it would be easy to infer that these particular characters are synonymous with failure. But taken together, these characters can also be said to constitute Morrison's heuristic of masculine success; each is secure in who they are, or think they are, dedicated to following a specified course of action, and undeterred in the face of disapproval aimed at them from inside the family or out in the community. However, their behaviors give credence to assertions that masculine success rarely translates into behaviors that enrich the community as a whole.[1] Though the freedom they seek is recognizable within the space of African American expressive culture, it is the product of individual endeavor that takes the shape of materialism, hubris, abjection, or consumption. As southern migrants victimized by relentless instantiations of trauma, these three characters, along with the characters discussed in Chap. 3, ultimately sustain the very systems of domination they hope to thwart.[2]

In this chapter and the one that follows, I will move across Morrison's body of work in order to focus attention on what I refer to as her

H. Beavers, *Geography and the Political Imaginary in the Novels of Toni Morrison*, Geocriticism and Spatial Literary Studies,
https://doi.org/10.1007/978-3-319-65999-2_2

"Southern men." In light of the remainder of the book's focus on a single Morrison text, the plan for the first two chapters of this study calls for traversing across several of her novels, paying special attention to works published prior to or just after *Beloved*. In this chapter, Macon Dead, Son Green, and Joe Trace help us to understand how Morrison's portrayal of performances of black manhood and the anxieties they occasion, ultimately proves to have consequences beyond their individual circumstance. Further, Morrison's Southern men offer an effective way to illustrate the workings (and limitations) to be found in tight space and the "arrested motion" I refer to in this chapter's title is meant to suggest that what seems, on its face, to be immobility is actually much more complicated. As I will demonstrate Macon, Son, and Joe are all *in motion*, but each discovers that there is a distinct difference between *motion* and *progress*.

Hence, in their struggle to navigate tight space, these characters actively, if not intentionally, inhibit communal progress. As I conceptualize it, tight space is generated out of a traumatic injury that creates a geography of estrangement.[3] Be it a house, a neighborhood, a town, or figurative location of the North, tight spaces are superimposed over the spatial and domestic geographies these characters inhabit. As black men with ties to the South, the tight spaces enclosing Macon Dead, Son Green, and Joe Trace and the strategies they employ to navigate them take on a range of configurations. As one might imagine, the claustrophobic nature of tight space induces them to find ways to project the illusion of mobility, but each succumbs to failures of the spatial imagination. In lieu of ascertaining the actual source of the tight spaces enclosing them, their aim of destroying the figurative cages confining them leads to physical forms of havoc that endangers the entire community.

Though each character is preoccupied with the effort to eradicate tight space and discover new forms of mobility, Morrison takes care to remind us that the white supremacist political imaginary is at work to thwart their designs. Indeed, rather than viewing Morrison's depiction of these characters as a polemic inveighing the shortcomings of black men, this chapter seeks to build on Susan Neal Mayberry's assertion that "Morrison's treatment of her male characters becomes a key to her success in countering the temptations of exclusionary feminism" (4). What this suggests is that even as Morrison often portrays trinities of black women, she does so, not to insist that such configurations are preferable or inevitable, but rather to insist that communal spaces free of patriarchal hegemony lead to radically different outcomes.[4] Inevitably, though, communities segregated along gender lines are neither preferable nor advantageous.[5] This chapter's focus on men is ultimately an effort to parse Morrison's belief that African American communities are models of interconnectedness; communal health is a product of symbiosis and interdependence that lead to the burdens of power and responsibility being borne equally by both men and women.

In order to foreground the behaviors unique to the three men treated in this chapter, it is useful to juxtapose the strategy employed by Pilate Dead, one of Morrison's most enduring female characters. This character is distinguished by her willingness to do the necessary work of self-maintenance and recuperative healing that leads to a healthy sense of place. By comparison, the black male characters to be discussed are prone to defer doing the necessary work because the tight spaces that enclose and estrange them prevent the improvisatory, political, and wholistic forms of critical thinking required to reconcile the quest for manhood with liberatory praxis. Consider, then, the epigraph above and the way it implies liberation is often a product of consensus. As such, it invites us to think about *movement* as a duality: the body in motion and the mobilization of a group or community for an expressed purpose. Though Pilate has very practical reasons for asking the question, it resonates at a collective level because it evokes both process and progress. And the answer to the question ("Ain't supposed to go nowhere") reminds us that bodies cannot achieve motion unless they can overcome the "friction of distance" and subsequently generate sufficient momentum to sustain it.

The momentum necessary to invent alternative imaginaries requires a change in habits of judgment. Thought of in relation to the notion of place, the characters discussed in this chapter are often distinguished by their propensity to understand place as an opportunity to impose their will to achieve individual ends.[6] Another way to characterize what it means to navigate tight spaces is to think about the geography of estrangement, where habits of judgment, systems of scale, and concepts of place intersect. [7] If Toni Morrison's fiction routinely portrays black communities seeking a way to "get where they want to go,"[8] the three southern men in this chapter dramatize habits of judgment that complicate the meaning of topophilia (Yi-Fu Tuan names perception, attitude, value, and world view as key aspects of topophilia). And he goes on to propose that topophilia may be a tactile phenomenon, where the individual may delight in the feel of air, water, earth, or other sensual events that bring pleasure.[9] Though these characters embody a vexed sense of place, it would be inaccurate to conclude that they are ignorant about their condition or that they eschew mounting a critique of their circumstance.[10] They are prone, however, to couch their responses to oppression solely in terms of race; believing that difficulties can be ameliorated simply by nullifying (or aping) white men's authority and influence. As we will see, these characters are conditioned to meet force with force, as if guile and evasion are outmoded and outdated weapons of limited effectiveness. In light of this narrow-minded view, we would do well to remember that. Morrison's investment in these characters reflects the notion that successful acts of place-making are often the consequence of a hard won victory.[11]

With her prized geography book and rocks collected from everyplace she's been, *Song of Solomon*'s Pilate Dead is a character whose difference is signified by absence (e.g. a navel, a husband, material possessions).[12] Recalling how her difference has resulted in banishment, one might readily assent to viewing Pilate as a symbol of estrangement. But such a position is refuted by the details Morrison provides to understand her. As a character whose name is folded in a box dangling from her ear and whose unstable circumstances lead her to ruminate on how she wants to be in the world, Pilate is the embodiment of resourcefulness and purpose:

> When she realized what her situation in the world was and would probably always be, she threw away every assumption she had learned and *began at zero*. First off, she cut her hair. That was one thing she didn't want to think about anymore. Then she tackled the problem of trying to decide how she wanted to live and what was valuable to her. When am I happy and when am I sad and what is the difference? What do I need to know to stay alive? What is true in the world? (149, my italics)

Pilate's willingness to "thr[o]w away every assumption and beg[i]n at zero," indicates a method for positioning herself in the world through acts of self-critique and reimagining. Just as the name dangling from her ear signifies a commitment to preserving her identity and protecting it in a world that is hostile because she is both black and a woman, the geography book she carries indicates that she has been "marked to roam the country, planting her feet in each pink, yellow, blue, or green state" (150). However, the book's deeper resonance may lie in Pilate's "deep concern about human relationships" (150), which gestures toward the field of humanistic geography and its effort to understand "the weaving together of social relations and human-environment interactions" as it occurs within the affective space of experience in order to create what Paul C. Adams, Steven Hoelscher, and Karen E. Till refer to as "textures of place" (xiv). One comes to understand the texture of place, as Yi-Fu Tuan reminds us, by acknowledging the importance of experience, which "implies the ability to learn from what one has undergone. To experience is to learn; it means acting on the given and creating out of the given" (9). Pilate's concern for others is grounded in the experiences of her girlhood and can be traced to her birthplace, Lincoln's Heaven, where "she had been treated gently by a father and a brother" and taught "a preferable kind of behavior" (150).[13]

Pilate's question about black mobility, placed in proximity with the process she uses to imagine a sense of purpose indicates that a strong sense of place is often coterminous with assertions of the political imagination. Refusing to be bound by conventional notions of place, Pilate's unconventionality involves rejecting the idea that life and death are radically opposed states of being. "Ain't nothing natural about death," she informs her sister-in-law, Ruth, "It's the most unnatural thing they is" (140). Pilate's belief, that "people themselves," should decide if they want to live forever, is radical in its own right. It is a belief buttressed by her sense that people "die when they want to and if they want to. Don't nobody have to die if they don't want to" (140). Though she has seen her father murdered by white men who coveted his land, she sustains a relationship with him across the conventional boundaries delineating life and death, which reflects her sense that "there was nothing to fear" (149). The "close attention [she pays] to her mentor—the father who appeared before her sometimes and told her things," means that neither he, nor she, has allowed death to interfere with their relationship. Resourced in this way, Pilate has no concept of what it means to be trapped in tight space and as the geography book is meant to suggest, her entire life is built around an unimpeachable form of topophilia. Its practicality notwithstanding, her radical outlook sets her apart from the men who constitute the focus of this chapter. Their inability to master their fear leads to habits of judgment that underwrite beliefs and behaviors that are, from a communal standpoint, not the least bit preferable.

It is important to note that a fair number of Morrison's characters have Southern origins (e.g. they have lived there or have parents from there), which means they have each wrestled with the question of identity, starting, with what might easily serve as a second epigraph, "Niggers get their names the way they get everything else—the best way they can" (88).[14] What we find is that Macon has been orphaned, Joe has been abandoned, and Son has adopted a lifestyle borne out of his status as an exile that requires a fluid approach to identity. In their distinctive ways, each character engages the question of "how…[black folk] get where they want to go," but none can be said to experience a sense of place. Indeed, in their efforts to manage their estrangement, they confuse topophilia with its opposite, topophobia, which sabotages their ability to engender a meaningful sense of place because they equate place-making with recompense for past injury.

But their topophobia is heavily informed by their pursuit of perfectability. This is by no means an easy conclusion to reach; each character displays tendencies that contribute to communal forms of dystopia. And if utopia is what they seek, it is one largely characterized by anti-social behaviors whose main goal is solitude or, the ability to conduct their affairs with a modicum of interference. Their past histories of trauma and betrayal would also seem to make them ill-suited for the kind of visionary, forward thinking necessary to imagine the future as a prominent break from the present.[15] But because their belief in perfection intersects with their past trauma, it becomes the engine of destructive forms of single-mindedness, inhibiting meaningful contact with others, as if reliving their original injury becomes its own form of redress. Because tight space links trauma and estrangement, the three characters treated in this chapter reflect Morrison's sense that "the damage done to her people—damage rooted in their history of enslavement—is at the same time the condition of their radical freedom" (9). Their estrangement from family, community, and self is evidence of Morrison's desire to achieve in her fiction what the blues accomplishes in music, namely to adopt a philosophical posture in which the *act of expressing pain* or, as Ralph Ellison described it, "fingering the jagged grains" is ultimately a gesticulation toward healing. As a writer whose intentions are undeniably political, Morrison fiction might be said to eschew a diagnostic posture in favor of a speculative one that requires her to "probe racial experiences that are painful to the touch."[16]

As it ranges across Morrison's work, this chapter focus on her southern men is the first stage of a critique of how the effects of the patriarchy, sexism, and misogyny endemic to hegemonic manhood are portrayed in individual works. As I examine each character, my analysis begins by looking at the circumstances that produce their names. Beginning with Macon Dead, we find that his ongoing cycle of expenditure, acquisition, and leverage can be traced to the bureaucratic error that resulted in the family name. Bearing "free papers," authored by a drunk Union soldier, Macon Dead Sr. (we later find that his original name is Jake) is an ex-slave literally written into being through an act of bureaucratic inscription that erases his past. Both Macon and Milkman are heirs to this legacy: land and title as manifestations of the self. For example, Macon's belief that owning self means owning people recapitulates, rather than repudiates, antebellum slavery. According to Railroad Tommy, Macon will never be a figure of wealth and influence on the order of Gilded-Age industrialists such as Andrew Carnegie, John D. Rockefeller, or Andrew Mellon, but he is nonetheless feared in the black community on the Southside because he owns the deeds to the homes in which blacks reside and is unmoved by their hardship. In the North, he has become a newer, more insidious turn on the proverbial "house nigger." And yet Macon Dead, Jr. cannot help but wonder if

> he and his sister had some ancestor, some lithe young man with onyx skin and legs as straight as cane stalks, who had a name that was real. A name given to him at birth with love and seriousness. A name that was not a joke, nor a disguise, nor a brand name. But who this lithe young man was, and where his cane-stalk legs carried him from or to, could never be known. No. Nor his name. His own parents, in some mood of perverseness or resignation, had agreed to abide by a naming done to them by somebody who couldn't have cared less. (18)

Believing that his identity is a product of a "literal slip of a pen," Macon's relationship to lineage is fabricated out of miscalculation. Where migration represents an opportunity to reimagine the self through a new form of spatial awareness, Macon's desire for "a name that [is] real," set against the bureaucratic error that renders his name a joke, means that despite cutting all ties with the South, the fact that he owns houses in an area of town known as Southside signals his failure to escape from it. Indeed, the act of misnaming is the product of a Union soldier's error, symbolizing an instance of Northern betrayal that inflicts an injury on Macon that he feels every time he, or someone else, utters his name.

But we come to understand Macon and his relationship to place by casting backward into his past where we discover that his iteration of tight space lies in marked contrast to life on his father's farm. With its one-hundred and fifty acres, its stream, fruit trees, and wild game, the farm is the one place where Macon would have had no need to make acquisition an end in itself. There would have been no need to accumulate property or engage in destructive forms of speculation because the farm, as the result of his parents' effort to transform their freedom into place, would have meant a radically different orientation to spatialized identity.

We cannot understand this, however, unless we return to the moment when Macon Dead, Sr. received his name. When the former slave endeavors to register as a freed person, Macon Jr. relates, he steps up to the desk where the Union soldier serving as clerk is drunk:

> He asked Papa where he was born. Papa said Macon. Then he asked him who his father was. Papa said, "He's dead." Asked him who owned him, Papa said, "I'm free." Well, the Yankee wrote it all down, but in the wrong spaces. Had him born in Dumfries, wherever the hell that is, and in the space for his name the fool wrote, "Dead, comma Macon." But Papa couldn't read so he never found out what he was registered as till Mama told him. (53)

But rather than telling him to change it, Singing Bird, the woman he meets on a wagon headed north, looks at his free papers and the name and says, "it was new and would wipe out the past. Wipe it all out" (54). In this instance, the name "Dead," is symbolic of how Macon, as freedman gets to "begin at zero," move forward in history, and shed the burden of the past. So that even when his inability to read road signs lead to a wrong turn that puts him in Pennsylvania, far from his original destination of Boston, Macon Dead's name functions as a talisman against the misfortune that arises when plans go awry.

Macon Dead, Sr. proceeds to develop a meaningful sense of place whose most important feature is that it is the physical manifestation of the destiny that came with accepting his name. Relating the story to Milkman, which "he had not said [to anyone] for years," Macon goes on to describe his boyhood:

> He called our farm Lincoln's Heaven. It was a little bit of place, maybe a hundred and fifty acres. We tilled fifty. About eighty of it was woods. Must have been a fortune in oak and pine; maybe that's what they wanted—the

> lumber, the oak and the pine. We had a pond that was four acres. And a stream, full of fish. Right down in the heart of a valley. Prettiest mountain you ever saw, Montour Ridge. We lived in Montour County. Just north of the Susquehanna. We had a four-stall hog pen. The big barn was forty feet by a hundred and forty—hip-roofed too. And all around in the mountains was deer and wild turkey. (51)

By calling his farm Lincoln's Heaven, Macon Dead offers reason to believe that Lincoln's decision to issue the Emancipation Proclamation need not, as some might have believed, be simply understood as a matter of expedience. As Macon's act of naming suggests, the farm recasts Lincoln's belief that freeing the slaves was a necessary bulwark against the South's military aims. By Macon Senior's reckoning, giving his farm a name that, in its way, gestures toward the *perfection* of Lincoln's political machinations in such a way that Lincoln's Heaven becomes the physical manifestation of a sense of agency, evolving into new kinds of labor and productivity. In keeping with the conceit, Macon inverts racial hierarchy by naming his hinney mule, President Lincoln. "That's what we called her: President Lincoln," Macon says, "Papa said Lincoln was a good plow hand before he was President and you shouldn't take a good plow hand away from his work" (51).

The bounty epitomizing Lincoln's Heaven invites comparison with the Bottom in *Sula*, which begins with "a nigger joke," racist whites play on the freed slave, who is duped into believing the hilly, rocky land looking down on the valley is "the bottom of heaven" and therefore "the best land there is." The Bottom is a synecdoche for all the economic advantages produced by the white duplicity that determines that they should receive the lion's share of everything. As "nigger joke," the Bottom is the antithesis of utopia. But Macon, who "worked right alongside" his father all through his childhood understands what it means to have a genuine sense of topophilia. Thinking back to a time before he owned his "hearse," he remembers the days when "just starting out in the business of buying houses, he would lounge around the barbershop and swap stories with the men there" (52). While describing Lincoln's Heaven to Milkman, Macon's topophilia is restored in a moment when "every detail of that land [is] clear in his mind":

> ...the well, the apple orchard, President Lincoln, her foal, Mary Todd; Ulysses S. Grant, their cow; General Lee, their hog. That was the way

> he knew what history he remembered. His father couldn't read, couldn't write, knew only what he saw and heard tell of. But he had etched in Macon's mind certain historical figures, and as a boy in school, Macon thought of the personalities of his horse, his hog, when he read about these people. His father may have called their plow horse President Lincoln as a joke, but Macon always thought of Lincoln with fondness since he loved him first as a strong, steady, gentle, and obedient horse. (52)

Several issues are clarified regarding Macon's past identity here. First, his father's decision to name the farm animals after Lincoln and his wife along with two Civil-War generals means that he has taken the intangibility of a historical narrative that largely excludes him and turned it into the vehicle for advancing his own personal narrative. Whereas the conventional history Macon learns in school constructs blacks as the objects of Lincoln's benevolence, his experience with the animals on his father's farm means his relationship to American history is a function of his affective ties to a geographical location. Recalling the spring when the family hog, General Lee, was slaughtered, Macon remembers, "General Lee was all right by me…Finest general I ever knew. Even his balls was tasty. Circe made up the best pot of maws she ever cooked" (52). The Dead family consuming all the edible parts of a hog named for the general who led the Confederate Army once again symbolizes the act of dismantling the past, making it an integral element of what is to come. For Macon, his time at Lincoln's Heaven is characterized by its reversal of the valences of power, historical narrative, and space.

Second, prior to acquiring his wealth, he was a member of the community, who valued the barbershop as a communal space of storytelling and camaraderie. While the north is a null space for many black migrants, Macon's initial experience is wholly positive and affirming. Talking about "the land that was to have been his," means that at one point in his life, he did have a sense of futurity that did not involve exploitation and greed. Macon's hatred of the North, the fact that his life there is a product of his displacement from Lincoln's Heaven reflects an insatiable topophobia that can only be fed by the acquisition of more property. Through the character of Macon Dead, Jr., Morrison shows how his physical displacements accompanies trauma and occasions the tight space he occupies as an old man, one structured on the basis of compensation.

Macon's tight space is equally typified by his fall into a state of cultural illiteracy and rootlessness. His story about Lincoln's Heaven is important because it demonstrates that the part of the story that Milkman knows, that "somebody shot [Macon's] father. Five feet into the air, (42)" is also when Macon misinterprets the narrative. Remembering that it took his father "sixteen years to get that farm to where it was paying. It's all dairy country up there now. Then it wasn't. Then it was...nice" (53), Macon believes that everything "bad that ever happened to [his father] happened because he couldn't read" (53). He sees his father's death as the point of demarcation between the life he could have had and the life he settles for. But more importantly, in seeing his father's murder, he believes he has witnessed his father's *death*. In contrast to Pilate, Macon is like his father, who "only knew what he saw and heard tell of," and interprets death as a state of finality. But here recall Pilate saying that death is a choice; Macon's miscalculation is that in a world governed by materiality, whether it be a piece of paper, a key, or a house, verifies his sense that his father's illiteracy contributes to his demise. His estrangement from Pilate can be traced to this fundamental difference in outlook.

Macon's effort to recover his lost sense of place requires that his location in time and space be structured on a grid of ownership. He expresses this ideology when he tells Milkman, "Own things. And let the things you own, own other things. Then *you'll own yourself and other people too*" (55; my italics). Macon's identity is verified through the accumulation of property and other material acquisitions, but again it indicates his faulty interpretation of Lincoln's Heaven, where the name his father embraces leads to the naming of other things, evidence once again of the efficacy of viewing his new name as a rebirth. By contrast, Macon Jr. has moved beyond the idea of self-ownership—admirable in itself, perhaps—to the more destructive idea of property as the primary index of human worth. His control over a small collection of dilapidated houses that he rents solely to blacks less financially endowed than he, is an indication of his complicity with the segregationist tactics employed by whites in northern cities and the sad truth that Macon *is*, for all practical purposes, dead. Unlike Pilate who embraces the idea of returning to zero in order to imagine the future, Macon's life is nothing more than a self-willed act of nullification. In this sense, he has made a radically different choice than both his father and his sister. Contrary to Macon's reliance on verifiable truth (e.g. his father's body), his father has chosen to persist as presence and guide for Pilate, and appears to her shortly after his murder, "wearing the coveralls and heavy shoes he was shot in"

(150). Subsequently, he comes to her "in a white shirt, a blue collar, and a brown peaked cap. He wore no shoes (they were tied together and slung over his shoulder), probably because his feet hurt, since he rubbed his toes a lot as he sat near her bed or on the porch, or rested against the side of the still" (150). And when he tells her "You can't just up and leave a body," we find out he holds the key to the family's history.

As a form of social death, Macon's materialism is fraught with the silences that shroud his father's "dead" body and evidenced when the Dead family go out for a Sunday drive. The neighborhood blacks refer to his beautiful green Packard as "Macon Dead's hearse." As the car rolls "slowly down Not Doctor Street, through the rough part of town… over the bypass downtown, and head[s] for the wealthy white neighborhoods, (32)" it symbolizes Macon's longing to escape his proximity to the dingy, dilapidated homes he owns in Southside. In 1936, at the height of the Depression, the Dead family's prosperity means their weekly sojourn anticipates the exodus of the black middle-class out of communities like the Southside for more comfortable and luxurious neighborhoods occupied by whites. But more immediately, the Sunday drive declares Macon's contempt for blacks of lesser means, as well as the unconscious way he equates wealth and freedom.

> Some of the black people who saw the car passing by sighed with good-humored envy at the classiness, the dignity of it. In 1936 there were very few among them who lived as well as Macon Dead. Others watched the family gliding by with a tiny bit of jealousy and a whole lot of amusement, for Macon's wide green Packard belied what they thought a car was for. (32)

With an identity so contingent on materialism, the "amusement" the Packard creates is ironic because for all the ways the car signals Macon's rise, it likewise marks a descent that severs his ties with people. In a town where a large portion of the population has southern origins, Macon's replacement of President Lincoln's mulepower with George and Will Packard's horsepower becomes a parody of motion:

> He never went over twenty miles an hour, never gunned his engine, never stayed in first gear for a block or two to give pedestrians a thrill. He never had a blown tire, never ran out of gas and needed twelve grinning raggle-tailed boys to help him push it up a hill or over to a curb. No rope ever held the door to its frame, and no teenagers leaped on the running board for a

> lift down the street. He hailed no one and no one hailed him. There was never a sudden braking and back up to shout and laugh with a friend. (32)

As Morrison describes the car, it "ha[s] no real life at all," and thus symbolizes how Macon's version of masculine success is summed up by his car, the keys to the houses he owns, and the tight space that squeezes all the life from the women in his family.

In spite of his memory of Lincoln's Heaven, with its failed promise of an endless bounty, Macon's greed nullifies his influence and stature, as signified by his belly's "sagging paunch" (63).[17] His marriage to Ruth is a matter of economic expediency, foregrounding patriarchy, caste politics, and class-consciousness.[18] In his view, the "real" world is purely speculative, a matter of acquiring leverage and sustaining it. But he fails to recognize the discursive underpinnings of this sentiment. Because he sees Lincoln's Heaven as a utopian space, Macon's topophobia results from his sense that his family was cheated out of paradise. However, his father's ongoing relationship with Pilate suggests that kinship transcends property and ownership.

In the case of *Jazz*'s Joe Trace, his name is self-generated, but it reflects despair rather than self-assertion. "I was born and raised in Vesper County, Virginia, in 1873," Joe states, "Little place called Vienna" (123). Though his story resembles the beginning of the classic slave-narrative, unlike Frederick Douglass, who states his confusion on the question of the month and year of his birth, Joe's certainty regarding the year and place of his birth is mitigated by being abandoned by his parents. Taken in by the Williams family as an infant, Ms. Rhoda tells Joe "You are just like my own" (123). Despite being young, Joe realizes that the word "like" signifies that though she did not give birth to him and treats him like he belongs, her use of the word nonetheless signifies his status as orphan. And so when Joe inquires as to the whereabouts of his parents, she replies, "O honey, they disappeared without a trace." Hearing this, his parents' disappearance comes to stand for *how* he means in the world. "The way I heard it," he states, "I understood the 'trace' they disappeared without was me" (124). Thus, when he begins school and recognizes that he "had to have two names," he adds the "Trace" to his first name to become Joe Trace.

But this act of self-naming, unlike that moment when Frederick Bailey becomes Frederick Douglass, is predicated on the belief that his mother will return which makes "Trace" a placeholder for his true name.

Further, as Joe conceives it, "trace" has to function as a verb; in order to sustain the notion that his parents are coming back for him; he must invest faith in the notion that they have the requisite tracking skills to "re-trace" their steps and find him. Hence, even as he understands that Ms. Rhoda is his surrogate mother, consider Joe's answer to Victory's question about his real mother's identity when he states, "Another woman. She be back. She coming back for me. My daddy too" (124). Joe's belief that he will be reunited into a conventional model of family constitutes his version of utopia. Estranged from this dream-wish of parental rescue, Joe believes his parents will immediately recognize he belongs to them and his life will finally begin in earnest. But unlike Pilate's decision to begin "at zero," Joe imagines a moment when he will cease to be an orphan and be admitted to a legitimate form of family membership. His abandonment leads him to consider his origin as an instance of erasure, a displacement from the realm of whole numbers. Just as he cannot locate the speck of glass he tried to remove from the side of his foot as a boy, Joe is never able to shed his sense of abandonment. "I don't know what happened to the speck of glass. I never did get it out. And nobody came looking for me either" (125). The minute pain caused by the speck of glass signifies the scale and scope of Joe's perpetual state of injury; though it is not debilitating, it remains lodged in a place Joe cannot locate.

After he names himself and imagines a time when the surname "Trace" will be replaced by his true name, Joe finds a surrogate father in Henry Lestory. Joe declares that he lives by the two lessons Lestory has taught him, one being that "the secret of kindness from white people—they had to pity a thing before they could like it. The other—well, I forgot it" (125). Under Lestory's tutelage, Joe becomes his near equal in hunting skill. In the process, Joe grows "more comfortable in the woods than in a town." and "get[s] nervous if a rail or a fence [is] anywhere around" (126). What is it, then, that overcomes the sense of place Joe finds in the woods?

As it turns out, the first lesson Joe learns from Henry Lestory proves to be a very useful tool for survival in the City, since the "light work" Joe does as a waiter involves doing service for whites whose adherence to the myth of racial superiority leads them to interpret black subservience as a posture that is both legitimate and sincere, rather than as the mask Paul Laurence Dunbar describes in the poem "We Wear the Mask." But the more substantive lesson Joe learns comes when Lestory states, "I taught both of you all never kill the tender and nothing female if you can help it. Didn't think I had to teach you about people. Now learn this: she ain't prey. You got to know the difference" (175).

Joe's inability to recall the second lesson speaks to the emotional and mental incoherence that induces him to go out in search of Dorcas. When Victory and Joe joke, "speculating on what it would take to kill Wild if they happened on her" (175), it denotes that he can only conceptualize a relationship with the woman he imagines as his own mother through the aegis of violence, as if she is a hunting challenge and it no longer matters that she is human. Looking directly at Joe, Lestory insists that even if Wild is "crazy" she may have her reasons for not wanting to live among people, stating further, "You know that woman is *somebody's* mother and *somebody* ought to take care." Lestory's act of signifying fails to have a lasting effect. Hence, the fact that Joe remembers only one of the *four* lessons the hunter's hunter taught him will have profound implications. Joe's estrangement is intensified when he goes on his last solitary quest to find Wild. His failure creates a state of cultural weightlessness that he struggles to overcome.

Place is transmuted into tight space; the topophilia Joe once felt in the Vienna woods is replaced by an overwhelming sense of topophobia. The labor he devotes to abandoning the South is not, as we might expect, a matter of altering his habits of judgment. The last time he searches for Wild and believes he has come upon her hiding place, Joe begs for any gesture that might serve as an acknowledgement that contact with the woman who gave birth to him will verify his *place* in the world. However, failing to receive confirmation, he concludes that he

> loved the woods because Hunter taught him how to. But now they were full of her, a simple-minded woman too silly to beg for a living. *Too brain-blasted to do what the meanest sow managed: nurse what she birthed.* The small children believed she was a witch, but they were wrong. This creature hadn't the intelligence to be a witch. She was powerless, invisible, wastefully daft. Everywhere and nowhere. (179, italics mine)

The blast that he aims at the white oak limbs hanging over his head constitutes an act of symbolic matricide. Though his shotgun is emptied of shells, it is Joe's *desire* to inflict violence on Wild, to confront the fact that she is "everywhere and nowhere," that informsthe act of "hunting" Dorcas. Believing that having a whore or drunkard for a mother would be better than having an "indecent speechless lurking insanity" is reason for Joe to eradicate Wild altogether.

It is an important turn in Joe's narrative that "no one [knows] what it was that permitted him to leave his fields and woods and secret lonely valleys. To give away his fishing pole, his skinning knife—every piece of his gear but one, and borrow a suitcase for their things (106)" to enable the move, first, to Baltimore and, finally, New York. That Joe and Violet's "Baltimore dreams [are] displaced by more powerful ones" (106), might reflect a renewed sense of possibility, but it more likely represents Joe's belief that he is entering a new wilderness in search of prey. Hence, the insanity that results "when the track's not talking to you," means that Joe misapprehends the highly bureaucratic and textualized urban enclave he inhabits for the blank page of the wilderness. As if it is a cipher lacking a code key, the cityscape only has meaning if Joe can project his search for Wild onto it. His description of what happens when he loses the track is telling: "[Y]ou might get up out of your chair to go buy two or three cigarettes, have the nickel in your pocket and just start walking, then running, and end up somewhere in Staten Island, for crying out loud, Long Island, maybe, staring at goats" (130). Of interest here is Joe's use of the colloquialism "for crying out loud," because it demonstrates that the City's idiom has invaded his speech, in a kind of spirit possession. Hence, we might argue that it is the City, not the trail which is speaking to Joe, a frightening thought perhaps, but not altogether far-fetched when we consider how the narrator—in her role as the City's "voice"—thrills at the sight of violence. As the narrator describes it, the excitement of the weekend is a time for, "connections, revisions, and separations even though many of these activities are accompanied by bruises and a spot of blood," as if foreshadowing the gunshot wound Dorcas will ultimately die of at Joe's hands. Note how Joe declares, "But if the trail speaks, no matter what's in the way, you can find yourself in a crowded room aiming a bullet at her heart, never mind it's the heart you can't live without" (130). Joe's "hunt" for Wild, which gets projected onto Dorcas, is reminiscent of Sethe's effort to "outhurt the hurter" in *Beloved*.

The state of estrangement that exists between Joe and Wild (and thus, Joe and himself) recalls Sethe's rage at Schoolteacher and underscores why she and the community become estranged. The manner in which Joe's rage turns inward should be familiar to readers of *Beloved* as he mirrors Sethe's brand of radical individualism. Murdering Dorcas becomes both an affirmation of his tracking skills and the consummation of his desire to eradicate the sense of loss he experiences at not having been mothered, making his version of the self-made man a product of what Richard Slotkin refers to as regeneration through violence. In this sense, Joe's masculine success—which includes initiating and consummating his relationship with Dorcas—rests on an unstable set of assumptions: e.g. moving through city streets is equal to the solitude to be found in the wilderness; the satisfaction of his desire is a problem unique to Joe, a matter of Henry Lestory's woodcraft, not petty jealousy; and finally that the city is indifferent to his actions. As the narrator proves, the gossip Joe's act of murder generates is an end in itself, a new way to conceptualize inside and outside. And finally, the satiation of desire is not, as Joe believes when he initiates the affair with Dorcas, synonymous with escaping the past.

Joe's topophobia for Vienna and the surrounding regions, issues from blaming the victim rather than seeking the cause. Having been made homeless by random acts of white violence back home, he fails to understand that Wild's behavior might, in fact, be the product of a violation so insidious that it renders her incapable of living among people. Morrison's trope of the two-story house is in evidence here. Because Joe is unable to grasp that Wild's injury might involve a story so harrowing that he would relinquish all claims on her attention, his sense of abandonment and estrangement leads him to opt, first, for confrontation that gives way to pleading which in turn gives way to symbolic violence meant to erase her story altogether. Joe's effort to escape the South is correctly read by friend, family, and even Violet, as an inexplicable attempt to leave the one place on earth he feels most himself. But in the wake of his three failed attempts to find the woman he believes to be his mother (and he never gets confirmation that Wild *is* in fact his mother), the South goes from being a point of departure to an aporia that cannot be redressed. As the following chapter will discuss, we see how Joe and Violet's estrangement constitutes a moment when Morrison deploys the trope of the Two-Story House. Joe's state of injury has to be understood in relation to Violet's spiritual malady, created by the suicide of her mother, Rose Dear, and exacerbated by her grandmother's stories of Golden Gray, who becomes a symbol of both idealization and idolization. If reverence for the woods involves an ability to both see *and hear* signs, Joe's self-involvement inhibits his ability to ascertain Violet's pain as anything but an inconvenience and an imposition. In their guise as Harlemites, Joe and Violet's Southernness comes to mean "from there" rather than "of there," which entraps them both in a tight space that reduces the question of "how do colored folks get where they want to go," with a single word answer: escape. But unlike slaves who head North to escape bondage, escape for Joe and Violet does not signify the journey to safety. Their move northward is enclosed in the idea of *escapism*, suggesting a turn from the real toward the fictional.

Tar Baby's Son Green (aka William Green; aka Herbert Robinson; aka Louis Stover) is a man with many names. In his presence, plants thrive, as if he is an Adamic figure, capable of living in—and enhancing—the ostensible paradise known as Isle des Chevaliers. But he is more aptly associated with the emotional volatility of Adam's son, Cain. As an "undocumented" man, Son bears the mark of Cain: like him, Son becomes "a fugitive and a vagabond" (Genesis 4:12) as a consequence of an act of violence inspired by jealousy.[19] His nostalgia for his hometown of Eloe, Florida is the counterweight to Jadine's cosmopolitan lifestyle. Ultimately, like Paul D and Sweet Home in the early and middle stages of *Beloved*, Son fails to recognize that Eloe is more memory than reality. As a man who revels in the joy of receiving his "original dime" (169), Son's nostalgia functions as a counter-balance to Jadine's bourgeois sensibility and thus it has much to do with evading the responsibilities that come with the provisional identity bestowed upon those who *opt into* the body politic. As a character who finds himself in the midst of wealth, we cannot help but equate him in the black vernacular, with a form of racial authenticity that should be comforting and reassuring.

The effort to understand Son Green's place in this discussion has to begin with how he understands himself. "He did not always know who he was, but he always knew what he was like," Morrison writes (165). Given the range of lifestyles and postures Toni Morrison's characters embody, what are we to make of a character who thinks of himself in this way? The most obvious move is to talk about constructions of the self. Unlike the other two characters discussed in this chapter, Son Green is a man constantly in motion; mobility is integral to how he sees the world and his place in it. The self that he imagines is one loosed from the strictures of singularity; what distinguishes Son is his commitment to being who he *needs to be* at any given moment. For example, when he boards Valerian's boat, he walks along the deck "with nothing in mind to say if anyone suddenly appeared." Just as the question of belonging is answered for the other four characters in specific locations, Son's identity remains a product of Eloe, Florida. But having been forced to abandon his life there, he adopts a life of pure exigency. "It was better not to plan," Morrison writes of Son, "not to have a ready-made story because, however tight, prepared stories sounded most like a lie. The sex, weight, the demeanor of whomever he encountered would inform and determine his tale" (5). As Morrison conceives it, Son's existence is improvisatory which means both that he eschews having a pre-figured design for his experience and also, in the way of musical improvisation, he seeks to harmonize with his surroundings. If we think of mainstream social conventions like authenticated identities, meeting contractual obligations and reciprocal behavior as the "melodic" aspects of society, Son embodies the counter-point to melodic structure. The problem with adopting harmony as a personal ethos is that it does not require a set of personal codes that transcend the moment and provide a moral guide for behavior. Son is thus a

> man without human rites: unbaptized, uncircumcised, minus puberty rites or the formal rites of manhood. Unmarried and undivorced. He had attended no funeral, married in no church, raised no child. Propertyless, homeless, sought for but not after. There were no grades given in his school, so how could he know when he had passed? (p. 166)

Son believes there 'was something wrong with the rites,' which denotes his unwillingness to acknowledge the importance of ceremony in favor of a looser approach to everyday experience. But Morrison's play on words, the way "the rites" bears the homophonic imprint of the words "the rights," needs to be taken into account. On one hand, it means that Son rejects the assessment of those who exercise arbitrary forms of power to label what is correct and incorrect while leaving no room for dissent. On the other, it suggests that Son abhors a life defined by conforming to a binding social contract.

While Joyce Hope Scott's assessment of Son as a trickster figure, "an outrageous figure of the margins yet somehow at the center of the tale," is compelling, reading him in this manner has the potential to place Son so far out of the realm of social convention that his behavior can appear illegible in relation to the other characters. However, it should be noted that for all his resistance to convention, Son is cognizant of and adheres to strict definitions of gender hierarchy. Not long after climbing aboard the Seabird II, Son hears women's voices and concludes he is "the only man aboard. He felt it—*a minus something*—which eased him" (7, emphasis mine). Hence, the name *Son* might be intended to signal his subordination under patriarchal authority. The name implies that the man who fathered and raised him wanted to retain his superordinate position and thus have progeny living in a perpetual state of subordination. But it is also suggestive of the Son as successor, as savior, even. In this respect, his presence can be thought of as regenerative.

The Street household seems renewed by his presence, especially after he sheds his dirty clothes and unkempt dreadlocks in favor of a Hickey Freeman suit and a haircut. It is difficult, however, not to recognize Son's sense of entitlement, which is buttressed by the illusion of reciprocity. For example when Sydney tells Son to "clean [his] life up," Son responds by playing to his ego and calling him "Mr. Childs," and "Sir," and asking if he can eat in the kitchen. But the obsequiousness is feigned. Though he says that all he wants is Valerian Street's help in securing a visa and identification, Son's life is based on working outside established channels. Though he pleads *mea culpa* for stealing, Son feels entitled to take whatever he needs, when the occasion requires it. Further, Son is not above reminding Sydney that it is Valerian, and not him, who holds the key to his destiny, stating, "I'm guilty of being hungry and I'm guilty of being stupid, but nothing else. He knows that. Your boss knows that, why don't you know it" (162)? In a perverted sense, Son has informed Sydney that both of them are subservient to Valerian's whim, which he underscores through his use of the word "boss." After he receives consent to eat in the kitchen, Son leaves, "pleased…that Sydney thought he was interested in Valerian's generosity," which indicates that it has all been a ruse and indicates further, perhaps, that what Valerian wants is irrelevant.

Morrison's use of the Tar Baby folktale as a structural cornerstone of the novel's plot, raises the question over and over, who is stuck on who? Is Jadine meant to entrap Son or is Son a trap for Jadine? If we read *Tar Baby* as a love story then the analogue text for *Tar Baby* is Hurston's *Their Eyes Were Watching God*, with its pairing of a middle-class, light-skinned black woman and a dark-skinned, working-class man. The analogy is strengthened when we consider that, like Janie and Tea Cake, few of the people who know Jadine and Son can ascertain the logic underlying the bond between them. This is evidenced during Son and Jadine's trip to Eloe. Son's two best friends, Soldier and Drake, consider what it means for Son to be with a woman like Jadine. At first, they enjoy Son's "presence and his prize woman." In their adoration of Son, they view Jadine as a commodity, "like she was a Cadillac he had won, or stolen, or even bought for all they knew" (254). Eventually, though, they wonder how to situate the relationship within the space of their understanding of how men and women relate to one another in a specific moment in time and space. Because Eloe is their main point of reference, they try to imagine what the future holds for Son and Jadine, leading Soldier to ask her, "You all getting hitched?" When Jadine demurs, Soldier adds, "He's good. You ought to snatch him" (254). Soldier goes on to tell Jadine the story of Son and his dead wife, Cheyenne. Though we have already been privy to Son's version of what happened between he and his wife, Soldier's version puts the relationship in a different light. Feeling competitive, Jadine asks Soldier if Cheyenne was "pretty," and he answers in a manner reminiscent of Jude's description of Sula, "Naw. I wouldn't say pretty. Not bad-lookin', mind, but nothing like pretty" (254). He concludes by saying that Cheyenne "wasn't pretty, but you had to hand it to her though. She had the best pussy in Florida, the absolute best" (254).

What Soldier omits from the story is the part Son has related to Jadine earlier in the novel. Son's version of the story is offered as explanation for his impromptu approach to identity, his sense of dislocation, and his memory of the violence that precipitates it. Unable to attend the funeral of his friend, Frisco, Son has to backtrack and explain why he could not be present to mourn the death of a person of such importance, the man who gave him "his original dime." Characterizing Cheyenne's death as "a mistake," Son has, "to leave Eloe on the run," because he has jumped bail after being charged with second-degree murder.[20] Under Jadine's interrogation, we find that Son, after he comes upon Cheyenne with a thirteen-year-old boy, has driven his car through the bedroom wall of his house. Cheyenne's death is caused when the car explodes and the bed catches on fire. "I pulled her out of the fire," Son states, "but she never made it. They booked me after that" (176). When Son declares he wanted to avoid prison because he "didn't want their punishment, [he] wanted [his] own," his statement recalls the pivotal moment in the Tar Baby folktale, when the farmer throws Brer Rabbit into the briar patch, the place "where he was bred and born." This is underscored when Jadine calls Son "a big country baby," who lives like he was "just born" (172).

When we return to the exchange between Soldier and Jadine, however, we find that he believes Son "Never should have married that woman. That Cheyenne. Every one of us told him that, or tried to. But he did it anyway to his grief and sorrow" (254). What Soldier insinuates is that Son's relationship to Cheyenne should have remained purely physical, which is underscored by Soldier's positive assessment of her sexual prowess, which likely means he is speaking from first-hand experience, making his advice not to marry her self-evident. So that when Soldier looks at Jadine and asks, "Who's controlling it?…The thing. The thing between you two. Who's in control" (255)? His question reveals how the Son/Jadine pairing dramatizes *Tar Baby*'s larger theme and substantiates the argument that Morrison's intention was not to write a love story, but rather to examine the nature of power relations and how they are informed by caste, gender, and class.

So as Soldier probes Jadine about her plans with Son and she seeks information on Cheyenne's relationship with Son, what is revealed is the schism between divergent approaches to inter-personal relationships. But that schism does not denote, as one might expect, the divide between masculine and feminine. Rather, Morrison's deeper intent is to call attention to the difference between myth and rhetoric. In so doing, Morrison's effort to distinguish myth from rhetoric recalls Philip Fisher's assertion that myth is "a fixed, satisfying and stable story that is used again and again to normalize our account of social life" (232). As such, myth clarifies the social dramas unfolding before us by insinuating the importance of symmetrical patterns moving across a temporal grid. By contrast, Fisher insists, rhetoric is "always plural" (232). So that rhetorics diverge from myth because they constitute "a tactic within the open questions of culture. It reveals interests and exclusions."[21] The exchange between Soldier and Jadine, when viewed through Fisher's observations on rhetoric, are tactical maneuvers that reveal how hegemonic masculinity utilizes myth to determine women's subordinate position as a form of common sense.

When Soldier relates that Son "wouldn't know a good woman from a snake" (255), he recalls the serpent's role in causing the Fall of Man. Son's inability to tell "a good woman from a snake," means that he is doomed to make the same mistake over and over again, as if his existence can only be clarified within a mythic frame. But the rhetorical aspects of the exchange are revealed when Jadine challenges that assessment with a put-down of her own. Soldier's rejoinder, "You a hot one, ain't you?" (255) signals that his understanding of relationships rests on the assumption that women who give off the figurative heat of self-assertion must be subordinated. Hence, his question of who controls the relationship intimates that he sees what happens between a man and a woman as a matter of heat transfer, where the man's dominance is the means by which the heat possessed by independent women such as Jadine needs to be subdued or overwhelmed with heat of even greater intensity. Soldier's declaration that "Son don't like control. Makes him, you know wildlike" similarly signals Soldier's incredulity at Jadine's insistence that "nobody controls anybody" (255). Though her defensiveness is disingenuous, Jadine's sentiment, when viewed through her cosmopolitanism, is recognizable. But because Soldier can conceptualize men's relations with women only in terms of heat, Jadine's assertion rests on a thermodynamic dilemma: When two objects with the same relative temperature are in proximity, how can work be done?[22] Knowing that Son has driven his car into the house he shared with Cheyenne, killing her and her lover, Soldier's declaration that control makes Son "wildlike" means that a woman who fails to make Son the center of her world, to love him exclusively, sends him into a state of conflagration.

Son's behavior is a model of expediency in which he resists being controlled by either institutional bureaucracy or wayward women. It means that for all his mobility, he must rely on the underground economy, inconsistent channels of information, and improvisatory zeal to survive. The result is that he exists in a tight space in which he must adopt a regulatory posture toward everything. While the advantage of this posture is that he can endorse or dismiss any epistemological scheme he encounters, it also has negative implications. Unlike Pilate who chooses how she wants to live in the world, based on her interest in others, Son is interested only in himself. His view of the world is a product of "the international edition of *Time*, by way of shortwave radio and the views of other crewmen" on the ships he works. He is "suspicious of all knowledge he could not witness or feel in his bones" (167). Unlike Macon Dead, Sr. whose life in freedom emerges from an act of incorrect documentation, Son is an "undocumented man" who occupies a subjectivity that is situated outside the textual boundaries of conventional knowledge. "The conflict between knowing his power," Morrison writes, "and the world's opinion of it secluded him, made him unilateral. But he had chosen solitude and the company of other solitary people—opted for it when everybody else had long ago surrendered, because he never wanted to live in the world their way" (166). As such, Son rejects the idea that he is answerable to external forms of authority which should make him heroic.[23]

Son's rejection of what he deemed to be the illusion of "making it" leads him to see the efficacy of dangling Jadine out the window to remind her of what constitutes the real, especially when he insists,

> The truth is that whatever you learned in those colleges that didn't include me ain't shit. What did they teach you about me? What tests did they give? *Did they tell you what I was like*, did they tell you what was in my mind? Did they describe me to you? Did they tell you what was in my heart? If they didn't teach you that, then they didn't teach you nothing, because *until you know about me, you don't know nothing about yourself*". (264, my emphasis)

As a member of "the underclass of undocumented men," Son's juxtaposition of academic knowledge and lived experience has a persuasive power suggestive of the attitude that views "book learning" as an instrument of delusion, if not racial disloyalty outright.[24]

Or is it? Son's corrective to Jadine's "incomplete" education is not a narrative that includes male and female experiences in a horizontal configuration. Son asks if college told Jadine what he "[is] like," which reprises Son's talent for mimicry but fails to assert what he stands for. Once again, women are the "minus" he can regard or disregard at his leisure. What denotes Jadine's miseducation is the absence of Son's story from her formal education. Indeed, viewed from a vantage point that eschews a patriarchal, masculinist version of African American experience, Son's claim about Jadine's education is counterfeit; his insistence that she is epistemologically deficient because she was not taught about him is specious and narcissistic. Indeed, Son's resistance to conventional forms of identification, his belief that the United States "seemed sticky. Loud, red, and sticky. Its fields spongy, its pavements slick with the blood of all the best people," means that by fiat his oppositionality rejects inscription into the dominant narrative.[25]

But the level of sympathy Son displays toward Ondine, Gideon, and Mary. Therese, a reflection of working-class solidarity, leads us to discount Jadine's anxieties about Son's unwillingness to conform to middle-class notions of respectability as the sign of her acquiescence to white supremacy. Son's model of history, with its insistence that progress can only be measured by how it honors a recapitulation of the past, is recursive. And because Son adheres to essentialist notions of racial separatism, we fail to locate him within the same system of authority inhabited by Valerian Street. But the character of Son points to the way Morrison dramatizes how black men's cultural nationalism, as it sought to resist white supremacy, ignored the question of male domination altogether. Son's diatribe marks his (and by implication, black nationalism's) anger at being excluded from the master narratives of patriarchy and masculinism. But Son's declarations announce his anxiety regarding a decline in his male authority. What seems on the face of it to be a call for a new order, is simply the insistence that the white masculine narrative expands its perimeter to include black men—provided, of course, that the stories be limited to those featuring heterosexual men who exercise total control.

We come to understand the rhetorical features of masculine hegemony when Jadine enters Valerian's greenhouse and finds Son and Valerian "laughing to beat the band" (127). Morrison's critique of masculine privilege is signaled by the joke that Son tells Valerian about "the three colored whores who went to heaven," and her omission of the punchline, which signals that at a moment when men are bonding across the lines of difference, Jadine is an outsider. Furthermore, the joke has been preceded by Son's pronouncement, "I know all about plants. They like women, you have to jack them up every once in a while. Make em act nice, like they're supposed to" (148). This statement anticipates that moment later in the novel when Son has to "put out [Jadine's] light with his fist" (264).[26] That moment, coupled with the window incident, demonstrates Son's propensity for violence. And it recalls Guitar's rejoinder when Milkman asks him, "Why worry about the colored woman at all?" and he replies, "Because she's mine" (223).

The tipping point in Son's and Jadine's relationship comes when he accuses her of being a race traitor:

> People don't mix races; they abandon them or pick them. But I want to tell you something: if you have a white man's baby, you have *chosen* to be just another mammy only you are the *real* mammy 'cause you had it in your womb and you are still taking care of white folks' children. Fat or skinny, head rag or wig, cook or model, you take care of white folks' babies—that's what you do and when you don't have a white man's baby to take care of, you make one—out of the babies black men give you. You turn little black babies into little white ones; you turn your black brothers into white brothers; you turn your men into white men and when a black woman treats me like what I am, what I really am, you say she's spoiling me. (270)

Morrison's novel, published in 1981, anticipates the rancor that would emerge in the 1990s, when black feminists took pains to call attention to the ways that leadership was a concept synonymous with blackness and maleness. Son's diatribe is distinguished, at root, by his assertion that black women are the main culprits in the sustenance and furthering of the brand of white supremacy that emerged during antebellum slavery. Of particular interest is the manner in which Son insists that the "mammy" is no longer a term associated with a working-class black women located in white domestic spaces; for him, the term is applicable across class lines, with its adherents assuming a variety of aesthetic postures that belie the mammy's stereotypical image and with sufficient social mobility to further their desire to serve as white men's concubines. Moreover, Son points to a definitive fault line in communities of women in which those who treat black men "like what [they are]" are worthy of black men's trust and fidelity. However, in light of Son's resistance to asserting a definitive public identity, which is asserted through the narrator's observation earlier in the text that "he always knew what he was like," what he is saying is that the black woman who aligns herself with what Son characterizes as an exigent form of social posturing is condemned by her emasculating sisters for assuming the role of domineering mother.

As this chapter nears its conclusion, it is important to unpack Son's formulation. What is buttressing his accusation that Jadine's intent is to "have a white man's baby," is the belief that black men are beset on all sides by women whose politics are shot through with maternal desire. Those women who assert themselves against men who, like Son, accuse black women (especially upwardly mobile black women like Jadine) of wanting black men to be eunuchs at worst, and at best, sperm donors recruited to help them make black babies destined to become "white men's babies" (270) are dismissed from his perspective on the world. Arrayed in opposition to these women, however, are black women dedicated to treating black men "like [they] really [are]," who endorse exigent masculinity as the sign of an authenticated form of black manhood. But this schism is a false one, a product of Son's imagination. Indeed, if we make a brief turn back to *Song of Solomon*, we find an exchange between Milkman and his lover, Sweet, after he has discovered that his grandfather, Solomon, "rode the air" all the way back to Africa. After he relates the narrative that he believes confirms—and thereby authorizes—his acquisition of a new form of selfhood, Sweet's question, "But who'd he leave behind," effectively re-opens the closed circle of myth Milkman has entered, in order to insist that male quests are inevitably of a singular, personal nature and as such, family and community are sacrificed.[27]

In short, men like Son, who rejects ties to bourgeois society and, indeed, anything or anyone seeking to confine—or redefine—him are exemplars of vertical acts of place-making.

Son's rejection of social decorum, his insistence that it is "better not to plan," is not, as most of the narrative has asserted, a sign of his outsider status. The accusation he levels at Jadine asserts that he is very much an insider; for all his resistance to being situated within conventional systems of record keeping, he sees himself as definitively inside blackness and authoritative notions of maleness, and he sees himself as a victim of Jadine's machinations to make him white (and by implication a eunuch). Son's exigency needs to be understood within Morrison's critique of the excesses of cultural nationalism. Though we might celebrate his unwillingness to engage in "company shit," Son is nonetheless a man who routinely concludes he has "gone too far." But Jadine's assessment, that Son lacks the ability "to forget the past and do better," proposes that his version of tight space is one in which his hubris makes it impossible to see the inadequacy of his rejection of the justice system's imposition of punishment. Though his exile can be said to be a form of punishment, he has come to see his estrangement as a virtue.

However, this observation is suggestive of the ways tight space can be characterized as a circumstance in which black men's efforts to mobilize the necessary political imagination to liberate themselves in a white supremacist nation ultimately rests on a troubling paradox. Macon, Joe, and Son are each, in their respective ways, alienated from the maternal impulse. Or, put another way, each eschews the opportunity to assume responsibility for or commitment to acts of paternity. Hence, Macon's attempt to abort Ruth's pregnancy, Joe's turn away from Violet when she begins to long for a child of her own, and Son's belief that the only agency black women possess lies in assuming the status of mammy, ultimately signal a resistance to futurity and an unequivocal (and seemingly impregnable) commitment to sustaining past and present in a state of equilibrium. As the next chapter will endeavor to argue, such thinking is fraught with the belief that the community's inability to sustain acts of place-making is intricately linked to southern men's inability to recreate Pilate's decision to "start at zero." As Macon, Joe, and Son are each meant to suggest, zero is not a starting point for them but a null space whose parameters are defined by masculine violence and which find conceptual (if not physical) form in the verticality of the two-story house.

Notes

1. Mayberry goes on to state, "Because of the dual-gendered emphasis of her personal and, however, and because her writing has become increasingly preoccupied with the 'relationships of black men and black women and the axes on which these relationships frequently turn,' all of Morrison's books explore masculinity and masculine types. They also examine the ways in which the stereotypes underlie men's individuation and affect how men and women 'complement each other, fulfill one another or hurt one another and are made whole or prevented from wholeness by things that they have not incorporated into their psyche" (Mayberry, p. 4).
2. Morrison is consistent in her depiction of circumstances in which her characters often utilize the very tools that dehumanized them—e.g. capitalism, difference, power—in the service of dehumanizing others. Indeed, she is often prone to create narratives that feature a minimal number of white characters, even as she underscores the undeniable power of white supremacy.
3. As I noted in the Introduction, tight space can be characterized as being "a product of either individual or collective trauma (if not both), tight space signals a character's spiritual and emotional estrangement from community, an estrangement that inhibits a meaningful relationship to place. Tight space induces strategies that play into vertical configurations of power, where individualism, materialism, violence, and abjection are key components of their confinement."
4. Though we could look at the household of Eva Peace and see a trinity of women whose bond is fraught with conflict, such that Hannah Peace can say of her daughter, Sula, "I love Sula, I just don't like her." Or, in looking at the trinity of women in the Dead household, Ruth, Magdalene, and First Corinthians symbolize the ways that women are impacted by men trapped in tight spaces.
5. As Mayberry states, "Viewed collectively, Morrison's male characters reveal that issues of gender, race, class, and age cannot be segregated; conflicts between African American men and women result not from sexual disease but from cultural dis-ease, the cure for which includes radical structural surgery." p. 14.
6. While Morrison's fiction is not bereft of male characters who engage in acts of selfless conduct (Halle, Paul D., Stamp Paid, Sixo from *Beloved* come quickly to mind, as do Romen, Reverend Locke, Billy, and eventually, Frank Money in later novels), more often than not, their effort to impose their will (or their failures to do so) are solitary gestures, driven by ambition and ego.

7. That so many of these characters fail has much to do with the ways that a variety of systems: economic, cultural, and political are arrayed against them, hampering their ability to create productive notions of home where they are. Domestic geographies are the site at which the social relations these systems occasion, commonly known as the politics of scale, unfold in unpredictable ways in the homes, public spaces, and means of public conveyance Morrison's characters occupy and utilize in their everyday lives.
8. Morrison's characters are firmly situated within the politics of scale, which Julie Cidell characterizes as the "ways in which political contests move up and down" avenues of power (196), whether it be at the local level (e.g. neighborhood or municipal) or in larger arenas of influence (e.g. state, national, or global). But in view of how each character sees their circumstance as a manifestation of identity politics, they have difficulty initiating forms of contentious politics, which Leitner, Sheppard, and Sziarto define as "concerted, counter-hegemonic social and political action, in which differently positioned participants come together to challenge dominant systems of authority, in order to promote and enact alternative imaginaries" (157).
9. As Yi-Fu Tuan argues, topophilia has several key elements that are integral for understanding how the individual relates to a physical location. He names perception, attitude, value, and world view as key terms (see Chap. 1, Note 9). And he goes on to propose that topophilia may be a tactile phenomenon, where the individual may delight in the feel of air, water, earth, or other sensual events that bring pleasure (93).
10. The Duncans go on to cite a number of research studies conducted in the field of humanistic geography in which "identity politics, both progressive and reactionary, [can be] based on attachment to place." They cite another study which explores "the negative externalities associated with the attachment to place arising from a search for distinction that depends on explicit comparisons with other places." They insist that "the nature of attachment to place varies and that such variation should be investigated empirically." While that is obviously not my intent, I do want to suggest that southern men in Toni Morrison's fiction exist in a state of comparison of the places they left in the South, whose aesthetic components remain mired in memory and their lives in the North, which are often heavily circumscribed by the limits to higher states of existence, with boundaries that are constantly policed. Cf. "Sense of Place as a Positional Good: Locating Bedford in Space and Time."
11. Sense of Place as a Positional Good, 42.
12. Toni Morrison, *Song of Solomon* (New York: Plume Books, 1978, rpt. 1987). All further references are to this edition.
13. I link Pilate's process of self-discernment to the geography book because it resonates in the work of humanistic geographer, Yi-Fu Tuan, who writes,

"In every study of the human individual and of human society, fear is a theme—either covert as in stories of courage and success or explicit as in works on phobias and human conflict. Yet no one…has attempted to take 'landscapes of fear' as a topic worthy of systematic exploration in its own right and for the light it may shed on questions of perennial interest: What is it to be human? What is it like to live in the world?" p. 3.

14. Moreover, in keeping with Morrison's propensity to draw on biblical sources, each of the characters embody five of the Seven Deadly Sins. For instance, Macon personifies greed; Cholly embodies sloth, Guitar exhibits anger (or wrath), Joe exemplifies lust, and Son is guided by pride.
15. Indeed, if trauma keeps them tied to the past, how, one might ask, is utopianism part of the equation? It is helpful to think of E. Ann Kaplan's insistence that thinking about trauma makes it necessary to distinguish "different types of trauma, and analyz[e the] different ways people relate to trauma." Kaplan asserts further: "Equally importantly trauma is one's specific positioning vis-à-vis the event. For this reason it is necessary to distinguish the different positions and contexts of encounters with trauma. At one extreme there is the direct trauma victim while at the other we find a person geographically far away, having no personal connection to the victim. In between are a series of positions; for example, there's the relative of trauma victims or the position of workers coming in after a catastrophe, those who encounter trauma through accounts they hear or clinicians who may be vicariously traumatized now that increasingly counseling is offered to people who survive catastrophes. People encounter trauma by being a bystander, by living near to where a catastrophe happened, or by hearing about a crisis from a friend." Cf. *Trauma Culture: The Politics of Terror and Loss in Media and Literature*, p. 2.
16. Given the propensity to categorize Morrison's approach to fiction writing as "magical realism," a term she rejects, it could be that her speculative bent is a way for her to utilize fictional techniques that indicate how the norms of black life differ radically from the norms associated with white life—and thereby asserted as the *norm for human behavior*. As Philip Weinstein aptly puts it, "Morrison's subsequent novels work out how black freedom involves something radically different from the white fantasy of freedom-as-unconfinement—fantasy born of innocence and false to the impediments of creaturely life itself. Rather, the freedom open to her people strenuously engages every obstacle in its path, taking on, as Morrison later puts it in *Song of Solomon*, 'the condition our condition is in (Weinstein, p. 9).'"
17. Here, I find useful Susan Neal Mayberry's characterization of Macon as a "fat cat," whose girth is a product, not of being the engine of economic opportunity, but rather the opportunistic collector of what is discarded or unwanted. He knows, "as a Negro he wasn't going to get a big slice

of the pie," but knows he can collect the pie filling "oozing around the edge of the crust." Mayberry aptly links Macon's greed to a sweet tooth, which means his body could signify another of the Seven Deadly Sins: gluttony.

18. As Bart Landry describes it in *The New Black Middle Class*, in the late Nineteenth and early twentieth century, men like Macon sought light-skinned women like Ruth as evidence of their ambition and increasing worth. Though such gestures were not universal, they nonetheless invite critical assessment of the ways that a wife's proximity to whiteness somehow meant they were destined to become men of influence and status.
19. Son is not meant to be associated with the role of savior, despite the implications of his name, Son is also Morrison's vehicle for challenging some of the assumptions of the Black Power movement of the late 1960s and early 1970s. Though he would like to rescue Jadine from her plight, Son is at root just as self-absorbed as Jadine. Though he is not as materialistic as she, his behavior is often just as reckless, if only because he worships folk culture despite the ways that it fails to accommodate a plurality of viewpoints.
20. Florida law determines that a charge of second-degree is appropriate "when the killing lacked premeditation or planning, but the defendant acted with enmity toward the victim or the two had an ongoing interaction or relationship. Unlike first degree murder, Second-degree murder does not necessarily require proof of the defendant's intent to kill." Cf. http://statelaws.findlaw.com/florida-law/florida-second-degree-murder-laws.html.
21. Fisher writes that understanding rhetorics requires that we "look at the action potential of language and images, not just their power or contrivance to move an audience but the location of words, formulas, images, and units of meaning within politics." Rhetoric, Fisher concludes, is the place where language is engaged in cultural work, and such work can be done on, with, or in spite of one or another group within. Rhetorics are plural because they are part of what is uncertain or potential within culture. *Redrawing the Boundaries: The Transformation of English and American Literary Studies*, p. 232.
22. In thermodynamic terms, work occurs when potential energy is transformed, usually through the expenditure of heat, into kinetic energy. In an open system, heat transfer means that expended energy is replaced. But in a closed system, with a limited store of energy, energy expenditure falling to zero means that the system is beset with entropy.
23. Once again, Douglass' narrative is paradigmatic in terms of its portrayal of a slave physically overcoming an overseer in combat. Rebelliousness in black male characters is often pitched as a necessary component of black manhood. But rebellion is generally not a declaration of anarchy, but

rather a signal that the black male subject is searching for a social structure that will not invalidate his authority.

24. Cf. Robert Stepto, "Distrust of the Reader in African American Narrative", p. 196.
25. Cf. Ross Chambers' argument regarding the efficacy of oppositionality, the manner in which it represents a posture that eschews viewing experience on a grid of winning and losing in favor of a liminal existence that seeks to play opposing views against one another. Reading Son through this lens would confirm Scott's sense of him as a trickster. But my point is that Son cannot have it both ways. He cannot reject a place in a world that values information transfer through conventional forms of media (e.g. schools, television, news organizations, etc.) and then invalidate that world because it does not have the inclination to locate his story alongside conventional historical events. While Son argues for the importance of dissonant versions of history, it is unreasonable for him to propose that Jadine's education needs to acknowledge his particular kind of dissonance.
26. Though the moment of violence dissolves into laughter and reconciliation it recalls the moment in *Their Eyes Were Watching God* when Tea Cake beats Janie after he sees her talking to the color-struck Mrs. Turner and beats Janie as an expression of jealousy. Though it is disturbing to read the exchange between Tea Cake and the other men on the Muck, where they deem Tea Cake "a lucky man," because "Uh person can see every place you hit her" (140). What makes the moment of a piece with *Tar Baby* is Tea Cake's declaration, "Janie is wherever *Ah* wants tuh be. Dat's de kind uh wife she is and Ah love her for it…Ah didn't whup Janie 'cause *she* done nothing. Ah beat her tuh show dem Turners who is boss" (141). The rhetorical function of violence is underscored when Tea Cake brags, "Ah jus let her see dat Ah got control" (141).
27. Cf. Michael Awkward's excellent interrogation of Morrison's effort to "break" the spell cast by the primordial myth of self-discovery. According to Awkward, "Morrison's position as black and female, however, problematizes her relation to myth because of the fact that traditional myths, like most other cultural forms preserved from an andocentric past, tend to inscribe as part of their truth a subordinate and inferior status for women" (486). And he notes additionally that "[c]oncurrent with Milkman's achievement of indispensable awareness of self and culture is Hagar's painful quest to achieve bourgeois American society's standards of female beauty. Indeed, Milkman's and Hagar's gendered situations in a patriarchal capitalist society ultimately delimit their journey's very nature and success" (492).

CHAPTER 3

From Zero to Nowhere: Tight Space and the Topophilia of Violence

Niggers get their names the way they get everything else—the best way they can
—Toni Morrison, *Song of Solomon*

"Well, it is a free country"
"Not yet but it will be"
—Toni Morrison, "Recitatif"

The previous chapter closed with the assertion that the unifying feature in the experiences of Macon Dead, Joe Trace, and Son Green was that each grew up having to contend with dead or absent mothers. I discussed Joe Trace's effort to retaliate against what he comes to believe is his mother's malicious act of abandonment. Scanning *Tar Baby*, we find only a scant reference to Son's mother; for him home is the space occupied by "Old Man," his father, who otherwise lives alone. This leaves Macon Dead, whose extended narration of what it meant to lose his father seems to constitute that moment when the relationship between property (as a material form of inheritance) and community and family becomes disproportionate in favor of the former. However, Pilate's birth coincides with the death of his mother and we are invited to pay close heed to his failure to offer any commentary on its impact on his life. So that even as Macon, Jr. is an active participant in Pilate's upbringing, the narration is silent on

H. Beavers, *Geography and the Political Imaginary in the Novels of Toni Morrison*, Geocriticism and Spatial Literary Studies,
https://doi.org/10.1007/978-3-319-65999-2_3

the quality of Macon Dead Sr.'s life as a widower. His relationship with daughter Pilate continues long after his murder and embodies "undying love" in its most literal form, but we have little to go on as to whether he sustains the resentful attitude toward God that leads him to name his daughter after the man who condemned Jesus Christ to death. Though we are told that Macon Sr. selects Pilate's name from the pages of the Bible at random, his conclusion that it is not an error in need of correction suggests that he sees the death of his wife as a malicious act on God's part. It is important to remember, though, that Macon Sr. was illiterate and so his selection of his daughter's name is not a conscious one; he requires Circe (?) the midwife to inform him of the symbolic importance of his selection. But it is his refusal to make another selection, to find a more "appropriate" name for his daughter that is suggestive of his obstinacy.

Could it be that the death of his wife led the Macon Dead, the elder, to adopt a materialist posture toward Lincoln's Heaven? Once again, he can be contrasted with Pilate, whose decision to "go back to zero" marks her transformation into an individual whose greatest aspiration is evidenced by the final words she utters before her death "I woulda loved more people." His father's anger—through an act of transference—becomes associated in the mind of her brother, Macon, Jr., with land. In other words, Macon's belief that acquiring all the property he can—to make owning things his *raison d'etre*—is an end in itself, reflects his father's unsuccessful attempt to make Lincoln's Heaven into a surrogate space meant to substitute for the absence of his wife. Just as the 8-Rock Men in Ruby make The Oven an object of their idolatry, I am arguing that Lincoln's Heaven becomes the aim of the father and son's idol worship such that the father's death is synonymous with becoming landless and thereby worthless. The fact that his mother's death has already compromised Lincoln Heaven's status as a domestic geography that hinges on a horizontal act of place-making, leads Macon Jr. to conclude that the farm is a null space against which all the property he subsequently acquires is judged.

Building on this assertion, I endeavor to investigate the question of whether tight space eradicates the ability to sustain our physical ties to place. If tight space is "nowhere," I propose that Morrison's Southern men's ability to reassess their circumstances and make decisions that result in horizontal forms of place-making is thoroughly compromised. This chapter's focus on Guitar Bains, Cholly Breedlove, and the 8-Rock Men is meant to be suggestive of the ways that tight space and the two-story house create symbolic architectures that are reliant on acts of violence to authenticate their actions in the space of the real. I am keenly interested in the ways Morrison's characters are prone to defer doing the work necessary for the creation of horizontal place-making because the tight spaces that enclose and estrange them prevent the improvisatory, experimentally political, and wholistic forms of critical thinking required to reconcile manhood and liberatory praxis. Moreover, because they deem manhood to be a closed practice, these characters' inability to set estrangement aside generates forms of topophilia that are antithetical to horizontality as a sustainable mode of belonging. In the case of these men, loving where they are is a contradiction in terms since *where* they are is a product of nullification. In this chapter, I examine several more southern men, specifically, Guitar Bains, Cholly Breedlove, and the town of Ruby itself, as it is conceptualized by the 8-Rock Men. What distinguishes them is their reliance on "exteriorized" behaviors that undermine efforts to constitute the horizontal forms of place-making necessary to sustain the interiority of intimacy.

In the Epilogue of *Invisible* Man, Ralph Ellison inquired, "Can politics be an expression of love," a question which proves to be pertinent to a discussion of *Song of Solomon*'s Guitar Bains. Of the five male characters discussed in Chap. 2 and this chapter, Guitar is the one for whom the question of "how do [black] folks get where they want to go," is most pressing. He comes north out of circumstances similar to the other four characters; we find the same direct line between parental loss and estrangement as we noted in the lives of Macon and Joe. Guitar's topophobia can be linked to a devastating injury that is equally pernicious in its effects. Easily the most politically sophisticated of Morrison's southern male characters, he exercises habits of judgment that lead nonetheless to a destructive form of stagnation. Perhaps more problematic is Guitar's belief that his turn to violence is doing political work necessary for the black community's survival. Seeing his work with the Seven Days as a corrective for the Civil Rights Movement's *agape*-driven mission of social change, Guitar rejects the movement's call for unification across racial lines.

Guitar is a teenager growing up in the 1940s when he meets Milkman Dead. Readers of *Song of Solomon* may have noted the implausibility of their relationship, evidenced when we discover in this chapter that Milkman is twelve when he becomes friends with the 18-year-old Guitar. The six years that separate them turn out to be the hinge that allows their friendship to swivel between Milkman's irresponsibility and

Guitar's single-mindedness and later, between the distrust and estrangement that sends the relationship into a death spiral of murderous violence.[1] But prior to the novel's conclusion, Guitar plays an important role as a vehicle of the plot in the early stages of the work, since it is he who introduces Milkman to his aunt, Pilate. He also provides the necessary contrast to Milkman's self-centered and narcissistic flights of fancy, lending clarity and substance to their conversations. However, if we only use his membership in the Seven Days as the thematic divergence from Milkman's genealogical quest and place him in the roll of foil, we miss an opportunity to discern the ideological labor he is meant to perform. Pragmatically speaking, Guitar's solution to racialized violence against blacks is elegant. But its elegance points to Morrison's rejection of easy solutions; the problem with Guitar's claim that the Days are playing a numbers game, "balancing ratios," and sustaining patrilineal forms of lineage is that for all its facility, it eschews political agency.

Just as the other characters discussed thus far have absorbing stories regarding their names, Guitar's is equally compelling. We find out how Guitar Bains received his name when Pilate asks him if he "plays the guitar any." Guitar talks about the instrument he saw in a window "down home in Florida," offered as first prize in a contest to see who can guess the number of beans in a glass jar. His response, "Not cause I do play. But because I wanted to" (45), reflects both incapacity and unrequited desire. Pilate's offhand comment that Reba could have won the guitar for him because she "wins things," is all the more resonant as a juxtaposition. Reba characterizes her life by stating, "I win everything I try to win and lots of things I don't even try to win." But in light of Railroad Tommy's long list of all the things black men will never have, all the ways they are excluded from the competition before it begins, Reba's characterization could be taken as the source of black men's rationale for distrusting black women; as if a black woman "winning" happens at the expense of black men.[2]

After Guitar's father is tragically killed in a sawmill accident, the sawmill foreman delivers a bag of divinity made by his wife for him and his siblings. When he tells Milkman the story, just describing the candy gives him the dry heaves and it validates his claim that sweets makes him "think of dead people. And white people" (61). This information takes on deeper resonance when, later in the novel, Guitar equates Pilate's "Jemima shoes" routine with his mother's warm response to the sawmill boss after his father's funeral. He remembers "how his mother smiled when the white man handed her the four ten-dollar bills. More than gratitude was showing in her eyes. More than that. Not love, but a willingness to love. Her husband was sliced in half and boxed backward" (224). Morrison's use of free indirect discourse emphasizes that though Guitar was not in close proximity to the catastrophe; he has heard the mill hands relate how his father's severed body is haphazardly placed into the casket for burial, the parts facing each other.

> He'd heard the mill men tell how the two halves, not even fitted together, were placed cut side down, skin side up, in the coffin. Facing each other. Each eye looking deep into its mate. Each nostril inhaling the breath the other nostril expelled. The right cheek facing the left. The right elbow crossed over the left elbow. And he had worried, as a child, that when his father was wakened on Judgment Day his first sight would not be glory or the magnificent head of God—or even the rainbow. It would be his own other eye. (224)

Here, free indirect discourse fixes our attention on this image: his father's eyes locked in an eternally probing gaze, the breath expelled from one nostril to the other, in a cycle of respiration and expiration that dramatizes the renewal of bodily functions, sustaining the defilement of his father's dead body till the Judgment Day arrives. At that moment, his father will be forced to meet his Maker in a dissected state, as if his father's body parts, one half positioned directly across from its likeness, generate the repellant force that results when like encounters like.

The indignity is compounded when his mother accepts the four ten-dollar bills with a gratitude and "willingness to love" that proves to be the source of Guitar's inability to eat sweets, his association of sweets with white people and the dead:

> Even so, his mother had smiled and shown that willingness to love the man who was responsible for dividing his father up throughout eternity. It wasn't the divinity from the foreman's wife that made him sick. That came later. It was the fact that instead of life insurance, the sawmill owner gave his mother forty dollars "to tide you and them kids over," and she took it happily and bought each of them a big peppermint stick on the very day of the funeral. (225)

Guitar's sense of place, signified by the peppermint stick he held at "the graveside, at the funeral supper, all the sleepless night" and finally discards in the outhouse's "stinking hole," is configured around acts of compensation that prove to be more injurious then beneficial. The sawmill owner's notion that his gift will "tide [Guitar's family] over," all but declares that he neither expects, nor is he concerned with facilitating, the Bains family's success. The physical displacement created by Guitar's father's death means that he lives in a state in which he loses the ability to understand the concept of proportionality. He understands that the injury meant to approximate concern for his family's well-being is in truth the public declaration that black lives are synonymous with devaluation and subsistence rather than surplus. But more than this, the incongruence of the response, the fact that the compensation his mother receives comes nowhere near an acknowledgement of his father's importance to the Bains family, makes her gratitude akin to a betrayal. Hence, Guitar's aversion to sweets is a consequence of the trauma inflicted by the white supremacist political imaginary, whose habits of judgment issue from the assumption that even in death, black people are not due sufficient recompense to sustain the important role the deceased played in the family and the community. Further, Guitar interprets the notion that black people should subsist rather than thrive, feeds directly into his sworn duty to "keep the numbers the same."

Though Florida's reputation as a bastion of racial intolerance and terror is rarely discussed in the same breath as Mississippi or Alabama, a conversation between Milkman and Freddie provides further context for Guitar's disaffection. When Milkman asks him if he is from Michigan, Freddie replies, "Naw. Down south. Jacksonville, Florida. Bad country, boy. Bad, bad country. You know they ain't even got an orphanage in Jacksonville where colored babies can go? They have to put 'em in jail. I tell people that talk about them sit-ins I was *raised* in jail, and it don't scare me none" (109, italics in original). Without recognizing it, Freddie voices the logic underlying the televisual representation of black bodies packed into jail cells during the Civil Rights Movement. He also asserts an essential aspect of Guitar's trauma: his mother's unwillingness to elevate principle over expediency orphaned him and, as his murder of Pilate attests, imbues him with a deep resentment of black women.

When Milkman tells Guitar about the sack in Pilate's house containing gold, Guitar's thoughts turn to "what the gold could buy when it bec[o] me[s] legal tender" (179). Rather than thinking of how the gold could help him further the aims of the Seven Days, Guitar fantasizes about "what he would buy for his grandmother and her brother, Uncle Billy, the one who had come up from Florida to help raise them all after his father died; the marker he would buy for his father's grave, 'pink with lilies carved on it'; then stuff for his brothers and sisters, and his sisters' children" (179). Guitar's sentimentality indicates he remains fixed on the idea of seeking adequate compensation for the deprivation and displacement that followed on the heels of his father's death. The guitar in the store, the bag of divinity, and his mother's "willingness to love," are symbols that combine to create a tight space constituted out of unrequited desire and inadequate compensation that can only be negotiated through a constant effort to create the kind of positional alignment—in the form of "racial balancing"—denied to his father.

Hence, when Guitar tells Milkman about his membership in the Seven Days and describes its mission to "keep the numbers the same," he intimates that by committing a random act of murder against a white person he has abandoned any effort to integrate his public and private selves into a complete person. Though he describes the Seven Days as an organization founded on the principle of loving black people, Guitar's belief that violence is a reflection of what he would die for is invalid because he can never lay claim to the acts he commits. One of the most important achievements of African American writing was its insistence that authorship and responsibility were synonymous. The necessity for escaped slaves to obtain documents that authenticated their words, speaks to the lengths required to manifest a self within the space of public utterance.[3] This is verified when Milkman equates the Seven Days to Malcolm X and the Nation of Islam's practice of using X as a surname in lieu of knowing their true names. But where the Nation used the "X" as a placeholder for the African names that were lost when Africans were kidnapped by Europeans, the Seven Days' practice of reducing the identities of its members to days of the week surrenders all claims to any public declaration of blackness' inherent value in time. The Seven Days relies on white supremacy's insistence that blackness is synonymous with worthlessness, which in turn requires its members to uphold the very superiority they claim to abhor. By adopting time and silence as weapons, the Days constitute the assertion that invisibility and anonymity are coveted aspects of racial identity. As a member of an organization whose greatest imperative is to avoid visibility, when Guitar asserts, "I don't give a damn about names," he nullifies his declaration that, "My whole life is love" (159), because loving involves a healthy perspective and the willingness to own it publicly.

Guitar's life is a model of spatial discipline. In his view, whiteness is the ultimate form of otherness, which means that to navigate life in the north, with its more porous boundary separating the black-and-white worlds, he must eschew imagination for a life characterized by its adherence to mimesis. Once he is initiated into the Seven Days, Guitar's life is structured according to the calendar and methods of killing, which come to serve as points on his moral compass. Thus, when Guitar tells Milkman, "I do believe my whole life's geography," he means on one hand that his life consists of mapping his place in the world using the racial atrocities of whites to guide him. As geographer Mark Monmonier points out, however, maps "have three basic attributes: scale, projection, and symbolization. Each element is a source of distortion" (5). Guitar's propensity for violence suggests that he over-determines symbolization. The act of taking the life of a white person by mimicking the method used to kill a black person is a purely symbolic gesture. If the Days are "indifferent as rain," then the true nature of their criminality lies in their unwillingness to participate in the assertion of an alternative imaginary.

Trapped in a symbolic matrix, Guitar cannot embrace his rights as a citizen, concluding that the electoral process is an ineffectual response to injustice lacking in scale. Guitar's inability to countenance the notion that small gestures like voting are multiplicative, small acts that, in a democracy, combine to create large-scale outcomes, leaves him with very little in the way of alternative habits of judgment. Feeling that his manhood is constantly contested, he cannot partake of the resources of the Southside because he must reduce it, for the sake of expedience, to an ever-shrinking universe where his values alone are ascendant.[4] For someone whose entire life is geography, Guitar begins *Song of Solomon* concerned with social relations and the impact they have on the individual's ability to connect with their surroundings. However, Guitar's version of tight space is characterized by his propensity for violence and his aversion to sweets and can thus be productively linked to his estrangement, not only from his community, but from his own sense of purpose.[5]

In his book *Achilles in Vietnam*, psychiatrist Jonathan Shay talks about the shrinkage of the soldier's social space and moral horizon. When this happens, Shay argues, concern for the larger community contracts until it encompasses only one's closest comrades. Hence, when Milkman expresses his fear for Guitar, the response, "That's funny. I'm scared for you too" (161), signals the space growing up between them. Moreover, as the "Sunday man," responsible for avenging black folk killed on the Sabbath, Guitar demonstrates Shay's sense that in a diminished moral-universe, the warrior's ability to distinguish right and wrong is eroded along with his belief in sacred rituals. Because combat trauma "destroys the *capacity* for social trust," Sunday cannot serve as a day of communion.[6]

Though it might appear that Guitar's quest for gold is a product of greed, in actuality the quest is driven by the warrior's indignant wrath. Because he believes himself to be otherwise disenfranchised, Guitar's participation in the Seven Days is inextricably linked to his life in the South as a hunter. As he relates to Milkman,

> I used to hunt a lot. From the time I could walk almost and I was good at it. Everybody said I was a natural. I could hear anything, smell anything, and see like a cat. You know what I mean? A natural. And I was never scared—not of the dark or shadows or funny sounds, and I was never afraid to kill. Anything. Rabbit, bird, snakes, squirrels, deer. And I was little. It never bothered me. I'd take a shot at anything. The grown men used to laugh about it. Said I was a natural-born hunter. After we moved up here with my grandmother, that was the only thing about the South I missed. (85)

With their coded language, exclusionary practices, and strict adherence to codes of conduct, the Seven Days clarify how violence allows the male body to assume material importance in a system of unstable signs (in this instance, whether the black male body is "authentic" in the category of manhood).[7] When Guitar recounts how he'd "take a shot at anything" he invalidates his claim that "his whole life is love," because as a young man "bound to change the rules," he determines that expediency requires that both blacks and whites be targeted.

This relation breaks down, of course, because the Seven Days are built on the inherently circumspect project of trying to flatten the criteria by which we assign value to human bodies in social space. Though their racial essentialism should make the targets unmistakable, the inability to distinguish between inside and outside leaves them room to expand the criteria from random white people killed on the designated day to anyone who stands in their way. Located in the tight space of cyclical violence, Guitar can make Milkman and Pilate the objects of his violent retribution because he assumes the right to delegitimize those forms of black personhood he deems inauthentic within the space of his cause. Not only is this

Morrison's way of articulating the weaknesses of 1960s cultural nationalism (in ways that anticipate the critique she mounts using Son Green), but it also suggests that the black community does not embody a monolithic notion of what constitutes manhood.[8] Whereas Milkman's quest for his name leads him to discover a new relation between the North and the South, violence serves this purpose for Guitar.

The one final observation on Guitar to be offered here is that he embodies what sociologist Deborah Lupton refers to as "edgework,"[9] which is useful for understanding how his sense of purpose occurs at the place where risk and pleasure intersect. It is productive to think about Guitar as a liminal figure, caught between convention and chaos. Remembering that Guitar embraces the status of stranger, he revels in his position straddling the boundary between inside and outside. Torn between his role as warrior and lover, Guitar's sense of place is distinguished as a border identity, whose most salient characteristic is its undecidability.[10] However, as a black man of action, he assumes a privileged vantage point that renders whiteness synonymous with strangeness. According to Lupton, there are two strategies for dealing with those whose marginality renders them strange: anthropophagic and anthropoemic. The former "involves annihilating strangers by devouring them and then metabolically transforming them into a tissue indistinguishable from one's own" (134). While the latter involves "vomiting the [strange] banishing [it] from the limits of the orderly world" and preventing it from entering the lives of those positioned "inside." Guitar's hatred of sweets and white people, where the thought of either literally makes him ill must be balanced against his figurative cannibalism, where in adopting their methods of violence to his own ends, he becomes the equivalent of the white supremacist imaginary which finally leaves him in the place "where black folks are supposed to go": nowhere.

Both this chapter and the preceding one, seek to focus on how black southern men in Toni Morrison's fiction have struggled to find a place to belong, a way to extricate themselves from the tight spaces that confine and confound them. One characteristic shared by Macon Dead, Joe Trace, and Guitar Bains is that each engages in a set of social practices aimed at emancipating them from the past. The point here is not that they succeed, or at least succeed in a way that does not prove to be injurious to others, but rather that for each (and one might include Son Green here as well) their false consciousness is reflected in the belief that the only forms of selfhood worth honoring are those wrought from the hard truths of northern life.

This is in evidence when Railroad Tommy launches into a litany of all the things that Guitar and Milkman will not be able to look forward to in the future. Though it is clear that Railroad Tommy has taken the proceeds of his labor as a railroad man and, with Hospital Tommy, opened a barbershop in Southside, he is clearly aware of the larger world, which is evidenced when he turns to those aspects of life associated with white men who have the economic, social, and cultural capital to have total control not only over their destiny but the destinies of thousands of others, many of whom they will never meet. The scale of their influence and power takes the form of a "private coach with four red velvet chairs," the "special-made eight foot bed," and especially the "governor's mansion [and] eight thousand acres of timber to sell" (60). His point is that for black men not only is the opportunity for such opulence out of reach, it is one of many opportunities that can never be acquired. He continues:

> And you not going to have no ship under your command to sail on, no train to run, and you can join the 332nd if you want to and shoot down a thousand German planes all by yourself and land in Hitler's backyard and whip him with your bare hands, but you never going to have four stars on your shirt front or even three. (60)

All black men can count on, according to Railroad Tommy, is a broken heart and a "whole lot of folly" (60).

Railroad Tommy's perspective reflects Tuan's equation of place and experience. What goes unvoiced is that there may have been a time in his life when he believed all those things black men will never have were within his reach if he worked hard and made progress. But as he confronted the systemic barriers placed in his path simply because of his race, the chasm between ambition and achievement proves to be one that can only be bridged in the shadows, at a greatly reduced scale. Though black men's decision to participate in the underground economy of bootlegging, prostitution, or drugs is a decision to ravage their communities, the lecture Railroad Tommy delivers to Guitar and Milkman is, in fact, the insistence that the tight spaces governing black men's existence, governed by the likelihood that "you never going to have it," is justification for these choices.

Turning to the character of Cholly Breedlove in *The Bluest Eye*, then, we must consider what it mean to achieve a state of emancipation when the most important lesson he has learned is that a sense of place, with its rootedness to family, neighborhood, and community is a contradiction in terms. As with the other four characters, we return to the act of naming. In Cholly's case, when he is only four days old, his mother wraps him in blankets and newspaper and discards him on a junk heap near the railroad tracks. Rescued by his Great Aunt Jimmy, who raises him after his mother runs away, it is she who names him "after [her] dead brother, Charles Breedlove. A good man" (133). But when he musters the courage to ask his aunt about the identity and whereabouts of his father, she tells Cholly that his father's name is Samson Fuller and that he "taken off pretty quick before" Cholly was born. Puzzled as to why he is not named after his father, Aunt Jimmy replies, "What for? He wasn't nowhere around when you was born. Your mama didn't name you nothing. The nine days wasn't up before she throwed you on the junk heap. When I got you I named you myself on the ninth day" (133). She concludes by referencing the biblical figure of Samson, stating, "Ain't no Samson never come to no good end" (133).

Given how things turn out for Cholly and his family, one could say that this is a prophetic moment. And, of course, by the end of *The Bluest Eye*, Cholly has raped and impregnated his own daughter, Pecola, suggesting he is his father's son. Though he has been named after a "good man," Cholly has little in the way of guidance to understand what being a good man means. The closest he comes is a man named Blue Jack, the drayman who drives a wagon delivering grain. Cholly loves Blue, recalling "[l]ong after he was a man…the good times they had had" (134). Blue is a storyteller, full of stories of the Emancipation Proclamation, the ghosts of headless white women, and talking his way out of a lynching. The best time he shares with Cholly is eating the heart of watermelon at a church picnic. For all the pleasure such a moment contains, there is little in the text to suggest that Blue passes on practical ideas about being a man since his main topic is himself. Blue offers Cholly little more than the benefit of vicarious experience.

When we think of how "Cholly," is a variant of the name "Charles," the name signals he is a poor imitation of a man. At the church picnic, waiting for the watermelon to be dashed on the ground, Cholly looks at the father holding the fruit over his head in a manner that signifies his strength and intent and "wonder[s] if God look[s] like that" and concludes, "No God was a nice old white man, with long white hair, flowing white beard, and little mean blue eyes that looked sad when people died and mean when they were bad" (134). Cholly decides that the image of a man holding a melon over his head, "whose big arms looked taller than the trees" and causing the melon to "[blot] out the sun," that it:

> must be the devil who looks like that–holding the world in his hands, ready to dash it to the ground and spill the red guts so niggers could eat the sweet, warm insides. If the devil could look like that, Cholly preferred him. He never felt anything thinking about God, but just the idea of the devil excited him. And the strong, black devil was blotting out the sun and getting ready to split open the world. (134)[11]

Of interest here is Cholly's image of God as a being with "little mean blue eyes," only capable of reacting to death and evil. As Morrison describes it, Cholly's conception of God anticipates his daughter, Pecola's, fascination with blue eyes, but where she interprets them as the instrument of her liberation, the key to a newfound sense of belonging, he sees them as vehicles of either remorse or judgment. As a figure associated with intentionality and pleasure, the devil becomes attractive to Cholly precisely because his ability to blot out the most prominent source of light creates a circumstance characterized by darkness and destruction. Specifically, he identifies most with the devil as the melon hangs suspended in the air because it symbolizes how manhood is most compelling when it holds destiny and anticipation in a state of equilibrium. Consider as well how the image of the man holding the watermelon above his head recalls the image of Samson, as a pillar of strength and confidence, the bringer of death and destruction to the Philistines. But, here, it is important to remember that for all his strength, Samson dies along with his enemies, a figure of resignation, not resistance. Cholly's conflation of Samson and the devil has much to do with what will become his legacy, power that, for all its individual merit, proves injurious to the entire community.

As Philip Weinstein aptly points out, *The Bluest Eye* represents an opportunity for Morrison, to explicate how "the damage done to her people—damage rooted in their history of enslavement—is at the same time the condition of their radical freedom" (Weinstein, 9). Cholly Breedlove, a man taken off a junk heap in a railroad yard, is a character who embodies the qualities of both. His aimlessness makes him the detritus of the community, but his "radical freedom" lies in his utter sense of kinesis. This is evidenced when, after his Aunt Jimmy's death and the episode where he is forced to have sex under the threatening guns of white hunters, he sits on her porch and in the midst of his fear that Darlene might be pregnant realizes that he:

> had to get away. Never mind the fact that he was leaving that very day. A town or two away was not far enough, especially since he did not like or trust his uncle, and Darlene's mother could surely find him, and Uncle O.V. would turn him over to her. Cholly knew it was wrong to run out on a pregnant girl, and recalled, with sympathy, that his father had done just that. Now he understood. He knew then what he must do—find his father. His father would understand. (151)

Cholly "[w]ith no more thought than a chick leaving its shell…*stepped off the porch*" (151, italics mine), but he does so with the intent of escaping his impending responsibility. His act establishes the dominant pattern of his life, which is to substitute acts of evasion for leaps of faith. The moment when he meets his father is a combination of disappointment, rejection, shame, and disintegration. In Samson Fuller's midst, he cannot remember his mother's name or even "Whose boy was he" (156); thus, his own father, close enough for Cholly to touch, makes him an orphan while standing in his father's midst. Unlike Macon, whose father is murdered before his eyes, and Joe, who has no clue to his father's identity or how even to ascertain it, Cholly is orphaned by an act of omission. The discarded orange crate he sits on at the mouth of the alley where he found Samson Fuller shooting dice becomes the site of the unhinging of Cholly's manhood. Even as he fights back the tears in hopes he "will be all right," he loses control of his bowels, soiling himself, "like a baby" (157). He winds up under a bridge in a fetal position, reduced to an infantile state, in a state of paralysis.

Critics often trace Cholly's unraveling to the scene where he is forced to have sex under the threatening gaze of white men with guns.[12] While these arguments are compelling, it is also possible that this singular emphasis diminishes the impact Cholly's meeting with his father has on how he sets about configuring a sense of self. The act of soiling himself in the moments following Samson's paternal denial allows us to equate his state with Kristeva's definition of abjection (Lupton, 138).[13] Though it would make sense to turn back to the scene with the hunters, it seems more prudent to press beyond that moment to understand what Cholly's life in the north means in the wake of the trauma he suffered prior to migrating. While the episode with the hunters strips him of the ability to direct his anger at whites, his acts of self-denigration come to be staged in the midst of those who look like him. Hence, prior to leaving the South, Cholly's life is a remarkable combination of self-loathing and license. In a provocative formulation, Morrison suggests that Cholly's subjectivity can only be contained within the blues, as if to insist that it resists articulation in a critical sphere. Thus, Morrison writes:

> Only a musician would sense, know, without even knowing that he knew that Cholly was free. Dangerously free. Free to feel whatever he felt—fear, guilt, shame, love, grief, pity. Free to be tender or violent, to whistle or weep. Free to sleep in doorways or between the white sheets of a singing woman. Free to take a job, free to leave it. He could go to jail and not feel imprisoned, for he had already seen his furtiveness in the eyes of his jailer, free to say, "No, suh," and smile, for he had already killed three white men. Free to take a woman's insults, for his body had already conquered hers. Free even to knock her in the head, for he had already cradled that head in his arms. (159)

Note Morrison's use of the word "free" ten times in the passage above. But the frequency of its appearance is not meant to be suggestive of an emancipatory space; it is meant instead to intimate that Cholly's life is beset on all sides by license. If he can be said to reside in a political imaginary at all, it is one whose most dominant feature is anarchy. Cholly's life is, as we see with Macon, Son, and Guitar, inner-directed, rendered contingent because his ultimate goal is both to re-enact and complete his failed act of copulation and to prove to his father that his manhood is a product of his own industry. When he opts to settle into marriage with Pauline, he does so while in this "godlike state," of self-containment. The interdependency of marriage; a symbiosis that reflects two people's intermingled attributes and shortcomings, never comes to fruition. Lacking this, Cholly, along with the other southern men in Morrison's fiction has a difficult time understanding that interdependence is integral to acts of horizontal place-making in a community.

"Abandoned in a junk heap by his mother, rejected for a crap game by his father, there was nothing more to lose. He was alone with his own perceptions and appetites, and they alone interested him" (160). In epistemological terms, the pursuit of knowledge is such a solitary event, Cholly cannot conceptualize domestic space as a site of the kind of reciprocity that parenting involves and upon which family depends. His inability to establish a relationship with his children, coupled with the collapse of his marriage, ultimately compromises his relation to domestic space. In that sense, the freedom Cholly Breedlove achieves means that he lives in a state of perpetual topophilia. Though this is counter-intuitive, I want to suggest that Cholly is able to disregard all the negative aspects of northern life that another man might experience as force acting upon his personhood. As Cholly ponders how he came to be trapped in a marriage that "[freezes] his imagination," he thinks instead, "of whatever happened to the curiosity he used to feel. Nothing, nothing interested him now. Not himself, not other people. Only in drink was there some break, some floodlight, and when that closed, there was oblivion" (160). Unique among Morrison's southern men, however, because he has absolutely no agenda, save the satiation of his desire for drink and his own sensations, Cholly revels in the "floodlight," as if the consumption of alcohol occurs at the point where pain and pleasure intersect. The moment with Darlene persists as an emotional pivot; any displeasure he might feel regarding his life in Lorain, Ohio is nullified by the fact that it is also the place where he discovered a means to render pain irrelevant. Though this is not an unusual sensation for black men to experience in light of the ways that capitalism has historically used and discarded them, the freedom Cholly Breedlove achieves is fed by his sense that all the things that make his life miserable are also the equivalent to beginning "at zero," with the difference that he is not led to indulge an interest in human relationships, rather, he seeks to evade them; Cholly's idea of zero begins and ends with nullification.

His sense of topophilia, then, is a product of his abdication of any desire to exert force on the landscape in a meaningful way. If we turn, momentarily, to *Sula* we find a passage that clarifies the ontology informing Cholly Breedlove's life. Sula Peace's impact on the Bottom is generated by the inhabitants' sense that she is "distinctly different. [Her grandmother] Eva's arrogance and [her mother] Hannah's self-indulgence merged in her and, with a twist that was all her own imagination, she lived out her days exploring her own thoughts and emotions, giving them full reign, feeling no obligation to please anybody unless their pleasure pleased her" (118). Though Morrison is describing Sula Peace, her words could just as easily be applied to Cholly Breedlove, particularly when we consider that Sula was as:

> willing to feel pain as give pain, to feel pleasure as to give pleasure, hers was an experimental life…She had no center, no speck around which to

> grow. She was completely free from ambition, with no affection for money, property or things, no greed, no desire to command attention or compliments—no ego. For that reason she felt no compulsion to verify herself—to be consistent with herself. (119)

It could be argued that a recurrent plot in African American literature is the necessity of routinizing selfhood by affiliating physical gesture and symbolic heft. Recalling Morrison's Nobel Lecture in which she declares that doing language "might be the measure of life," looking at Sula and Cholly, neither has the ability to take imagination the noun and cross into the territory constituted by *acts of imagining*. It means that both characters' distorted sense of topophilia stems from their sense that who they are bears no relation to where they are. Put another way, the wreckage they leave in their wake co-exists alongside the fact that they are virtually impervious to *being in* a place.

The sadness and loss that led Cholly into a circumstance where he is on the verge of discovering what it means to achieve intimacy with another person is disrupted; in that moment with white men's guns trained on his back, inducing him to "perform," sexual desire constituted a kind of spiritual emptying out, leaving him bereft of the ability to enact a strategy of self-verification, to use his imagination to improvise a coherent self. In light of this, imagination lacking an outlet becomes a weapon. Turning once more to *Sula* and the havoc that ensues when the imagination and purpose fall into a state of estrangement. Morrison writes:

> In her way, her strangeness, her naivete, her craving for the other half of her equation was the consequence of an idle imagination. Had she paints, or clay, or knew the discipline of the dance, or strings; had she anything to engage her tremendous curiosity and her gift for metaphor, she might have exchanged the restlessness and preoccupation with whim for an activity that provided her with all she yearned for. *And like any artist with no art form, she became dangerous.* (121, my italics)

It is obviously not my intent to suggest that the *sources* of Cholly and Sula's sense of dislocation are equivalent. Gender difference should not be overlooked in this instance; part of Sula's problem is that at the time the novel is set, the idea of a woman declaring she wants to "make [her]self," is antithetical to domestic convention. But what is of interest here is the manner in which Morrison clarifies that community cannot be sustained if it is organized around the performance of injury in spaces bereft of conversation. A jazz musician playing the blues does so in a dialogic space where what gets stated is met by a counter-statement; the jam session constitutes that place where the collision of statement and counter-statement represents the act of making play and competition synonymous, the ultimate form of conversation. The blues is not meant to eradicate misfortune, but in rendering trouble dialogical, it seeks to engage it by situating it within the space of collective and widely accessed metaphor.

But because Cholly's life is locked into a provisional mode, his relation to others can never fully take root. With nothing to say, having lived by his own set of dictates, he exists on the margins of community, his "value" to the community generated by his insistence on embracing worthlessness. Ironically, he becomes the measure of how the community calculates worth. That worthlessness, it turns out, is intricately linked to spaces outside of the home: a junk heap in a railyard, a sexual encounter in the woods, and a crap game in an alley. Even when he is indoors he is ultimately outdoors because his understanding of the world has taken root in the open. Cholly proves incapable of associating human connectedness to the interiority of the house, which simply means that his life in the North mirrors his life in the South, where personal license resists containment and resists as well the decorum necessary to make home a private space. Ultimately, the Breedlove family is "outdoors" because they exist in a tight space that is public. Hence, Cholly's body can relate to his daughter, Pecola, as both father and lover not only because he lacks the necessary habits of judgment to distinguish between the two roles but also, more poignantly, because his life in the South has never allowed him to map out a form of masculinity that does not link sexuality and exploitation as essential mechanisms. Though the moment with Pecola begins as a reprise of his courtship of Polly, Cholly is alienated from the kinds of emotional interiority associated with familial intimacy.

Indeed, taking all of Morrison's "southern men" together, each reflects the privileging of acts we associate with exterior spaces as sites of vertical place-making. I have just discussed Cholly Breedlove's provisionality as being of a piece with being outdoors. But thinking of Guitar, we find that his membership in the Seven Days has its roots in his of hunting, which he associates with the South. When Joe Trace stalks Dorcas, she is a surrogate for his mother, Wild, whom he seeks at the place he believes she resides in the woods. Son Green's life as an undocumented man essentially makes it impossible for him to be comfortable in the interiorities Jadine covets. As I will discuss below, the 8-Rock Men are said to be "hunting" the women in the Convent. Macon Dead is fixated, not only on the advantages that come with property, but also how people he considers beneath him are reminded of their "inferior" status, which he accomplishes by driving his hearse on Sunday afternoons through the neighborhood. The sign of his authority lies in his ability to put people like the Bains family outdoors.

Hence, Cholly's abjection is toxic because of how it comes to be projected outward into the black community itself. To be sure, Pecola's madness is a product of incompetent parenting, but in the light of the long-standing belief that child-rearing was a collective, communal practice, it would seem that the neighborhood is culpable as well. Furthermore, Morrison, through Claudia, the narrator links Pecola's fate to abjection, but in this instance that abjection is generated and sustained by the community itself. As Claudia recalls, Pecola's destruction is a product of communal endeavor and not, as we might conclude, of Cholly and Pauline's horrific parenting.

> All of our waste which we dumped on her and which she absorbed. And all of our beauty, which was hers first and which she gave to us. *All of us—all who knew her—felt so wholesome after we cleaned ourselves on her. We were so beautiful when we stood astride her ugliness.* (205, italics mine)

What does it mean, Morrison asks, if our sense of place, our conception of topophilia, can only be achieved at the expense of our neighbors? How, she wonders, are black folks supposed to "get where they want to go" if the journey can only be made when black bodies are made to serve as the fuel? It is important, then, to understand how white supremacy and racial identity work symbiotically, like parasite and host. Morrison emphasizes this parasitic relation through Claudia's condemnation of Lorain's black community for its role in Pecola's destruction:

> Her simplicity decorated us, her guilt sanctified us, her pain made us glow with health, her awkwardness made us think we had a sense of humor. Her inarticulateness made us believe we were eloquent. Her poverty kept us generous. Even her waking dreams we used—to silence our own nightmares. And she let us, and thereby deserved our contempt. (205)

Cholly Breedlove's transgressions notwithstanding, the tight spaces that enfold her male characters is an indication that liberation is a collaborative project. If Morrison's writing can be said to be "political," it could be because she has demonstrated a fascination for peeling the layers away from words like "community" or "freedom," or, for that matter, "self," to suggest that none of these words have substance if we fail to acknowledge what we find at the intersection of individual memory and collective responsibility is not simply a matter of *place* as noun, but ultimately the verb, *place-making*.

If the characters discussed in this and the previous chapter are the product of systems of devaluation that indicate the political stakes attached to acts of naming, they are also indicative of how identities established in traumatic circumstances require alternative imaginaries out of which new habits of judgment can emerge that emphasize collectivity as integral to acts of place-making. Though the Deadly Sins figure as core elements of her characters' personalities, arguments that Morrison is scapegoating these characters (and in the process, black men), miss the point.[14]

At a more immediate level, Morrison's recurring use of the Deadly Sins to orchestrate plot is integral to understanding of how her characters manifest their respective forms of estrangement.[15] Recalling Sargisson's assertion that estrangement "is integral to utopianism," the presence of sin would seem to invalidate the possibility of utopia until we consider a novel like *Paradise* in which the murderous rage expended on the women in the Convent is a product of the 8-Rock Men's belief that their actions are justified, a course of action deemed necessary because the Convent threatens the sanctity of Ruby's self-containment. Understanding their behavior as mandated by an Old Testament that sanctions judgment, wrath, and destruction, the men are blinded to the nature of their sin. Therefore, the greed, sloth, wrath, lust, and pride we see in Macon, Cholly, Guitar, Joe, and Son are, by their lights, a sign of how deeply committed they are to perfecting their circumstances. Whether it is material acquisitions, incest, retributive violence, extra-marital sex, or anarchic individualism, each character endeavors to imagine utopian forms of progress, but in doing so, transgress against both God and the community.

Though both *Tar Baby* and *Paradise* end in ways that suggest Morrison's tendency to eschew neat methods of closure, what is striking is that she sees those moments when meaning undergoes destabilization as the most favorable conditions—if we consider her readers—for human freedom and innovation to thrive. It is the reason the Convent represents such an obvious threat to the men of Ruby. Populated by women, many of whom are defined as outcasts, cast-offs, or malcontents, the Convent is actually the space that undermines Ruby's ability to remain a totally closed system.

Ruby's progress toward becoming a closed system has been documented in Pat Best's history project, which she uses to reconstruct events that have transpired since the Disallowing, the founding and abandonment of Haven and the establishment of Ruby. She notes that after World War II, the 8-Rock men are integral to the establishment of the town of Ruby, which allows them to consolidate their family lines to ensure that nothing and no one can pollute the purity of their heritage. What should be a town energized by past injury to embrace an ethos of empathy and inclusiveness, is finally a space fraught with the same imperative as *Beloved*'s Sethe, to hold the past at bay. As she sets about augmenting her narrative, Pat realizes several troubling aspects of the 8-Rock's ascendancy in Ruby. First, she realizes that the 8-Rocks are engaged in acts of intermarriage and affiliation that are meant to sustain their purity, diminish the risk that anyone reminiscent of the blacks who undertook the Disallowing will remain in their midst or "pollute" their lineage. Hence, Pat's mother, Delia, is allowed to die while giving birth simply because she is fair-skinned and married to a member of one of the "first" families. Second, Pat is stunned by the realization that none of the 8-Rocks who remain in Ruby have died, their immortality tied to the symbolic geography they seek to sustain against all intruders. This impulse is reflected in the Christmas play that superficially re-enacts the birth of Christ. But Pat notes that the play's principle characters, ostensibly the nine families who founded Ruby, are considered so only if they have done nothing to jeopardize the town's purity. In truth, the play dramatizes the Disallowing and the establishment of Ruby, erasing those families who have violated the injunction against bringing in outsiders and, by implication, iterations of blackness that seek to complicate racial identity rather than relying on simplistic binaries.

But such a practice is rendered all but impossible in Ruby, where Richard Misner concludes that he is "herding a flock which believed not only that it had created the pasture it grazed but that grass from any other meadow was toxic" (212). Fresh from the Civil Rights Movement, where he has witnessed the heroism of "ordinary folks," Misner sees Ruby as a place where "Booker T solutions trumped DuBois problems every time" (212). However, this is why Pat Best's role in the novel is so fraught with contradictions. Though her meticulously documented history of Ruby reveals it to be a space where outsider and enemy are synonymous, Pat opts never to share it with anyone. After a spirited conversation with Misner about what constitutes the nature of home, in which he insists that home is not "some fortress you bought and built up and have to keep everybody locked in or out," or "some place you stole from the people living there," Pat leaves the school and concludes that "the deep weeping pleasure the audience took from the play disgusted her" (214). However, she underestimates the coercive power of Ruby, for without even recognizing it, she burns all the papers that might render an alternative narrative. Given Pat's realization that the 8-Rock Families are distinguished by their immortality; the fact that their relationship to the town is nearly symbiotic, it would seem that the town is an exemplar of the "magical realism" critics attributed to Morrison's fiction in criticism produced in the 1980s. But I submit that Ruby is by no means a "magical" space, certainly not in any mystical sort of way. It is perhaps more apt to understand that the town is a machine. Hence Pat's act of destroying the documents, the manner in which she does it without conscious thought, bespeaks Ruby's ability to find the necessary fuel to sustain itself; the inhabitants of the town are cogs in a system of racial superiority whose automaticity is ratified by the Disallowing, which holds uncertainty at bay by rendering dissenting claims as heresy, as disruptions of mechanical efficiency.

The volatility that resides beneath the surface of the town's manifestation of safety comes to the fore when Ruby's young men state a desire to change the inscription on the Oven from "Beware the Furrow of His Brow" to "Be the Furrow of His Brow." Hearing this, the elders object with disdain and revisit the process of the Oven's construction and its dismantling and reconstruction. As Philip Page brilliantly points out, what Morrison depicts here is significant; not only "are there multiple meanings of the text—multiple signifieds—but here are multiple texts, multiple signifiers" (639). Here, she suggests that the dialogue the Oven generates is a new form of heat, a way to reinvigorate Ruby's waning power, at the very least a discussion that should signal that the young are ready to take their place among the town fathers (9).

But the dispute, whether the Oven begins with "Be," "We," or "Beware," also signals a fluctuation of meaning. In the Morrison's universe, this is a good thing, for she is at her most distrustful of state power when meanings are stable, unimpeachable. Thus, when Steward Morgan declares, "If you, any one of you ignore, change, take away, or add to the words in the mouth of that Oven, I will blow your head off just like you was a hood-eye snake" (87), he shifts from the compensatory rhetoric associated with narratives that privilege inclusiveness to the strategic rhetoric we associate with a repressive state that has created an illusion of divine authority. For his threat forecloses upon the possibility dialogue creates and points to the Oven as a false idol wrought from a reified past, whose mythology is authenticated by violent force.

However, in the days after the massacre at the Convent, Morrison offers readers an opportunity to ruminate on what it means when a community's habits of judgment occur at the intersection of aspiration and scorn. What does it mean; Morrison proffers, to reside in a community whose aspiration to thrive issues from their unwillingness to confront how injury figures into the effort to create a meaningful posture toward the future? Here, we might draw parallels to those moments after the Feast in *Beloved*, where Baby Suggs' neighbors turn away from her despite the fact that her Calls in the Clearing have been an integral source of healing because they have emphasized the importance of black embodiment.

Reverend Misner's character, as a newcomer and an outsider, is one of the few characters adequately positioned both to assess Ruby as a product of the political imagination. He observes, "They think they are protecting their wives and children, when in fact they are maiming them" (306). The roots of this transgression lie buried in Ruby's history and thus he concludes the town' birth came:

> out of an old hatred, one that began when one kind of black man scorned another kind and that kind took the hatred to another level, their selfishness had trashed two hundred years of suffering and triumph in a moment of such pomposity and error and callousness it froze the mind. Unbridled by Scripture, deafened by the roar of its own history, Ruby, it seemed to him, was an unnecessary failure. (306)

If a propensity for violence has, in effect, been constitutive for Guitar Bains and Cholly Breedlove, Morrison's depiction of Ruby completes a corpus of characters who can be said to be "nowhere." The progression from hurt individual to damaged community is meant to suggest that political imaginaries formed as a declaration of racial allegiance are doomed to fail. However, not in ways one might expect. *Paradise* offers us a "what-if" scenario in which Morrison tasks readers with remembering that tight space is a condition that creates *an obligation* to deploy the imagination when she writes, "How exquisitely human was the wish for permanent happiness, and how thin human imagination became trying to achieve it" (306).

Misner's sense that Ruby soon, "will be like country towns: the young thinking of elsewhere, the old full of regret," is declarative of how black communities seeking to determine "where they want to go," are a recurring instance in Morrison's fiction. Ruby is meant to confirm her sense that it generally involves an effort to balance practical concerns against idealistic ones and that collective forms of movement bring higher purpose, tactical awareness, and logistical insight together in an open-ended narrative.[16] Achieving a sense of place and belonging, as Morrison portrays it, has little to do with utopias. She posits forms of communal mobility mediated by the conflicting agendas that emerge out of praxis. The radical individualism of Morrison's southern men means their sense of place is fashioned in a conceptual vacuum where their estrangement from the community's larger concerns informs their pursuit of destructive willfulness.

Though estrangement is a term most often associated with alienation, linking it to utopianism provides a useful framework for understanding how Morrison's southern men structure their relation to place and placemaking. From a conceptual standpoint, utopias are "distanced from the now," and so Morrison's characters might be understood as individuals whose efforts at self-realization are stymied in the present. In light of the traumas her characters have suffered in the South, their inability to distinguish topophilia from topophobia leads them to turn the vitriol of their inner struggles against those whose circumstances most resemble their own.[17]

But *Beloved* invites us to think more broadly about the issues facing "the black community," by reflecting Tommy Shelby's sense that "racism, institutional or otherwise, is not the only significant obstacle that blacks now face, and for many it is not even among their more urgent political concerns" (121). Readers may recollect the conversation between Baby Suggs and Sethe in which they hold divergent views as to whether whites qualify as "real humans," a conversation that ends when Baby Suggs' insists, "Don't box with me. There's more of us they drowned than there is all of them ever lived from the start of time. Lay down your sword. This ain't a battle; it's a rout" (282). To a large degree, Baby Suggs' words are prophetic, capturing with incredible accuracy what life in the north will become. But unlike Railroad Tommy's lecture, they do not tell the whole story; where the lecture, with its reliance on sensual details, is about all those things black men will never have, Baby Suggs' historicist posture insists that the obstacles to black people's liberation function at a global scale. The conversation is further contextualized as a moment Denver recalls just prior to deciding whether she should leave the confines of 124 Bluestone Road and seek assistance for Sethe. "Denver stood on the porch," the narrator states, "and couldn't leave it." Just then, she hears Baby Suggs' voice "clear as anything" asking:

> You mean I never told you nothing about Carolina? About your daddy? You don't remember nothing about how come I walk the way I do and about your mother's feet, not to speak of her back? I never told you all that? Is that why you can't walk down the steps? My Jesus my. (288)

And when Denver restates Baby Suggs' insistence that "there was no defense" against the unpredictability of whites, the old woman ends the discussion by insisting further: "Know it and go on out the yard." It is important to note, this "exchange" recalls Pilate's relationship with her father as it occurs across the spatio-temporal boundary separating the living and the dead. We also see how the exchange challenges assumptions that political discourse is rooted in the physical realm, a manifestation of "real" concerns, but also because it argues that a political imaginary often coheres through audacious leaps of faith. Unlike the flight mechanism that spurs Cholly to step off his Aunt Jimmy's porch to escape the responsibility of fatherhood, Denver's newfound mobility is made possible because she listens *across* the boundary separating the living from the dead to seek a new iteration of place.

Denver's travels spark, in turn, acts of remembering on the part of the community, many of whom recall Baby Suggs' kindness and a time when 124 was "a way station, the place they assembled to catch news, taste oxtail soup, leave their children, cut out a skirt" (293). Without even recognizing it, it is Denver's physical movement, from one house to another, that induces the community to abandon the contentiousness that followed the "party with the twelve turkeys and the tubs of strawberry smash," in favor of a more conciliatory posture. They situate Sethe's murderous act in an encomium of communal solidarity and collective memory in which Baby Suggs' role as binding force is restored. Their conversations with Denver lead to the important recognition that perhaps:

> they were sorry for the years of their own disdain. Maybe they were simply nice people who could hold meanness toward others for just so long and when trouble rode bareback among them, quickly, easily they did what they could to trip him up. In any case, personal pride, the arrogant claim staked out at 124 seemed to have run its course. (294)

The restoration of the system of mutual concern and protection that should have hindered Schoolteacher's effort to reclaim Sethe and her children is signaled by the phrase, "when trouble rode bareback among them, quickly, easily they did what they could *to trip him up*" (294, my italics). The personification of trouble, a gesture that finds its most keen expression in the blues, is also an assertion of a political imaginary in which reconciliation, on both personal and collective levels, is a key element.

This personal aspect of reconciliation is embodied in Ella, a woman whose time as a slave was "spent in a house where she was shared by father and son, whom she called 'the lowest yet,'" sets about "convince[ing] the others that rescue was in order" (301). Like Lady Jones, Ella is an essential character, because her past experience has led her to adopt a strategy for dealing with the past, simply by comparing present difficulty with "the lowest yet." By using her own traumatic past as a template for understanding the scope evil can attain, Ella can assume a tactical stance toward Sethe's transgression:

> Whatever Sethe had done, Ella didn't like the idea of past errors taking possession of the present. Sethe's crime was staggering and her pride outstripped even that; but she could not countenance the possibility of sin moving on in the house, unleashed and sassy. Daily life took as much as she had. The future was sunset; the past something to leave behind. And if it didn't stay behind, well, you might have to stomp it out. Slave life; freed life—every day was a test and a trial. Nothing could be counted on in a world where *even when you were a solution you were a problem*. (302, my italics)

Thinking about Sethe, Ella recognizes that freedom is "a test and a trial" because it so often requires the freed person to eschew acts of self-sabotage in favor of intervention. One consequence of this decision is that it nullifies the necessity of waiting to be asked. The thirty women that gather outside 124 to exorcise the ghost symbolizes the power of collective resistance to overcome individual forms of crisis but it does not involve asking Sethe whether she requires intervention. What distinguishes this moment, however, is that upon their arrival, "the first thing they saw was not Denver sitting on the steps, but themselves" (304). Each of the women returns to the Feast, that moment just prior to the community's fall into collective crisis. In what constitutes nothing short of the kind of spatiotemporal travel made possible by stepping into a time maching, the women are returned to 124 Bluestone Road they frequented before Sethe's arrival. At Ella's signal, the thirty women "took a step back to the beginning. In the beginning there was no words. In the beginning was the sound, and they all knew what the sound sounded like" (305).

Just as Pilate "began at zero," as a first move toward self-determination, the thirty women outside approximate her gesture by making a figurative return to an originary moment that predates language. Perhaps Morrison means to suggest that they have returned to those moments during the Middle Passage when, prior to speaking a common tongue, all that was available to African captives was a sound that served as a medium through which to communicate empathy and solidarity in a liminal space in which they have ceased to be human but have not as yet become commodified and transformed into currency or property. And like Pilate, who realizes that there is nothing to fear, the thirty women's collective act of taking "a step back to the beginning" is akin to returning to a moment before human beings learned that language could be used as a vehicle for communicating fear and difference.

As Edwards might suggest, what the thirty women eschew is their status as a charismatic mass, whose powers of discernment and religious piety elevate them above Sethe. Rather, they recall how 124 Bluestone Road provided them with a space for collaborative forms of self-invention. If charisma constitutes a form of exemplarity that privileges some voices over others, Baby Suggs' house, the thirty women recall, is the place where they were required to be nothing more than themselves because 124 is synonymous with horizontal place-making. When considered alongside the re-materialization of their bodies in the Clearing, the women are reintroduced to the idea of sufficiency. Baby Suggs' notion that "good [is] knowing when to stop," informs her ministrations to the community. And it is with this in mind that the thirty women outside 124 Bluestone Road implicitly understand that Sethe needs to give vent to her rage, but they do not allow her to stab Mr. Bodner with an ice pick. Morrison's point, however, is that if anger is not directed at its' rightful source, then it festers to become a wound that endangers the collective body.

In the final pages of *Beloved*, then, we see a community restore its ability to utilize horizontal forms of place-making to ward off an impending threat. But such a move would not have been possible if the community of women outside 124 had failed to recover their sense of place.[18] Alongside the exercise of the political imagination necessary to reintegrate Sethe into the community in spite of her transgression, the affective ties to 124 as it symbolizes a *home* capable of nurturing the collective good are equally important. Here, it's important to take a moment to ponder the second epigraph at the start of this chapter. Taken from Morrison's short story, "Recitatif," the exchange between Twyla and Roberta speaks to the ways that, in a conversation between two black women whose class differences are belied by their common origins, freedom is the product of aspirational energy. In light of this realization, not how the 30 women, as they approach, "accumulating slowly in groups of twos and threes," the resulting gathering is the very embodiment of topophilia because the women's fusion of memory and purpose suggest that an attachment to place that incorporates acts of resistance against the established order—whether it be racial or gendered—must include "all of the human being's affective ties with the material environment" (93).[19]

Notes

1. I have been surprised by the number of critical readings of *Song of Solomon* that read the phrase, "and it did not matter which one of them would give up his ghost in the killing arms of his brother," as evidence that Milkman dies at the end of the novel, despite the fact that the preponderance of readings see it as a transcendent moment. Perhaps the most persuasive is John Brenkman's argument in "Politics and Form in *Song of Solomon*." Brenkman characterizes the end of *Song* as a confluence of magical romanticism and tragic realism. He writes, "The stylistic shift is motivated by the novelistic rather than the romantic imperatives of the text. It refutes Milkman's voice, even as it lets its authenticity be heard. It articulates the psychology of a tragic self-misunderstanding rather than the heroics of romance renewal. The register of tragic realism unmasks the metaphor of prowess, freedom, and continuity. Fratricide breaks the community's continuity with itself and Milkman has failed to find a fit emblem of his own freedom or a genuine activity for his own self-realization" (p. 73).
2. Black men's investment in "charismatic leadership" reflects a zero-sum game approach to power relations: e.g. for black men to have power, black women must be stripped of theirs.

3. I make this point, not as a new revelation, but rather to suggest that Guitar's violent gestures of love, in all their anonymity, are finally acts of self-aggrandizement.
4. Psychiatrist Jonathan Shay notes, "Annihilation of convention (Homer's *themis*) by another's acts can destroy...stable character...It can, quite simply, produce bestiality, the utter loss of human relatedness." Cf. Jonathan Shay. *Achilles in Vietnam: Combat Trauma and the Undoing of Character.*
5. The etymology of the word *estrangement* is intriguing; it grows out of cognate terms that imply difference and distance, combining the old French word *estranger* (or *etranger* in modern French) and the Latin *extraneare.* Estrangement "evokes the stranger and the extraneous, the unknown and the outside" (Sargisson, p. 394).
6. Shay, pp. 33–5.
7. Tommy Shelby terms this posture "community nationalism," a state in which "blacks possess a determinate collective volition regarding their status and future in America" (120). However, as Shelby points out, "advocates of community nationalism try to reduce all forms of black disadvantage to racial oppression or white supremacy thus linking every important political question that arises for blacks to this form of subordination" (121).
8. Cf. Ralph Story, "An Excursion into the Black World: The 'Seven Days' in Toni Morrison's *Song of Solomon*". Reading the novel through the lens of Addison Gayle's concept of the Black Aesthetic, Story reads the Seven Days as revolutionary, seeing for example, the suicide of Robert Smith at the start of the novel as an example of how Morrison "unites both Eastern and Western trains of thought." He states further, "For black folk to 'love so much they would kill is a profoundly radical idea yet one which can be clearly discerned in the poetic works of the Black Arts Movement of the 1960s..." Linking the Seven Days to the black secret societies that grew up in the nineteenth century, Story sees the Days as "a group grounded in both contemporary and nineteenth-century Afro-American history." I should take care to note here that Story's essay was published in the late 80s, which means it exhibits the remnants of cultural nationalism associated with the Black Power Movement. In the present moment, however, his reading of the text fails to account for the hegemonic masculinity Guitar (and the Days) embodies and uses a long discarded distinction between "street" (Guitar) and "house" (Milkman) to signal how black male resistance is inflected as working class.
9. As Lupton describes it, edgework "takes place around cultural boundaries: such as those between life and death, consciousness and unconsciousness, sanity and insanity, and an ordered sense of self and environment and an unordered sense of self and environment. Edgework is characterized by

an emphasis on skilled performance of the dangerous activity, involving the ability to maintain control over a situation that verges on complete chaos that requires, above all, 'mental toughness,' the ability not to give into fear" (pp. 151–2).

10. Lupton, p. 134.
11. This passage anticipates August Wilson's character of Levee in Ma Rainey's Black *Bottom*, where he expresses his desire to work with the devil to collect souls.
12. Both Mayberry and Suranyi, in works that were both published in 2007, link Cholly's disaffection to the moment with the hunters. My point is not to refute their arguments outright, but rather to suggest that if Cholly has been emasculated, the process originated with the hunters and was completed by his father. Though the moment with Darlene is humiliating, creating the template for how he will regard black women in the future, it is not, in and of itself, grounds to equate it with abjection.
13. Quoting Kristeva, Deborah Lupton defines abjection thus: "Abjection, she argues, is a powerful feeling which is both symbolic and experienced as a bodily sensation. Above all, abjection is a 'revolt of the person against an external menace from which one wants to keep oneself at a distance.'" Lupton, p. 138.
14. This chapter is indebted to Pereira's call for more careful attention to be paid to efforts to periodize Morrison's fiction. For my purposes, it means that the work done in the subsequent chapters of this study are focused, almost exclusively, on the project of de-colonization. Cf. "Periodizing Toni Morrison's Work from *The Bluest Eye* to *Jazz*: The Importance of Tar Baby" (p. 72).
15. Morrison's most memorable enactment of the Seven Deadly Sins comes in *Beloved*, where, during the feast at 124, all seven sins come into play as past trauma disrupts the community's optimism and inclusiveness, resulting in the radical autonomy that leads to Sethe's act of infanticide.
16. In view of how African American slaves in the nineteenth century came to adopt the Exodus narrative as an analogue for black struggle, which becomes an important component of the Civil Rights Movement's rhetorical practice, the belief in a "higher purpose" serves to bolster the resolve of oppressed people. But as *Paradise* is meant to suggest, a sense of higher purpose, in the absence of mutability, can quickly become self-righteous and dangerous.
17. Morrison's portrayal of the inability to generate a meaningful sense of place and how it subsequently inhibits her characters' ability to equate mobility with futurity recalls the need to be mindful of how a politics of scale is at work here, because her characters fail to understand how their local dilemmas are the product of assumptions and decisions that issue

from larger jurisdictions. One reason why the white supremacist political imaginary can place such a pervasive check on black mobility and futurity is because it has the power to control outcomes outright, influencing what will happen, generating a state of automaticity in which communities ultimately resemble the workings of a machine and outcomes are synonymous with common sense.

18. And the evidence of that is the fact that they restrain Sethe from using an icepick to kill a man she believes to be Schoolteacher, but who, in fact, is Mr. Bodner arriving at 124. Knowing where they are allows them to eschew the possibility for violence that can be explained away because of the misguided conclusion that whiteness is a "one size fits all" proposition. Also, stopping Sethe from hurting Mr. Bodner, does not mean that they don't ascertain the act as indicative of a mental state healthy enough to identify the actual source of her trauma.
19. He goes on to state, "These differ greatly in intensity, subtlety, and mode of expression." The response to environment may be primarily aesthetic; it may then vary from the fleeting pleasure one gets from a view of the equally fleeting but far more intense sense of beauty that is suddenly revealed. The response may be tactile, a delight in the feel of air, water, earth. More permanent and less easy to express are feelings that one has toward a place because it is home, the locus of memories, and the means of gaining a livelihood. The thirty women who arrive at 124, by substituting themselves on the steps of the house for Denver likewise regain their affective ties to place, what had been a source of anguish and dissolution is restored as the site of mutuality, purpose, and agency.

CHAPTER 4

The Housing of Hurt: The Optic of Tight Space in *Jazz*

Thus because jazz finds its very life in an endless improvisation upon traditional materials, the jazzman must lose his identity even as he finds it.
—Ralph Ellison, "The Charlie Christian Story"

Let our scars fall in love.
—Galway Kinnell, Book IV, *The Book of Nightmares*

The previous chapter revealed Morrison's commitment to dismantling the relationship between charisma and masculine authority as they combined in her southern male characters. Macon Dead, Guitar Bains, Son Green, and Cholly Breedlove fail to understand the importance of beginning "at zero" and in so doing remain trapped in the assumptions that confine them to the tight space that constricts movement of any sort, physical or conceptual.[1] An ambivalence toward northern life runs through Morrison's novels set there. Morrison does not characterize life in the North as a total failure that requires a turn back to the South, but her novels portray the North as the site of individual and collective trials that call for a level of tactical dexterity sufficient for generating the escape velocity necessary to break free of the pull of tight spaces. As the closing pages of both *Song of Solomon* and *Beloved* suggest, tactical dexterity of this sort is rarely achieved by solitary means. Indeed, if the struggles of Morrison's

H. Beavers, *Geography and the Political Imaginary in the Novels of Toni Morrison*, Geocriticism and Spatial Literary Studies,
https://doi.org/10.1007/978-3-319-65999-2_4

southern men teach us anything, it is that they often possess the fatal flaw of rejecting the idea that authentic forms of manhood can be achieved collaboratively, as if topophilia is contingent on acts of self-making.

Though *Jazz*'s Joe Trace is kin to the other southern men discussed in Chap. 2, he also represents a departure from them. After *Beloved*'s Paul D., few male characters living in the North in Morrison's fiction demonstrate that it is possible to discover a sense of personal renewal characterized by a collaborative posture, but Joe Trace perhaps comes closest. But this posture is not easily arrived at, and by the end of the novel, a trace of ambivalence lingers, signaling our fear that the lapse of judgment that leads Joe to violence could recur. The narrator informs us early on in the novel that the city can induce all sorts of behaviors by creating the illusion of self-determination and desire alongside the abandonment of common sense.

For example, in the early pages of *Jazz*, a teenage girl accuses Violet of stealing her baby brother out of his carriage. When a crowd gathers in response to the young girl's screaming they find that the teenager asked Violet to watch the baby so that she could run back into her apartment for "The Trombone Blues," a record she wanted to play for a friend. Though the narrator relates this occurrence as proof of Violet's descent into mental instability, it is also a moment that marks popular culture's growing influence in everyday life, where stimulation counter-mands the responsibility to kin. As the neighbors excoriate the girl for her lapse in judgment, we begin to understand the calamitous circumstance that arises when opposing principles collide. The scene illustrates the generational schism growing up between adults raised in the South with little in the way of diversion, who value personal connections developed over time, and young people's investments in the mass-produced dramatizations to be found on race records, which offer ministrations on romance and heartbreak, pleasure and pain. As Anne-Marie Paquet-Deyris points out, music in *Jazz* "seems to function as a substitute voice," speaking for individuals who do not feel able to put words together in a way that is "sweet" or "beautiful," as if an honest expression of feeling is no longer enough.

The feeling Paquet-Deyris describes—the need to defer to someone who can say it better—pervades Morrison's *Jazz* (1992). And perhaps it explains why the novel's narrative proves so enthralling. With a narrator who vacillates between omniscience and sentience, *Jazz* gives us characters who wear their hearts on their sleeves for all to see. However, for the bulk of the novel, they struggle to articulate what is troubling them. Morrison returns to a familiar theme: the manner in which selfhood can be compromised when aspiration becomes dislodged from memory. Part of the problem, though, is that the novel's 1920s setting is meant to signify how urban modernity can make acts of remembering, whether they are personal or collective, difficult to sustain and even harder to contextualize.

The central predicament in *Jazz* involves the difficulty of separating injury and identity. As an extended meditation on how tight space enables the housing of hurt, *Jazz* shows how the past proves to be poisonous to body and spirit. Though the threat no longer comes in the form of night riders with torches or back-breaking labor under an unforgiving sun, the danger lurking in the city assumes a new silhouette so attractive that pleasure and danger appear very near to being identical twins. Shirley Ann Stave has aptly stated that even as *Jazz* is set in Harlem and uses the Renaissance "as the backdrop for the novel's diegesis, Morrison interrogates a cultural space that has heretofore been regarded as a cultural Mecca for Americans of African descent" (60). But the novel's exegesis uses the 1920s to understand the cultural politics that accompany volatile social circumstances.[2] Though whites do not play a role in *Jazz*'s central plot, it is clear that the novel is attentive to the transformations occurring across Manhattan's populace, including the new forms of public visibility and consumption that cut across racial and class boundaries. Morrison reveals impulses that clarify the expanding role popular culture will play in how newly arrived migrants from the South reimagine spatial relations and the underlying systems of accountability.

But it would not be wholly accurate to describe *Jazz* as a historical novel. Harlem in 1926 proves to be a rich source for fictional material, but as a postmodern text, the novel's use of flashbacks and unreliable narration gesture toward the present moment's fascination with reality television and its invalidation of "behind closed doors." It is intriguing, then, to consider how the 1920s is that moment when "home" ceases to be a domestic space built around privacy and inaccessibility and becomes a visual tableau that announces—indeed, insists—that we look at what goes on behind closed doors, talk "underneath people's clothes," and make value judgments about what we see.[3] *Jazz* is a novel concerned with how quickly the new arrival can become acclimatized to the ways of the city and thus become inured to the new black cultural imaginary emerging in Harlem. As David Schiff relates, in the "early years of the twentieth century the tempo of life sped up sharply, as if someone had stepped on a global gas pedal. Urban life seemed faster, noisier, less predictable. The hopped-up pace felt exhilarating and dizzying" (50).[4] Burton Peretti argues that during the 1920s, entertainment "was even more of a mass phenomenon, transmitting forms of post-Victorian leisure to thousands and even millions" (39).

Where Chap. 2 made only brief mention of the recurring trope of the two-story house, this chapter elaborates on the ways that trope is suffused throughout the text. At its most practical, the trope is intended to direct our attention toward dwellings inhabited by individuals who have stories to tell. But at a more symbolic level, the two-story house denotes the spatial and domestic geographies in which Morrison's characters seek to create a sense of place (topophilia) in the wake of personal trauma. Further, the trope is useful in our effort to ascertain domestic power relations, especially in the case of Joe and Violet Trace, who migrate from country to city, where they encounter complex social mechanisms and unfamiliar codes of behavior. Manhattan in the 1920s constitutes a setting in which international, national, state, municipal, and corporate systems of governance complicate efforts to establish an attachment to place. As Neil Brenner asserts, the politics of scale is useful in identifying the spatial expression of social functions.[5] What is clear is that 1920s Manhattan is not yet a place where black bodies are valued on the same level as white ones. As early as 1914, Harlem's population had grown so rapidly that the quality of life deteriorated. Harlem residents paid 25% more than other New Yorkers for comparable apartments. One of Joe Trace's many changes come when he is forced to deal with the economic inequality impinging on his quality of life: "When the rents got raised and raised again, and the stores doubled the price of uptown beef and let the whitefolks' meat stay the same, I got me a little sideline selling Cleopatra products in the neighborhood" (128).

The novel's depiction of scale is further evidenced by Alice Manfred's refusal to call the police to investigate her niece's murder even though she knows Joe Trace pulled the trigger because she "didn't want to throw money to helpless lawyers or laughing cops when she knew the expense wouldn't improve anything" (4). Alice Manfred is aware that the proper conditions do not exist for her to benefit from services whites take for granted. Though she does not see herself as situated in a political imaginary, she knows that white habits of judgment in the North would consider the matter an example of "what those people in Harlem" do on a Saturday night. The narrator's reference to "laughing cops" expresses the incredulity that would meet Alice Manfred's plea for justice, the distance between her position as a resident of Harlem and the social mechanisms that serve whites but rarely if ever serve blacks. Instead, she contents herself with the thought that killing Dorcas has caused Joe so much pain that he cries all day, an outcome that is "as bad as jail" (4).

The two-story house therefore indicates the necessity of ascertaining the relationship between narration and power relations. In a manner that is remarkably consistent across Morrison's canon, she often deploys the trope in ways that involve men and women vying for space in the narrative to relate their experiences. The two-story house asserts the need to devote attention to those narratives that are vertically configured as a hierarchy sustained by acts of erasure and silence. But as Paul D. and Sethe demonstrate, Morrison's characters can evolve and become acclimatized to spaces in which narratives are configured horizontally, where it is possible for men and women to tell and listen to each other's stories.

But one of the major problems for all the characters in *Jazz* is that they struggle to loose themselves from improper approaches to storytelling. As the novel's title suggests, acts of storytelling take place during a moment when the growth of popular music and the medium of radio are expanding exponentially. The 32-bar song form, as it emerges from Tin Pan Alley, initiates an approach to songwriting that requires composers to fashion narratives that unfold within the space of three verses and a bridge (otherwise known as the AABA song form). Hence, *Jazz* is set in a moment when the sale of 78 rpm records to be played on the cheaper and more accessible phonograph routinizes music as a cultural technology that invites listeners to believe that singers of popular songs are speaking both to and for the audience. The relatively new musical genre of jazz arrives on the cultural scene and is interpreted as alternately exotic and scandalous. Because the music attracts whites seeking to transgress the tightly policed racial boundary, popular song comes to be seen as an innovative medium for the enhancement of personal encounters.[6] Moreover, popular culture persuades the populace to abandon the notion that personal experience cannot be reduced to two minutes on a 78 rpm record and to embrace the idea that performers of popular song are expressing how they feel with such accuracy that one's place in the world can be ascertained simply by memorizing a song's lyrics. As the phrase *knowing the lyrics by heart* intimates, singing along with the record is akin to coopting the words and using them as a vehicle for telling one's own story. But in doing so, Morrison suggests, New Yorkers were prone to shift concepts of value away from the material and the concrete toward the fictive and speculative. As Benedict Anderson recounts in *Imagined Communities*, "Cultural shifts in the understanding of time and the development of print journalism allowed for people to imagine themselves connected to others through … 'simultaneity.'"[7] Reading about celebrities' public escapades in magazines and "tattlers" gave people the sense that they, too, were caught up in the spectacle.

The novel's opening line, "Sth. I know that woman," indicates the manner in which urban modernity creates a conceptual space where speculation becomes synonymous with knowledge. As readers of *Jazz* quickly surmise, the novel is full of characters who engage in dangerous acts of misconduct: marital misconduct, social misconduct, criminal misconduct, and finally narrative misconduct and the attendant risks of that conduct are central features of the novel's plot. Here, we might ask, by portraying misconduct in 1926 Harlem, is Toni Morrison seeking to exert critical pressure on that moment's two grand narratives: the Jazz Age and the Harlem Renaissance? Both narratives are reliant on notions of increased pace: swifter trains and automobiles, technologies that speed up communication, the speed at which acquisition and expenditure occur, how an individual's status can change overnight. And we find that one of the most important settings for the swifter pace of social transactions is within the vocabulary of culture itself. What both narratives occlude—and what *Jazz* seeks to restore—is the human cost involved in acts of accumulation and expenditure of all sorts, whether they be cultural, social, economic, or political in nature. As the second installment of Morrison's trilogy that begins with *Beloved*, one of *Jazz*'s most important achievements lies in the way it reveals the psycho-social underpinnings of the controversy generated by the arrival of jazz music on the American scene, as if faster dance rhythms spelled inevitable doom.[8]

Jazz in the 1920s was considered alternately scurrilous and disreputable because, as Rudolph Fisher suggests, it rendered black life exotic, made it a commodity that wealthy whites scrambled to consume.[9] But the wrangling over whether jazz constituted a source of cultural prestige or a signal of impending collapse needs to be understood in terms of—cannot be understood apart from—the local context in which it occurs. The novel's setting foregrounds how, in moments of cultural or social disorder, great emphasis is placed on generating criteria for blameworthiness. Morrison likewise engages the intersection of two distinctly isolated historical constructs, the Jazz Age and the Harlem Renaissance. In

1926 New York, as the imperatives of rhetoric overwhelm the authority of myth, the Jazz Age and the Harlem Renaissance are often framed as moments of tremendous possibility felt not only at the level of sensation but also spatially. But the events in *Jazz* occur a year after Alain Locke, stated in an essay on New York City Mayor Fiorello LaGuardia's relationship to Harlem that "the rosy enthusiasm and hopes of 1925 ... were cruelly deceptive images" (224). The cultural and economic forces of the time have much to do with the modernist formulations of the individual at a societal moment when the boundaries between public and private were rapidly disappearing. The rhetorical postures of the 1920s were distinguished by the need to position the individual as an entity growing apart from cultural tradition, where the medium through which cultural tradition was disseminated became so incredibly rife with information that the fixed identities associated with a concrete sense of values were abandoned in favor of *the plasticity of value*. And what makes this unique to the twentieth century is that celebrity becomes a measure of social progress, where being able to watch a love affair unfold in a magazine leads people to believe they are *participants* in a culture that emphasizes spectatorship.

Jazz chronicles the arrival of a new consciousness regarding modernity in which "popularity" and "access" are the staging grounds for the enclosure of human experience in a rhetoric of desire whose completion does not bring about a new level of mastery and control. The novel describes a moment when the interiority enjoyed by the initiated gives way to a tight, less kinetic space where a transient form of value is tied to the marketing and consumption of goods and services. The rise of advertising meant that individuals could be induced to buy because they were assured that a new and tangible state of belonging would result from the purchase. Coinciding with the rise of Hollywood cinema, the 1920s saw individuals enclosed in the tight space created by a media that sought to avoid any hint of miscegenation. Morrison's narrator provides example after example of the city's ability to induce individuals to believe that their choices are the product of their own volition and thus points to the ways that popular culture created an illusion of social transparency, as if the popular and the air were one and the same. In *Terrible Honesty*, Ann Douglas describes the 1920s as an "Aerial Age" when "radio shows were on the air, planes toured the heavens, and buildings competed with the clouds. Everywhere people were netting the sky and finding in the air an androgynous free-for-all of spiritual energy" (196). *Jazz* chronicles the ways that the estrangement and disillusionment explored in Chap. 2 are best assuaged by indulging desires that can be traced to popular culture.

But attention also proves to be an important consideration in the acquisition of visual literacy. The 1920s sees the rise of style as a way to predicate behavior and to reward public visibility to those best able to manage and display it. On the one hand, the language we attribute to the term suggests an individual's idiosyncrasy, the choices one makes to be considered unique. But with the rise of advertising, the very idea of uniqueness is conscripted into the service of uniformity. *Jazz* foregrounds the ways style and attention structure the tactical sensibility we use to negotiate the everyday and from there how we structure concepts of respectability.[10]

As *Jazz* portrays it, respectability turns on the act of aiming a socially constituted gaze at individuals cohabiting in a particular social location. More importantly, it has to do with discerning whether a passerby in the throng deserves only a passing glance or a more intensely focused gaze that can, ostensibly at least, penetrate an individual's carefully managed surface traits in order to locate and discern his or her inner essence. To be respectable, then, is not a matter of *appearing to be* something; rather, it means that someone who becomes the object of an appraising gaze rises or falls in the social firmament according to the distance between surface and substance, such that *what they appear to be* and *what they are able to conceal* becomes indistinguishable.

But if there is a diagnostic bent in this novel, there is also a restorative one. Morrison's novel calls attention to the role music plays on the cultural scene, and the narrative treats a moment when audiences are wary of jazz music and its implications, making it impossible to read *Jazz* and not consider the roles speculation and consumption play in the constitution of the black urban subject. Looking first at the ways that Joe and Violet Trace fall under the spell of New York City, it is clear that traveling from the rural South to the urban North involved a drastic increase in those things demanding an individual's attention. Set at a time when fashion, advertising, and slick magazines were becoming the order of the day, *Jazz* depicts how Harlem was on one hand a *black* space in which African Americans sought to pursue the American Dream and on the other hand a location that was not immune to fluctuations in the economies (both financial and symbolic)[11] affecting everyday life. As such, Harlemites were just as prone as white Manhattanites to associate celebrity with a fully constituted public self that could be emulated, if only by wearing a particular makeup or style of hat. Set in the year prior to the emergence of talking films, *Jazz* offers the reader a glimpse into how millions of African Americans migrating north left behind the immobility that plagued their lives in the South in hopes of becoming more fully themselves.

Morrison's characters find themselves in a moment when the symbolic geography of the Harlem Renaissance and the antecedent conceptual geography of the Jazz Age are manifest. In both instances, we are presented with images of decadence and moral decline, but we are just as quickly seduced by the illusions of opulence and political possibility that take the form of advertising, radio, modern cinema, and popular entertainment.[12] The speed with which these changes beset the average person is likely to have intimidated many new arrivals to a point where they might have been tempted to board a train headed back South. But when Joe and Violet Trace arrive in New York, they have very little desire to return "home." Though they live a different existence than they did in Virginia, the two-story house is apparent in their respective traumas, which create an overriding sense of estrangement, a tight space the characters manage to escape to the extent that they regain domestic tranquility by the novel's end.

As previously stated, a political imaginary is the representation of both possibility and the limits on possibility that recognizes the gap between acceptable and unacceptable behavior as well as the affective moments that inform outliers of the need to come into sync. with their surroundings. If the greenhorn's behavior is distinguished by "slow" forms of understanding, the scope of that mental disconnect is communicated through jokes, disapproving looks, weak smiles, or no smile at all, vocal inflections that communicate annoyance or displeasure.[13] As a novel that features characters who endure embarrassment or shame for falling out of step with their fellow inhabitants, *Jazz* is a story about finding community among strangers, a story of carving a sense of place from the tabula rasa of space.

The 1920s represents a moment when the rise of slick magazines and advertising created the concept of celebrity almost overnight. Hence, Morrison's decision to set her novel in that moment might reflect her sense that one of the challenges for newly arrived migrants in the North was how to manage the rush of demands placed on their attention. The relationships that emerge in a city with millions of inhabitants occur in the midst of new forms of stimulation that newcomers feel obligated to treat as a regular aspect of everyday experience. African Americans associated with the New Negro Renaissance period such as Claude McKay, Zora Neale Hurston, and Langston Hughes have produced works that feature the greenhorn, that figure whose failures of judgment are a product of inexperience and a lack of social literacy. The greenhorn lacks the ability to focus in the midst of overstimulation and is thereby ripe for exploitation because he or she cannot discern which aspects of urban life demand full attention and which should be ignored.

For example, in Langston Hughes's "The Morning After," we find a speaker who wakes up next to a woman he met the night before after drinking "bad likker."[14] The poem reads:

> I was so sick last night I
> Didn't hardly know my mind.
> So sick last night I
> Didn't know my mind.
> I drunk some bad licker that
>
> Almost made me blind.Had a dream last night I
> Thought I was in hell.
> I drempt last night I
> Thought I was in hell.
> Woke up and looked around me—
>
> Babe, your mouth was open like a well.I said, Baby! Baby!
> Please don't snore so loud.
> Baby! Please!
> Please don't snore so loud.
> You jest a little bit o' woman but you
> Sound like a great big crowd.[15]

Hughes's poem recounts a moment when a refugee from the south, having relocated to Harlem, with its higher population density and unfamiliar codes of social decorum, realizes his neighbors are in such close proximity that his moral transgression is evident to anyone in earshot. As he will likely discover, that transgression will soon be known not only by his neighbors but ultimately the neighborhood, demonstrating how urban-dwellers lives reflect the more complicated social relations enacted across different spatial scales. The speaker's dream of being in hell likely signals his sense that his partner's snoring offers ample proof about his lapsed morals.

His realization that he has entered a radically different circumstance where the boundary between public and private is proven to be specious suggests the scale of the transformation of social relations in the black community that has come with migration. This is evidenced by the poem's concluding couplet: "You just a little bit o' woman / but you sound like a great big crowd." The woman's loud sleeping habits demonstrate how intimate acts (or their aftermath) occur in the midst of a large audience. Equating his companion with a "great big crowd," the speaker anticipates the manner in which a private encounter will become known among an ever-widening circle of strangers. In the crowded space of Harlem, hearsay represents the manner in which the link between conduct and visual evidence is no longer a requisite for assessing an individual's character. The aural evidence of a social transgression in "The Morning After" overwhelms the deficit of visual information until what people can hear nullifies the need to personally witness the transgression. What they can hear—and thus infer—is that the "voice" of the woman confirms the speaker's questionable morals and misconduct. The spatial politics of urban life are in evidence here; Hughes's poem reflects the manner in which the community's understanding of intimacy and thereby what constitutes communal cohesion is undergoing a set of profound changes. In Harlem, the village is re-imagined as the neighborhood, which means that an individual's influence in the physical world is limited to what might well be an equally small geographical location like a street or a city block, but gossip magnifies that influence because hearsay no longer requires a physically verifiable source, which means it can travel beyond the immediate confines of a street and take on a life of its own.

The question becomes how Toni Morrison works out the implications of such a development. What is the impact of gossip on communal cohesion? Does access to gossip represent a kind of moral authority simply because the urban inhabitant finds herself in the loop—that is, included in a circuit of information that allows her to "know" people beyond her immediate vicinity? The novel ascertains the answers to these questions through the narrator, who arbitrates what constitutes respectable behavior and what does not on a visual grid.[16] *Jazz* exemplifies what I am calling promiscuous narration: when a narrator willingly privileges excess over restraint, the narrator trades on promiscuity to produce what feels like definitive outcomes. Promiscuous narrative is properly understood in relation to Stuart Ewen's observation regarding the "universal language of the eye." For Ewen, the problem with the emergence of a social practice that privileges the visual is not simply a matter of calling attention to the seeing/not-seeing binary but also the manner in which acts of speculation, starting in the nineteenth Century, saw "the pre-eminence of *hard goods*" give way to "that of abstract value, immateriality, and the ephemeral" (157). Through careful attention to the novel's narrative structure, we begin to understand how Morrison's *Jazz* is a commentary on the 1990s, especially in light of the stock market crash of 1987, which Ewen characterizes as "a by-product of the economy of abstraction." Morrison's refashioning of the resignation that ends Fitzgerald's *Gatsby* and the optimism we so often attribute to the Harlem Renaissance is equally informed by the visual economy of abstraction.

As the reader quickly becomes aware, *Jazz* is a narrative built—in ways reminiscent of jazz—on acts of elaboration and re-elaboration, with the narrator oscillating between what Nancy Peterson refers to as "the detachment and overarching knowledge typically associated with a reliable omniscient narrator" and "the limited knowledge, biases, and involvement associated with an unreliable first-person narrator" (64). There are numerous instances of free indirect discourse, where the narrator adopts a communal voice, as well as others when she adopts a singular perspective. For example, at the luncheon Alice Manfred hosts in her apartment, the narrator launches into a commentary on how nicely Alice

> could lay a table. Food might be a tad skimpy in the portions, and I believe she had a prejudice against butter; she used so little of it in her cakes. But the biscuits were light, and the plates, the flatware, sparkling and arranged just so. Open her napkins wide as you please and not a catface anywhere. (72)

Speaking in the voice of a member of the Civic Daughters, the narrator offers an assessment of Alice's food that suggests that the narrator may have been present at the lunch the first time Joe saw Dorcas, which gives the narrator license to offer a negative and knowing assessment of the girl. But the narrator quickly assesses Dorcas's veracity by linking physical movement to visual details in a manner that equates physical movement with the articulation of erotic desire:

> *I always believed* that girl was a pack of lies. *I could tell by her walk* her underclothes were beyond her years, even if her dress wasn't. Maybe back in October Alice was beginning to think so too. By the time January came, nobody had to speculate. Everybody knew. *I wonder* if she had a premonition of Joe Trace knocking on her door? (72; emphasis added)

The intimacy the narrator implies, however, is mediated by an interiority that seems at times cloying. "I lived a long time, maybe too much, in my own mind," she states; "People say I should come out more. Mix" (9). She takes on the characterization of a flesh-and-blood narrator when she says, "*I agree that I close off in places*, but *if you have been left standing, as I have*, while your partner overstays at another appointment ... it can make you inhospitable if you aren't careful" (9; emphasis added).

Notwithstanding the question of whether the narrator's omniscient posture is physical or ethereal, she intimates that the source of her seemingly unimpeachable narrative-authority emanates from the city itself, making her presence both ubiquitous and ephemeral. The narrator's eye for nuance is rooted in Manhattan—the way that it came to stand for an active and restless modernity, the way the city constitutes a focused intensification of attention and consciousness. Hence, the narrator makes such declarations as, "I like the way the City makes people think they can do what they want and get away with it," and "Do what you please in the City; it is there to back and frame you no matter what you do. And what goes on in its blocks and lots and side streets is anything the strong can think of and the weak will admire" (8–9).

In this sense, the entire subject of *Jazz* is topophilia. All of the characters, with the exception perhaps of Alice Manfred, love being in New York, with a sky possessing the ability to "empty itself of surface, and [be] more like the ocean than the ocean itself, go deep starless" (35). With a nightlife sparkling with neon light, New York is a visual Babylon, where people go to see "the sights." But the "night sky booming over a glittering city" becomes both sound and emptiness. Though it could be argued that the city, as the narrator portrays it, is most skilled at distorting everything in its midst, it clearly speaks from the same kind of affective bond to place as people born in a small town so familiar with every detail and nuance that they come to embody where they are. In the years following World War I, soldiers returning from overseas could brag that they had "seen the world," even if that world turned out to be a trench in Germany or France. The idea of being closely identified with one place is mediated by the advent of the movie theater and the photograph. The narrator's sense of the intimate details underlying a man's ostensible desire for a woman on a stoop insists that *seeing*, as it is concretized as the gaze, has everything to do with the identificatory protocols that images of far-off places institute. From one's lonely station in a dilapidated building, one can make judgments on the larger world simply by employing the eye in ways directed by the cultural technology that privilege visuality.[17]

The dichotomy the narrator draws between strength and weakness is intricately linked to the cityscape. "A city like this one *makes me dream tall and feel in on things*," the narrator declares; "Hep. It's the bright steel rocking above the shade below that does it. *When I look over* the strips of green grass lining the river, at church steeples and the cream and colored halls of apartment buildings, *I'm strong*" (7; emphasis added). The narrator's "strength," if we can call it that, lies not in her physicality, which is confirmed when she states, "I haven't got any muscles, so I can't really be expected to defend myself. But I do know how to take precaution. *Mostly it's making sure no one knows all there is to know about me*" (8; emphasis added). How are we to take this? Literally, as if the narrator is lacking in physical stature and is therefore not a threat? Or as an indication that the dangers of city life are at her command? Could she be the embodiment of attention, meaning that her narrative capability is a product of the focalization of public behavior? Or could it be that behind all the glib assessments lies an insecure person whose main asset is the empty vessel of a life she fills with the failures and mishaps of those who enter her critical gaze? As Erika Spohrer aptly observes, *Jazz* is a "book of pictures" whose plot revolves around acts of spectatorship and the gaze.[18]

If the narrator's strength is not synonymous with physicality, it nonetheless issues from a gaze powered by our readerly desire to *know* the details of a moral transgression in a definitive way. In this respect, the narrator is reminiscent of Walter Benjamin's *flaneur*, a figure who delights in "inmersing [her]self in the crowd" (Lauster 140). The narrator seems to approach the task of narration with a relish that can be understood in relation to the *flaneur*'s role as a strolling spectator whose gaze is directed into the apartment and office buildings rising above street level, "someone who collects mental notes taken on leisurely city walks … who takes pleasure in abandoning [her]self to the artificial world of high capitalist-civilization" (Lauster 140). The narrator's declaration that trying to determine the Other's state of mind is "risky" must be juxtaposed against the fact that she tells the story of Golden Gray twice—first in an omniscient version that recounts Gray's journey from Baltimore, his discovery of Wild on the side of the road, and his arrival at Henry Lestory's cabin, and later in a version that features the narrator's ambivalence regarding how she gleans Gray's motivations for seeking out the father he has never known. In so doing, the narrator reveals her own motives: "Now I have to think this through, carefully, even though I may be doomed to another misunderstanding. I have to do it and not break down. Not hating him is not enough; liking, loving him is not useful. *I have to alter things*" (161, emphasis added).

The narrator's admission of her arrogance and presumption creates space in which to ponder Morrison's effort to deconstruct several iterations of modern black womanhood: the "crazy black woman," the "respectable black woman," and the "loose black woman." When Golden Gray rescues Wild from the side of the road, it constitutes a moment when Wild's "uncivilized" behavior stands in stark contrast to that of women residing in the metropole. But it is equally suggestive of how a lack of restraint was mapped onto black femininity to the extent that it became an index of racial conduct. Golden Gray's ambivalent attitude about his own racial identity leaves him to wonder if Wild's (and later Henry Lestory's) racial attributes will contaminate what he has heretofore believed to be racial purity. He dreads contact but wonders whether the decision to leave Wild on the side of the road to die will disrupt his ability to claim racial superiority because as a white man he is, by definition, more civilized. Is his act noblesse oblige or racial solidarity? We should be mindful, then, of how the labels attached to black womanhood reflect masculine anxiety. The labels provide cover for black (and white) men's transgressions against women and thus point to the ways *Jazz* historicizes a moment when configurations of black womanhood, all of which can be traced back to slavery's contortion of the black female body, became so widely accessible that the community is sure of what these labels mean as they relate to individual circumstance. Hence, Violet, Alice Manfred, and Dorcas offer the reader access to the emotional territory obscured by the stereotypes these terms insinuate. The narrator's adherence to observations that implies it issues either from direct experience or the illusory strength of omniscient narration carries with it an obligation to fashion an image of what these figures *look like.*

Relocating to New York meant that black female migrants were subjected to a social gaze that mediated their presence, creating a taxonomic system that might justify their presence in the spatial geographies to be found in the city. The woman in Hughes's poem lacks a coherent subjectivity, but she is an important indicator of the speaker's predicament because he makes her snoring synonymous with that predicament. And because her snoring is so loud that she can be heard all over the building, she becomes the "loose" woman by default because "respectable" black women are distinguished by their quiet ways. But Morrison foregrounds female characters' voices and feelings, thereby making those moments when the narrator provides details about them a product of omniscience rather than interaction. The problem with labeling women, Morrison suggests, is that it fails to understand that a complex individual might embody the three guises of black womanhood on display and thus reflect how behavior is often contingent on circumstance.

The narrator of *Jazz* invites us to pay attention to the ways that the characters behave in real life according to what popular music is promoting in the 1920s. This is suggested by the configurations that emerge at various instances in the text. We gain a sense of the difficulty of managing the different templates of womanhood in the scene where Dorcas, at sixteen, accompanies her friend, Felice, to a house party. In this moment, promiscuity and respectability acquire companionable weight. We also need to consider promiscuity's adjectival cousin, *promiscuous*, a term applied to individuals—most often women—engaged in a series of transient sexual-couplings.[19] Dorcas's promiscuous inclinations are signaled by her obsession with "finding something foxy enough to wear" (64). Knowing that the party is an opportunity to see and be seen, Dorcas's expectations for what kind of time she will have are shaped by her sense "that a badly dressed body is no body at all" (64). Without silk stockings and with shoes that are "those of someone much younger or very old," Dorcas feels ill-equipped to manifest an erotic persona that on one hand neither too young nor too old and on the other, dressed in a manner that declares that one is unavailable.

But here, we would do well to recall the Clearing and the manner in which the invitation to dance (along with laughter and tears) seeks to reawaken the notion that flesh and selfhood are not polar opposites as they were in bondage. Note how the house party indicates that aurality and visuality have fallen into a nearly seamless relation, with the music compensating for Dorcas's sense of disquiet regarding her appearance. The music intensifies the social gaze but does so by reversing respectability's visual imperative; the gaze no longer works in service to a morality steeped in "traditional" values but now supports an imperative in which corporeality and carnality are sutured to promiscuity's root word, *promise*, which denotes the act of "giving good grounds for expecting." This is communicated when Dorcas dances "not as fast as the others but ... graceful, in spite of those shaming shoes, and she is provocative" (66).

A pivotal moment in the party comes when the attention of everyone in the dining room focuses on two brothers, who move "like taut silk or loose metal," The boys' notoriety precedes them, which makes them the object of Dorcas' admiring gaze. Walking into the hallway adjacent to the dining room, Dorcas has an "unrestricted view of the brothers as they bring the performance to a rousing close. Laughing, they accept the praise that is due them: adoring looks from the girls, congratulatory punches and slaps from the boys" (66). When Dorcas notices the brothers "commanding the attention of a crowd in the dining room," she feels what the narrator describes as the "stomach-jump" that "is the sign of real interest and possible love" (66). Noting the brothers' "wonderful faces," Dorcas offers an invitational gaze that is met by the brothers, who's "eyes seem wide and welcoming to her" (66). But this visual transaction occurs within the illusory and volatile space created by the music, so that in the silence right before the record on the turntable begins to play, the romantic narrative set in motion by eyes meeting across a crowded room breaks down:

> The brothers turn up the wattage of their smiles. The right record is on the turntable now; she can hear its preparatory hiss as the needle slides toward its first groove. The brothers smile brilliantly; one leans a fraction of an inch toward the other and, never losing eye contact with Dorcas, whispers something. The other looks Dorcas up and down as she moves toward them. Then, just as the music, slow and smoky, loads up the air, his smile bright as ever, he wrinkles his nose and turns away. (67)

As the narrator observes, Dorcas has been erased in "the time it takes for a needle to find its opening groove" (67), illustrating music's power as a vehicle of both desire and rejection.

Having been the object of a gaze in which she has been "acknowledged, appraised, and dismissed," Dorcas finds her veins blocked by the "ice floes" created by rejection, concluding that the "body she inhabits is unworthy" (67). Despite the fact that Dorcas is "graceful" and "provocative," when she dances, outside of the encomia the music creates, the visual promise of the glowing ember at her navel proves to be an empty one.

The visual logic underlying Dorcas's rejection is easily understood as part of a critique of forms of masculinity characterized by sexism and misogyny that makes the objectification of the female body standard practice. But Morrison also demonstrates the taxonomies that create barriers between women that get played out spatially, where just being seen in a specific location has the power to define. In this light, we see how the relationship that develops between Alice Manfred and Violet defies such oppressive logic, especially if we persist in viewing them as the prototypical "crazy black woman" and "respectable black woman," content to play their assigned roles. But using a musical analogy, the relationship between Alice and Violet is perhaps better understood in terms of the blue note, which inserts a minor interval when a major interval is the expected approach to resolving the chord, Alice and Violet can interact in a way that grows organically out of their different forms of lovelessness.

Morrison emphasizes this by making their initial contact a matter of acting out of their respective "natures." Violet arrives at Alice's apartment and greets her by stating, "I don't have a thing to say to you. Not one thing" (75). As a black woman involved in the club movement, Alice "would not be caught dead" in a speakeasy: she is not "that kind of woman." Conversely, situating Violet in the space of "crazy" absolves her neighbors from directing a gaze that eschews a surface assessment of her and instead seeks to determine the source of her disaffection. But Alice is deeply aware, thinking about how Joe, "a nice, neighborly, everybody-knows-him-man," could kill her niece, that Violet 's attack on Dorcas is of a piece with the murder. From Alice's standpoint, Violent, as she has come to be called, is simply one more example of how black women are "armed; black women were dangerous and the less money they had the deadlier the weapon they chose" (77).

In a manner that reveals the "respectable black woman" for the artifice it is, Alice comes to look forward to Violet's subsequent visits to the apartment: "When Violet came to visit (and Alice never knew when that might be) something opened up." Alice realizes that in Violet's presence she is different:

> The thing was how Alice felt and talked in her company. Not like she did with other people. With Violent she was impolite. Sudden. Frugal. No apology or courtesy seemed required or necessary between them. But

> something else was—clarity, perhaps. The kind of clarity crazy people demand from the not-crazy. (83)

Alice comes to relate how she shared her husband, Louis, who was killed during the East St. Louis race riot, with another woman until Alice forces him to choose and he leaves. Though she does not tell Violet about how his departure made her feel, Alice recalls,

> What she neglected to say—what came flooding back to her—was also true: every day and every night for seven months, she, Alice Manfred, was starving for blood. Not his. Oh no. From him she planned sugar in his motor, scissors to his tie, burned suits, slashed shoes, ripped socks. Vicious, childish acts of violence to inconvenience him, remind him. But no blood. (86)

Instead, Alice recalls a different target for her rage:

> Her craving settled on the red liquid coursing through the other woman's veins. An ice pick stuck in and pulled up would get it. Would a clothesline rope circling her neck and yanked with all Alice's strength make her spit it up? Her favorite, however, the dream that plumped her pillow at night was seeing herself mount a horse, then ride it, and find the woman alone on a road and gallop till she ran her down under four iron hooves, then back again and back again until there was nothing left but tormented road dirt signaling where the hussy had been. (86)

Thinking about this, looking at Violet's hat "pushed back on her forehead," and noting how it "gave her a scatty look," Alice observes Violet's inner struggles and realizes that she can name them because she has also endured them. Though she has opted not to act on those feelings by slashing a dead girl's face, "the dream that plump[s] her pillow at night" involves the violent erasure of the woman who "stole" Alice's husband.

But the women in *Jazz* are distinguished by their willingness to do the necessary work of self-fashioning as a way to resist the immobility of tight space. After leaving Alice's apartment, Violet goes to a drugstore, "sucking malt through a straw wondering who on earth *that other Violet* was that walked about the City in her skin; peeped out through her eyes and saw other things" (89). Her desire to know and understand "*that* Violet" who disrupted Dorcas's funeral by trying to cut the dead girl's face is the recurrence of the trope of two-story house, which takes the form of Violet's psychic doubling. By recognizing that the woman who perpetrated such a disreputable act is not the woman she understands herself to be, Violet moves closer to the moment at the end of the novel when she decides to dispatch *that Violet* in favor of herself. The Violet who emerges at the end of the novel is self-possessed enough to ask, "What's the world for if you can't make it up the way you want it?" This question cleaves neatly to the attitude of Morrison's southern men, who engage the question by taking the world as they find it and attempting to fit themselves into it. Recognizing that she has been confined to the tight space of the "crazy black woman," Violet endeavors to break free. In one of the novel's most poignant moments, she asks,

> "'How did you get rid of her?'"
> "'Killed her. Then I killed the me that killed her.'"
> "'Who's left?'"
> "'Me.'" (209)

Morrison's use of quotation marks reveals this to be an exchange between Felice and Violet. Though it appears that Felice is talking because it follows directly on Felice's realization that "it seemed wrong" (209). But in fact the exchange is actually meant to follow what Violet said two paragraphs earlier. Felice is inclined to state, "I started thinking maybe the hairdresser was right again because of the way she looked when she said 'me.' Like it was the first time she heard the word" (209).

Cast in the role of the "loose woman," Dorcas seeks to gain the attentions of a man who will treat her nicely, an effort that can be interpreted to mean that she is most attracted to men who satisfy her hunger for change, for "something to do." This idea speaks of how simulation and stimulation are intricately linked. After she leaves Joe to be with Acton, Dorcas justifies the move by stating, "He didn't even care what I looked like. I could be anything, do anything—and it pleased him. Something about that made me mad" (190). Though she does not realize it, Dorcas rejects Joe's willingness to give her space to become who she wishes to be.[20] But if urban life creates tight spaces for its inhabitants, the 1920s represent a moment when changing one's appearance is a way to approximate a strategy for loosening social constrictions. Morrison's novel reminds us to be attentive to how African Americans' transition from their rural origins to urban space demanded the reorganization of social protocols, generating new ways to appraise the body, to understand how it relates to the *moment*. According to Dorcas, Acton relates to her in a very different way:

> Acton, now, he tells me when he doesn't like the way I fix my hair. Then I do it how he likes it. I never wear glasses when he is with me and I changed my laugh for him to one he likes better. *I think he does.* I know he didn't like it before. And I play with my food now. Joe liked for me to eat it all up and want more. Acton gives me a quiet look when I ask for seconds. *He worries about me that way. Joe never did. Joe didn't care what kind of woman I was.* (190; emphasis added)

To be sure, Dorcas's willingness to change herself into what a man wishes her to be is familiar to us. Dorcas differs from Pilate, who begins "at zero" and remakes herself into a person ready to engage others in substantive ways. In this, Dorcas is a reprise of Pilate's granddaughter, Hagar, who looks in a mirror and declares, "Look at how I look. I look awful. No wonder he didn't want me. I look terrible. I need to get up from here and fix myself up. No *wonder!*" (308). If respectability for women is a manifestation of a visual politics that has the power to enliven or destroy, Dorcas's declaration, "I have a look now," indicates her fall into a tight space akin to cultural weightlessness.[21] Further, Dorcas's claim to have "a look" and her willingness to contort herself into the girl she believes Acton wants her to be also anticipates *Tar Baby*'s Jadine, who has a modeling career based solely on her ability to "look so much younger when she chose that she didn't even have to lie to the agencies, and they gave what they believed was a nineteen-year-old face the eyes and mouth of a woman of three decades" (45). As Spohrer points out, "What Dorcas needs to fit and cohere her disparate parts is a controlling and colonizing gaze" (81), and that gaze is provided by her new lover, Acton. As the "prototypical male spectator," Acton can see Dorcas only when she "mimes the helpless position of the white female of Hollywood cinema," which seduces Dorcas into believing he is the man of her dreams. "I wanted to have a personality," Dorcas intimates, "and with Acton I'm getting one" (190). Though this statement is laughable in terms of the power it imputes to the masculine gaze, it is also disheartening because it reflects the impact of the magazine culture that trumpets the beauty of the white female while ignoring or distorting the attributes of black femininity. Her anger at Joe, "who didn't care" about her appearance, is one reason why she leaves him for Acton. Here, Morrison suggests that the social mechanisms that create our modern understanding of the "loose woman" have a great deal to do with how popular culture invited women to embrace a form of plasticity that would allow them to cast off one persona in favor of another, to embrace whatever iteration of the "ideal woman" was in vogue.

Perhaps this is why Violet's use of the persona of Violent to rid herself of the persona of "crazy black woman" has monumental implications. Her use of the personal pronoun *me* seems "like it was the first she heard the word," because it constitutes a moment when the behaviors she adopted to manage the injury she suffered as a girl after her mother's suicide, when hearing the story of Golden Gray introduces Violet to a narrative that emphasizes what it means to live in a state of adoration. Because her grandmother, True Belle, relates the stories in the wake of Rose Dear's suicide, however, Violet internalizes the narrative as a template for how she should move through the world and the sorts of expectations she should have as a woman. When she states, "Then I killed the me that killed her," she is taking ownership of her life by rejecting a template that does not suit her.

Jazz takes great pains to parse the role music plays in the construction of oppressive templates of womanhood during the 1920s, a moment when visuality and aurality are interpreted in radically divergent ways. For example, during the parade commemorating the lives lost in the race riots she escaped in East St. Louis, Alice Manfred watches the procession moving down Fifth Avenue and concludes that "what was meant came from the drums." The mourners in a parade intended to memorialize the tragic dead re-enact a counter-pointed present and past where music is a vehicle through which to exorcise the trauma of racial violence. For Alice, the music resides in a performative space in which disaffection and dissent are repurposed as communal rituals whose commemorative posture obscures the residual anger and frustration produced in a body politic that refuses to acknowledge, much less punish, acts of racial violence and the ways it invalidates the contributions blacks have made to the democratic project. The parade is distinguished as a moment when political dissent is expressed. But because it is band music and not a political treatise or demonstration, the drums become a surrogate for the rage and political outcry that should accompany instances when random violence takes lives. Further, irrespective of the drums' provocation, Alice does not understand them as a promissory circumstance that will soon give way to mindless celebration.

When music appears in Morrison's fiction, it is used to articulate the everyday workings of community or as a metaphor for agency or its lack. In *Beloved*, Paul D. and the other prisoners on the chain gang use the power of song to transcend the physical limits imposed on their incarcerated bodies:

> With a sledge hammer in his hands, and Hi Man's lead, the men got through. They sang it out, beat it up, garbling the words so they could not be understood; tricking the words so their syllables yielded up other meanings. They sang the women they knew; the children they had been; the animals they had tamed or seen others tame. They sang of bosses and masters and misses; of mules and dogs and the shamelessness of life. They sang lovingly of graveyards and sisters long gone. Of pork in the woods; meal in the pan; fish on the line; cane, rain, and rocking chairs. (128)

In this iteration, singing is a medium through which to assert an historical narrative, so substantive it renders the men's imprisonment invalid. Morrison's use of semicolons denotes how no man's experience is more valid than another man's and how the history created is a product of collective effort. But song is just as easily an assertion of resistant agency that challenges their dehumanization:

> And they beat. The women for having known them and no more, no more; the children for having been them but never again. They killed a boss so often and so completely they had to bring him back to life to pulp him one more time. Tasting hot mealcake among pine trees, they beat it away. Singing love songs to Mr. Death, they smashed his head. More than the rest, they killed the flirt whom folks called Life for leading them on. Making them think the next sunrise would be worth it; that another stroke would do it at last. (128)

Life on a chain gang is the very embodiment of tight space—cut off from loved ones, traumatized by arbitrary forms of discipline, the eradication of all those things that make a man an individual among the many. The chain gang in Alfred, Georgia, demonstrates what Guthrie Ramsey, in his book *Race Music*, refers to as "blackness as practice": blackness can be seen "as a dynamic process of cultural and ideological shape shifting. It can in fact, operate as both structure and resistance in a theory of practice" (36). As such, black vernacular musical forms like the work song emerge "as a most conspicuous mode of signification" in African Americans' effort to assert ethnic identities that stand apart from stereotype or fantasy.[22]

Ramsey's observation informs the manner through which *Jazz* interrogates the role music plays in how black folk understand their circumstances. During those instances where speech is either inadequate or recklessly transgressive, music can assume the task of stating the feelings of the group. For example, during the parade down Fifth Avenue, Alice

Manfred notices “a tide of bold black faces, speechless and unblinking because what they meant to say but did not trust themselves to say the drums said for them, and what they had seen with their own eyes and through the eyes of others the drums described to a T” (54).

In light of such a moment, though, the “new music” seems fitted to doing a different kind of cultural labor. If the chain gang’s work song can be thought of as the manifestation of a spatial logic that radically re-imagines the symbolic geography of imprisonment, then the music arriving on the cultural scene in Harlem represents the emergence of an erotic geography in which bodies spun into motion by the music on a phonograph challenge-convention. If music had once been a “beautiful noise,” its popular iteration and the movement it occasions is nothing if not a sign of “Imminent Demise.” The body plays a substantial role in this process, where “not just ankles but knees are in full view,” creating a circumstance in which “you couldn’t tell the streetwalkers from the mothers” (56). And in what amounts to the articulation of how popular music is nothing short of a remapping of the body, Alice and other women of her generation:

> did not know for sure, but they suspected that the dances were beyond nasty because the music was getting worse and worse with each passing season the Lord waited to make Himself known. Songs that used to start in the head and fill the heart had dropped on down, down to places below the sash and the buckled belts. Lower and lower, until the music was so lowdown you had to shut your windows and just suffer the summer sweat. (56)

The narrator’s use of free indirect discourse asserts that the good time the new music ushers onto the scene is a source of anxiety. “Lowdown music” is intended to evoke an erotic geography in which traveling south “below the sash and the buckled belts” of women and men under its influence is the expected result. But consider the way that Morrison’s phrasing denotes the manner in which the music itself constitutes the deployment of an erotic gaze as it also points out the irony to be found in a situation where black migrants living in the north have gazes that turn unceremoniously southward again. As the generational divide that formed with the advent of hip-hop suggests, jazz and the blues created a stir because they tapped into anxieties that equated respectability with hypervisibility.

Further, Alice attributes the violence and disorder in Harlem and other parts of New York directly to the music: "It was the music," she thinks, not "the droves and droves of colored people flocking to paychecks and streets full of themselves." Her "peace," in the form of "Clifton Place, with a leafy sixty-foot tree every hundred feet, a quiet street with no fewer than five motor cars parked at the curb," is disturbed by music so loud it is better "to close the windows and shutters" (59). But what comes through in Alice's assessment of the music, interestingly enough, is not the invasiveness of unwanted sound but rather a pollutant that threatens the security of all. Listening to the music makes "her aware of flesh and something so free she could smell its bloodsmell" (58–59).[23] Despite Alice's best efforts to shield Dorcas from the music's effects, the parade on Fifth Avenue is the occasion for her to ascertain the promise it offers.

Whereas her aunt hears the drums "saying what the graceful women and marching men could not" (53), Dorcas hears something quite different. Desiring the stimulation and release promised by life in a city that seeks both to fetishize and commodify pleasure, Dorcas hears the drums at the parade and understands that they "were only the first part, the first word, of a command. For the drums were not an all-embracing rope of fellowship, discipline, and transcendence. She remembered them as a beginning, a start of something she looked to complete" (60). Alice ascertains the drums as instruments communicating black resilience; Dorcas, by contrast, hears them as a mechanism able to instrumentalize her physical desire. In this respect, Alice and Dorcas are at opposite ends of the spectrum, with Alice believing that the music has undergone a transformation in which she hears "a complicated anger" and thus coming to hate its "appetite. Its longing for the bash, the slit, a kind of careless hunger for a fight or a red ruby stickpin for tie—either would do" (59). In her view, the music "faked happiness, faked welcome"; it does "not make her feel generous" (59).

Alice is therefore highly suspicious of jazz because it eroticizes the urban subject and diminishes the individual's grasp on the tenets of respectability and responsibility. Her trepidation reflects a common attitude of the time, since jazz was often associated—however unfairly—with dangerous places. But as Charles Hersch points out, the cultural politics that surrounded jazz in its earliest incarnations had much to do with "the many battles to roll back constraints and exercise some power over, or create some space within, the institutions and social relationships that dominate our lives" (12). The anxieties 1920s popular music incites in Alice Manfred reflects how the shift from the Victorian sensibilities of the late nineteenth century, which emphasized sobriety and restraint, were being displaced by what Peretti describes as an "adolescent revolution in courtship, public behavior, dress, and female behavior" (38). Even as the moment included "built-in limits," the loosening of restrictions on public displays and bodily adornment as it played out in settings such as Harlem ran up against a politics of respectability that turned a critical gaze on individuals whose actions threatened the overall reputation of the black community. "Alice Manfred had worked hard to privatize her niece, but she was no match for a City seeping music that begged and challenged each and every day, 'Come,' it said, 'Come and do wrong'" (67).[24]

On closer inspection, however, Alice's sense that music "had dropped on down, down to places below the sash and the buckled belts," is indicative, once again, of *Jazz*'s critique of visual politics. Alice's assessment depends on the male gaze to substantiate its claims. When she talks about the music dropping down, she is anticipating the ways that dances that involve moving the hips will attract the male gaze toward women's sexual parts. The point here is not whether Alice is correct about the imposition of new ways to map the female body, the ways that an erotic geography could invalidate efforts to de-emphasize the body in favor of women's intellectual attributes or their social consciousness. The problem is that both she and Dorcas are guilty of viewing the music as a monologic endeavor, where either/or is privileged over both/and. For Alice, the music invites the individual to sin; for Dorcas, it promises a solution to the boredom that accompanies idleness. Since to be idle is to be out of step with the quickened pace of adolescence, the anxiety Dorcas feels at being badly dressed, her feeling that she will be considered a "nobody," indicates the sense that music is apprehended instinctively, not intellectually.

The dynamics of erotic geography insist on the need to equate place and conduct. Malvonne's apartment, where Joe and Dorcas carry on their affair, is part of that geography; so is the party where Joe sees Dorcas for the first time. The anxiety that listening to "sooty music" creates in Alice Manfred is also part of the erotic geography informing Dorcas's corporeal logic, not only because jazz, as "race music," is associated with sexual congress and orgasm but also because the 1920s is a moment when the dissemination of the Hollywood notion of white beauty is asserting itself.[25] There are several instances when the black female body arrests the black male gaze, but the novel's most insistent claim is that one has to understand the difference between looking and seeing. The tight space in which Joe and Violet find themselves for the majority of the novel has much to do with Joe's inability to see Violet the way he sees Dorcas as well as with Violet's inability to integrate her visual practice into a singular method of focus. As Spohrer argues, Violet is erased by popular magazines and cinema, but she capitulates to this view of herself, so that like Polly Breedlove in *The Bluest Eye*, Violet "passively absorbs images of self-hate" (89). However, the end of the novel proves that Violet is capable of resisting the allure of white femininity and situate herself within the intrinsically valuable space of three-dimensional personhood.

In *Jazz*'s closing pages, Morrison shifts from the omniscient narrator to Felice, providing contrast between narration related for the sake of self-indulgence and dialogic narration that takes other voices into account. Joe, Violet, and Felice constitute a triumvirate of individuals who have suffered incalculable loss but who, through the rise of a community that is as improvised as the music in a jam session; find their way back to themselves. The place that emerges out the tight space of injury and loss is one in which they can own their misguided habits of judgment but not be held to account to an extent that requires exile from human contact. Even more important, perhaps, the place constructed in Joe and Violet's Harlem apartment is configured around a commitment to distinguishing between accountability and disability. Hence, Felice begins her exchange with Violet with an admission that she knows what it is like to have "another you inside you that isn't anything like you" (208). She continues:

> Dorcas and I used to make up love scenes and describe them to each other. It was fun and a little smutty. Something about it bothered me, though. Not the loving stuff, but the picture I had of myself when I did it. Nothing like me. I saw myself as somebody I'd seen in a picture show or a magazine. Then it would work. If I pictured myself the way I am it seemed wrong. (208–209)

Felice articulates the schism that exists between idealized notions of the black female self and the self that emerges out of lived experience. Though department stores catering to middle-class tastes or magazines offering an opportunity for members of the working classes to imagine themselves as "modern" (e.g. middle-class) women, what is essential to both Felice and Violet and what Felice invalidates, is the link between eroticism and spectacle. At the party, Dorcas is subjected to an appraising gaze by the two brothers and then dismissed with a look "just as the music slow and smoky, loads up the air" (67). As Spohrer points out, "Literary critics have long studied *Jazz* in relation to music and sound. Few, however, have delved into its complex investigation of the sense of sight and its sophisticated exploration of spectatorship and the gaze" (80). Spohrer's assessment has tremendous merit but leads to the question of whether it is possible to link visuality with an assessment of jazz music that can inform what Morrison is seeking to achieve in *Jazz*.

In a 1948 photograph by Herman Leonard, Ella Fitzgerald is performing with the camera positioned behind her, at waist level. But because the viewer is looking past Fitzgerald, the bottom right quadrant of the frame shows two of the most storied performers in jazz, Duke Ellington and Benny Goodman, enjoying Fitzgerald's performance. Both men wear dark suits with white shirts that seem to leap from the gray background, and both men are smiling.

The photograph's title, "Duke Ellington and Benny Goodman Listen to Ella Fitzgerald," signals that they, not Fitzgerald, constitute the photograph's subject.[26] It not clear whether Leonard set up the shot knowing that Ellington and Goodman would be seated directly in front of the stage, close enough for him to position them in the center of the frame, or whether he was shooting Fitzgerald and looked up to discover a monumental opportunity. We also have no way of knowing how the men came to be in the club: Did Fitzgerald invite them? Did they agree to meet there? Did they just happen to bump into each other? And we do not know how the circumstances affected Fitzgerald's performance. What we do know is that the photograph's conceptual aim inverts the frame's physical reality, so that the spectatorship of Ellington and Goodman is the subject. Even if we look at the photograph and focus our gaze first on Fitzgerald and then allow it to travel down to Ellington and over his shoulder to Goodman, we are nonetheless participants in the photograph's enactment of a dramatic moment. The light coming from stage left settles on the audience nearest to the stage and illuminates the center of the image, so that even though we see the light near the top of the upper left quadrant of the photograph, its effect is evident in the lower right quadrant, where it reflects off the right side of Ellington's forehead and to a lesser extent off Goodman's face.

The transience of this moment in 1948, the fragility of circumstance that likely led to Goodman and Ellington going their separate ways—literally and figuratively—at the end of the evening, underscores the fact that blacks and whites, their shared love of jazz notwithstanding, are not necessarily motivated to replicate this circumstance in a restaurant or movie house or at a Thanksgiving dinner. The photograph's logic rests on our awareness that the pleasure of this wonderful instance will be quickly exhausted, rendering its preservation all the more compelling and necessary.

The title of the photograph announces its conceptual and rhetorical agenda: jazz is constituted around perfect moments, instances where disparate elements align to create a circumstance whose greatest value lies in the fact that it is fragile, provisional. The photograph obscures the ephemerality of the jazz moment by creating a visual rhetoric that says jazz not only attracts an audience, it attracts celebrity. But the photograph's coherence, however fleeting, performs various kinds of cultural work. The cultural work performed by Leonard's portrait is most poignantly felt in our understanding of the everyday. The title infers that what we see is not an everyday occurrence, in part because it is rare that the spectacle of a live performance becomes as much about *who* is watching as *what* is being performed. Leonard turns the camera on the audience and captures two jazz giants *listening* to Ella Fitzgerald, but the question that lingers here is whether the image documents a moment that is the product of chance or whether the photographer realized that a special set of circumstances had emerged that would allow him to compose the shot in a way that would confirm his overall mode of seeing without seeming too contrived.

Whatever the circumstances, Leonard's photograph points us toward a conclusion. Morrison's *Jazz*, with its promiscuous, unreliable narrator who experiences what is either an epiphany or a breakdown, seeks to disrupt the relationship between narration and timelessness. The image rests on the mythic construct of the photograph as a moment frozen in time. But what needs to be interrogated—and what is pertinent to the conclusions regarding *Jazz*—is that the photograph asserts that Goodman and Ellington seeing Fitzgerald perform is *both* a singular moment and a timeless one that Leonard has managed to record for posterity. But as Susan Sontag observes, "Any photograph has multiple meanings" (23).[27] What is left unstated in the photograph is that whatever Fitzgerald opted to sing—"A Tisket a Tasket," "Beguin the Beguine," "Lush Life"—what Ellington and Goodman heard that night was a singular moment, never to be captured or repeated again. The Ella Fitzgerald on display on the evening the photograph was shot disappeared long before the film was exposed to light.

At no point in *Jazz* does the narrative ever mention, let alone represent, a live performance of jazz, as in James Baldwin's "Sonny's Blues," John A. Williams's *Night Song*, or more recently Nathaniel Mackey's multivolume *From a Broken Bottle Traces of Perfume Still Emanate*. Though Shirley Stave and other critics have insisted that Morrison's greatest achievement in the novel "lies in her choosing to define the City in terms of jazz, which functions both as the pulse of life, the metronome determining human actions, and the rhythm of the narration, which interfaces with the music in a shimmy of sound and vibration" (63), the narrator never takes the reader inside a speakeasy or other nightclub where the music is being played. There is the moment when a distraught Joe Trace walks down the street and listens to a blind man sitting on a crate, playing the blues on the guitar, but this is as close to a live performance that the novel gets. Jazz is either used as a metaphor or relegated to the background as atmosphere. Overall, the music is absent from the visual and aural tableau the narrator establishes.

There is tremendous merit in Alan Munton's assessment of the tendency to read techniques used by jazz musicians into Morrison's prose. In too many instances, Munton insists, the assertion that Morrison's fiction employs a jazz aesthetic is fraught with errors and overstatement.[28] In an interview with Salman Rushdie, Morrison states that *Jazz* features an approach to improvisation that takes two distinct forms: a writerly improvisation in which plot is first presented straightforwardly, like a simple melody, but she notes that improvisation provided a template through which to understand the lives of her characters, where they moved "from the South on into the city, where there were endless possibilities" (242). So the first page of the novel, where the narrator gives us what appears on its face to be the story of Joe, Dorcas, and Violet in its entirety, would be an example of writerly improvisation. But beyond that, "the relationship between fiction and jazz in Morrison's writing is as precise, and as limited as people "trying to improvise life" (242). As Munton proposes, however, jazz "and fiction should be kept separate" because jazz is not, as some critics seek to argue, a *language* that can be equated with prose. "Spoken language and the 'language' of jazz differ fundamentally, and it is not possible to derive the latter from the former" (250).

Jazz features Joe and Violet Trace's transformation from rural inhabitants to urban dwellers, from landowners in the South to renters in Harlem. But conceptually, Joe and Violet's ordeal has much to do with how their ability to engage their environment visually is colonized. Their reconciliation is made possible, then, by the act of liberating the gaze from its confinement in an external system of value and turning inward to consult their own blueprint of reality. That act enables Violet to "kill" her destructive *other* Viole(n)t because she no longer requires the template of white femininity as a way to configure her own sexuality or worth. As Spohrer puts it, "Only after abnegating absolute reliance on the passive gaze" ... does Violet assume visual presence. Joe can see her, because he is able to restore the vision that issues from what Felice refers to as his 'double eyes. Each one a different color.' Joe has a "sad one that lets you look inside him, and a clear one that looks inside you." Felice continues, "I like when he looks at me. I feel. I don't know, interesting. He looks at me and I feel deep" (206). In recovering what can be characterized as active, dialogic modes of looking, Violet and Joe return to a place that does not erase the traumatic past as much as it abandons the necessity of using it as a vehicle for self-punishment.

Indeed, the only way for the reader to understand the characters in *Jazz* is to eschew the assumptions about modernity's commodification of space and instead embrace jazz music's resistance to permanence. The narrator misjudges the characters because she has failed to see jazz as a musical practice, a philosophy, a structure of feeling, in which there is little or no investment in constructing a permanent structure. If anything, jazz music is akin to tearing down the building the minute it is completed in order to erect another structure that is the same but different. In jazz, the two-story house is neither hierarchical nor permanent; it is truly a house of many stories, each one as important as the others. The locality of jazz insists that the intersection of place and moment need not be totalizing. One possible answer to the question of how the individual could navigate a circumstance in which the air itself has become a commodity is by eschewing the idea of place as a permanent, physical location.

In *Jazz*, Morrison suggests that conventional approaches to narrative need to be rethought; she uses jazz music's ephemerality as a way to frame a quotidian approach to place that allows for a sense of futurity whose main asset is that it emphasizes being in the moment while jettisoning the past. *Jazz* ends with an altogether different triangle than the one related when the novel began. Where that triangle involved Joe, Violet, and Dorcas in a manner that could become legible to us only through Morrison's trope of the two-story house, the novel ends with the characters in a state of horizontality, where their respective stories can lie next to one another.

This is not to suggest that place is meaningless or that bodies cease to matter. But as Keally D. McBride informs us communities occur at a conceptual point where the "tension between the normative understanding of community and the everyday experience of them." *Jazz* is ultimately concerned with Morrison's insistence that we need not be prisoners of narrative's tendency to totalize our location in time and space. In a more comprehensive sense, Morrison resists the notion that literary realism is the most definitive approach to storytelling. Rather, we can opt for a more ephemeral, improvisatory relationship to past and present. Though this might mean that existence is fluid and unstable, the journey from property to personhood informs us that such a state is never virtual. Hence, when we look at our hands, we find that they are reaching out to touch that which is real, realizing that what makes us human resides, as Baby Suggs knew, in the flesh.

Notes

1. Turning back to Erica Edwards' apt characterization of what she terms the "charismatic scenario," Morrison's fiction is in step with what she sees as African American literature's propensity to register "the fault lines in black politics since Reconstruction, contesting how the charismatic scenario has often structured black political desire, the social life of black politics, and black political history as a field of knowledge itself" (Kindle vers. loc. 107 or 3543).
2. I make this assertion mindful of the ways that cultural historians of 1920s New York have de-emphasized Harlem's location on the island of Manhattan, save as a way to describe the sojourn whites made from downtown Manhattan to satisfy their attraction to the dark primitivism of its nightclubs. I am equally mindful that Modernist studies have been invigorated by assertions that there was not a singular "Modernism," but rather "a plurality of Modernisms," and I would insist that Morrison's novel undertakes to illuminate the complexity of such an assertion.
3. The late nineteenth and early twentieth centuries offered us writers like Henry James and Edith Wharton, whose novels of manners revealed the corrupted morals and risky behaviors of the middle and upper classes. James' *The Golden Bowl* and Wharton's *The House of Mirth* are texts which employ the social gaze as a metaphor for the ways the visual field is an active source of insight into the characters inner constitutions.
4. Schiff states further that the twentieth century, "unfurled in an unceasing progression of technological marvels from the airplane to cellphones. In the field of entertainment, three periods stand out: the 1920s for radical transformations in recordings, radio, and movies, the 1940s for television; and the 1980s for digitalization."
5. Neil Brenner, "The Urban Question as a Scale Question: Reflections on Henri Lefebvre, Urban Theory and the Politics of Scale". As Andrew Herod puts it, "Scale is arguably geography's core concept, for only through its resolution can we negotiate the boundaries between difference and similarity. It is scale which enables us to differentiate geographical landscapes, to delimit inclusion or exclusion in such social constructions as home, class, nation, rural, urban, core, and periphery." Or, the politics of scale could be thought of, in keeping with Helga Leitner, Eric Sheppard, and Kristin M. Sziarto, as "contentious politics," which entails the ways individuals and communities act to develop "strategies and practices that advance alternative imaginaries." Cf. Herod, "The Production of Scale in United States Labour Relations,"*Area* 23, no. 1 (March, 1991): 82–8. And Leitner, Sheppard, and Sziarto, "The Spatialities of Contentious Politics," *Transactions of the Institute of British Geographers* 33, no. 2 (April, 2008): 157–72.

6. Cf. Rudolph Fisher, "Whites Come to Harlem."
7. Quoted in Keally D. McBride, *Collective Dreams: Political Imagination and Communities*, 13.
8. In an essay published in *Ladies Home Journal* in 1921 titled "Does Jazz Put the Sin in Syncopation," in which Anne Shaw Faulkner wrote an expose announcing the negative impact jazz was having on American culture, stating, "We have all been taught that 'music soothes the savage b[r]east'," she writes, "but we have never stopped to consider that an entirely different type of music might invoke savage instincts" (Faulkner, 32). Reading Faulkner's piece, it is no great revelation to state that whites' reception of jazz music was shaped by their fears of miscegenation, which were linked to jazz's seeming ability to "dissolve inhibitions," with the guardians of public morality blaming "[jazz] for a variety of evils from the rise of illegitimate births among middle class white women to the bourgeoning traffic in white slaves".
9. One thinks here of Theodore Adorno's essay, "On the Fetish Character of Music and the Regression of Listening" and his [in]famous dismissal of jazz, when he states, "Regressive listening is tied to production by the machinery of distribution, and particularly by advertising. Regressive listening appears as soon as advertising turns into terror, as soon as nothing is left for the consciousness but to capitulate before the superior power of the advertised stuff and purchase spiritual peace by making the imposed goods literally its own thing" (287). Though Adorno believed he had a bead on why jazz appealed to a mass audience, his quarrel was not with jazz musicians, but rather with the rise of popular music—and its dissemination through records and radio. His fear that "exchange value disguise[d] itself as the object of enjoyment" was well-founded. But the fact that he wrote at a remove from jazz's existence as a local phenomenon, situated in a specific neighborhood; communicating the specificity of place, led him to paint with much too broad a brush.
10. As Chip Rhodes has observed, the 1920s, with its intersecting narratives of the New Negro Renaissance, the Roaring Twenties, and the Jazz Age, is "the most chronicled and caricatured decade in US history," because it can evoke notions of prosperity, mobility, and amiability on one hand, debauchery, alienation, and disillusionment on the other.
11. In their book, *New York Modern: The Arts and the City*, William B. Scott and Peter Rutkoff report that in 1925, the same year Alain Locke's *The New Negro* appeared, "Harlem had already begun to resemble Hell's Kitchen and San Juan Hill, inundated by impoverished West Side blacks" many of whom had migrated to New York from Virginia, the Carolinas, and Georgia (141). Disembarking at 125th Street, many of

these southern migrants, as part of an influx of poor newcomers, hoped they would find sanctuary from the racial violence and disenfranchisement they had known in the south (141). As early as 1914, the growth of Harlem's population was so rapid that long before Duke Ellington and Billy Strayhorn would exhort blacks to "Take the A Train," the quality of life had deteriorated to sub-legal standards. Harlem's transformation from rural and suburban enclave for wealthy whites into an "inner city" slum almost completely occupied by blacks was precipitated by real estate speculation in which what had been mansions for the rich were sold to absentee landlords who chopped them into apartments too small and too badly maintained to be safely habitable, even as Harlem residents paid 25% more than other New Yorkers for comparable apartments (142).

12. What distinguishes the two moments, however, is that the former signifies as black opportunity, while the latter signifies as white opportunism and exclusion. As Harvey Cohen relates, "Jazz Age New York art included only Americans of European descent New York's African American artists, with rare exceptions, continued to live and work in a world apart" (103).
13. Allan Tullos, *Alabama Getaway: The Political Imaginary and the Heart of Dixie* (Athens, GA: University of Georgia Press, 2011), 5.
14. Hughes recounts this circumstance in the form of a blues poem, a poetic form that few poets were practicing beyond Sterling A. Brown, given that blues music had only recently traveled northward from Mississippi to Chicago and from there to New York. In so doing, he reminds us that the blues—as a cultural form described by Ralph Ellison as tragi-comic—often captures moments of profound sadness, but does so in a way that seeks to metaphorize the source of that sadness and in so doing to re-ignite a sense of possibility.
15. Langston Hughes, *The Collected Poems of Langston Hughes*, ed. Arnold Rampersad (New York: Random House, 1994), p. 248.
16. When we trace etymology of the word "respectability," to its original source, we find that its root word, "respect" issues from the Classical Latin word *respectus*, which refers to the act of looking around or looking back, to give something one's regard or consideration. What *respectus* is inextricably linked to is the gaze. Thus, the phrase "in respect to," refers to the act of directing one's gaze *toward* someone or something.
17. Even with the advent of radio, one could argue that it relied on the listener's ability to visualize performers, or given the popularity of radio westerns, soap operas, and comedy shows, to "see" what was happening through the use of sound effects of easily identified objects the listener could use to form a coherent image.

18. Erika Spohrer, "Colonizing Consciousness: Race, Pictorial Epistemology, and Toni Morrison's *Jazz*," 80.
19. Both "promiscuity" and "promiscuous" have their etymological roots in the seventeenth century, deriving from the Latin word *promiscuus*, which in turn was derived from an earlier word *miscere*, to mix, consisting of elements mixed together.
20. It would not be appropriate, given the act of violence he directs at Dorcas, to call Joe's sensibility feminist in the strict sense, but what makes his act so devastating is that he is distinguished by his empathy for the women he encounters and his nonjudgmental acceptance of how they think. To be sure, this affinity is also why as "a backdoor man," Joe can use his charm to cajole women into buying his wares.
21. Characters who experience cultural weightlessness in Morrison's fiction are legion, with Pecola, Plum, Guitar, Son Green being among the best examples. So that it might be more appropriate to say that Baby Suggs falls into a widening state of depression in the aftermath of Sethe's violence and her sense that the excess of the Feast on the day before Schoolteacher's arrival marked her as complicit in the malfunction of the community's mechanisms. Her fixation on color is her attempt to find a way back to a world in which futurity is manifest, in which she can access the emotional, psychological, and mental energies she exercises in the Clearing, a space in which the antiphonal practices that characterize life in the modern black church provide the rituals of healing, reflection, and corporeality necessary to rebuild subjectivities compromised by slavery.
22. Ramsey states further, that black vernacular forms of music "and the various cultural practices surrounding them have existed as historically important modalities through which African Americans have expressed various components of "ethnicity." This relationship does not simply represent, as some would argue, black folks' yearning for a transhistorical, romanticized, uncontested, or even fictive past. The process of repetition and revision that characterizes these musical styles shows how black musicians and audiences have continuously established a unified and dynamic 'present' through music." *Race Music*, p. 36.
23. In her books *Purity and Danger* and *Risk and Blame*, renowned anthropologist Mary Douglas seeks, in the former, to account for the ways "that rituals of purity and impurity create unity in experience" (3). In the introduction to *Purity and Danger*, Douglas argues "Pollution ideas work in the life of society at two levels, one largely instrumental, one expressive. At the first level, the more obvious one, we find people trying to influence one another's behavior. Beliefs reinforce social pressures; all the

powers of the universe are called into guaranteeing an old man's dying wish, a mother's dignity, the rights of the weak and innocent." And Douglas continues, "Similarly, the ideal order of society is guarded by dangers which threaten transgressors. These danger-beliefs are as much threats which one man uses to coerce another as dangers which he himself fears to incur by his own lapses in righteousness" (3). Ultimately, Douglas concludes, "dirt is essentially disorder" and thus, it "offends against order. Eliminating it is not a negative movement, but a positive effect to organize (sic) the environment" (2). By Douglas' lights, the "whole universe is harnessed to man's attempts to force one another into good citizenship."

24. In *Risk and Blame*, Douglas turns to systems of blaming as a way to understand how individuals create systems of accountability. "In short," she notes, "the stronger the solidarity of a community, the more readily will natural disasters be coded as signs of reprehensible behavior (sic). Every death and most illnesses will give scope for defining blameworthiness." Douglas' work in both volumes clarifies why the response to jazz music *in the black community* was so incredibly ambivalent, ranging from the belief that jazz musicians "were fomenting a musical revolution," to the sense that jazz was the product of radically compromised morality, where the act of venturing outside the cultural norm established by European music, produced slipshod musicianship that required shaming techniques to re-establish moral order lest the belief in black inferiority be affirmed.
25. Erika Spohrer's insistence that *Jazz* is a pictorial book rests on her use of Laura Mulvey's classic essay "Visual Pleasure and Narrative Cinema," which established the notion of the male gaze and spectatorship as an object of scholarly inquiry and identified the "intended audience of classical Hollywood cinema as male" (79).
26. *Seeing Jazz*: Artists and Writers on *Jazz*, ed. Elizabeth Goldson (San Francisco: Chronicle Books, 1997), 128.
27. She goes on:
    Through photographs, the world becomes a series of unrelated, free-standing particles, and history, past and present, a set of anecdotes and *faits divers*. The camera makes reality atomic, manageable, opaque. It is a view of the world which denies interconnectedness, continuity, but which confers on each moment the character of mystery. Any photograph has multiple meanings; indeed, to see something in the form of a photograph is to encounter a potential object of fascination. (23)
28. For example, Alan Rice asserts, "All of [Morrison's] novels have been informed by the rhythms and cadences of a black musical tradition." He states further, that Morrison's "jazz aesthetic is created by visible stylistic devices that approximate those used in the musical tradition. This tradition foregrounds many aesthetic values such as functionality,

audience participation, improvisation, rhythm, and non-closure, and it is these which make up the total jazz aesthetic on which Morrison draws." Munton is especially critical of those moments when critics make statements like "Son's 'style of discourse' resemble[s] the improvisations of John Coltrane'" (Berret) or that there is "a jazz patterning with words repeated" (Rodrigues) or that there is anything that resembles a "jazz aesthetic."

PART II

South

CHAPTER 5

A Measure of Last Resort: Limerence and the Geometrical Shape of Community in *Love*

My playhouse is underneath
Our house, & I hear people
Telling each other secrets.
—Yusef Komunyakaa, "Venus Fly-Traps"

In this chapter, we turn to Toni Morrison's eighth novel, *Love* (2003), which is set in the town of Silk, South Carolina. There, Bill Cosey is the sole proprietor of Cosey's Resort and benefactor of Silk's black population. Even when he is not physically present, Cosey embodies Sula Peace's observation that black men are "the envy of the world" (104). But reading *Love* requires sustained attention to issues of space and place, especially as they relate to the concept of leverage. Where *Jazz* took place in a smaller section of the metropolis, events unfold in *Love* against the backdrop of the town. Though there is not a moment in the text where whites utter a single line of dialogue, they nonetheless exercise dominion over the black community as a direct result of their ability to exercise leverage; their silence is the measure of their influence and power. Over the course of the novel, which runs from the 1940s to the 1980s, Silk moves toward integration, signaling doom for Cosey's Resort, because it thrived on segregation and the limits it imposed on blacks occupying public space.

Cosey's Resort is a domestic geography where a number of troubling issues converge. First, its location in the Jim Crow South means that

H. Beavers, *Geography and the Political Imaginary in the Novels of Toni Morrison*, Geocriticism and Spatial Literary Studies,
https://doi.org/10.1007/978-3-319-65999-2_5

once its patrons are now free to seek lodging at any hotel or inn in the area, irrespective of race, the resort becomes doomed to antiquity as a novelty. Second, the resort has been built off of Bill Cosey's father's ill-gotten gains; the money Cosey has amassed results from a betrayal that both acknowledges and sustains white supremacy. And finally, the resort manifests the illusion of racial progress: Bill Cosey's success is an indication to other blacks that they, too, can achieve their dreams of ownership and prosperity but in ways that prove to be illusory.

In effect, Cosey's Resort has thrived because it had once been able to use segregation as a means to sustain its leverage over its customers who had little in the way of other choices if they wanted to vacation in the South. Although it is clear that we might apply Edwards's ideas regarding charismatic leadership to a reading of *Love*, closer examination of Bill Cosey's success requires a deeper understanding of the concept of leverage.[1] Looking at how events unfold in *Love*, leverage proves to be an important aspect of how the characters negotiate the tight spaces that seek to immobilize them. Leverage is important to Macon Dead, who uses the properties he owns as collateral for mortgages on more houses he will rent to blacks. But he and the majority of Morrison's other southern men lack the ability to gain leverage without causing injury. Cholly Breedlove's abjection gives him a form of leverage that assumes the shape of freedom, inducing him to rape his daughter. Son Green uses racial essentialism and violence to exercise leverage in his relationship with Jadine. Leverage gives these characters ways to manage tight space by creating mechanical advantage (figuratively speaking) that creates the illusion that they can exert force in order to create a desired outcome.

Perhaps this is why Morrison's turn southward is worth noting. Though the setting implies that there are a different set of issues surrounding characters living below the Mason-Dixon Line, closer inspection reveals that the concerns engaged in the first three chapters are equally manifest in *Love*. But those concerns are played out in a manner that departs from the previous discussion in profound ways. For example, a large portion of the novel happens at Cosey's Resort, a sanctuary for well-heeled blacks from the middle class who are not welcome at whites-only establishments. This signals a de-emphasis on the concept of home, since being at the resort represents membership in a community whose core principle is transience. Though the previous chapters focused on how horizontal place-making and the sense of belonging that it brings is often synonymous with finding a permanent home in which to dwell, Cosey's Resort represents the liminal space between home and elsewhere.

Further, by titling the novel *Love*, Morrison invites us to consider the role the erotic and the corporeal play in acts of place-making. The setting of the novel once again heralds the return of the two-story house, where an omniscient narrator vies with L for narrative space, which reflects the characters' struggle for narrative hegemony as they seek to assert ownership over the definitive version of the truth. Further, Morrison utilizes conceptual doubling to complicate our understanding of place, dramatizing how the present is beset by the implications of past habits of judgment whose impacts are still keenly felt. On a thematic level, conceptual doubling offers Morrison a way to revisit issues raised in earlier works, as characters reprise concerns that take on different contours and emphasize different imperatives. It may also involve instances in which double-meaning inheres—for example, in the way Cosey's Resort is a symbol of *both* achievement and immobility. Or it may involve the existence of an alternative imaginary residing in the background behind an existing political imaginary. One example would be a political imaginary in which black men assert the need for racial unity and liberation for the entire black community. But because the problems black men have with racism and bias are viewed as a function of an uncomplicated form of systemic racism, the identificatory practices of a black political imaginary that does not consider the intersectionality of women thereby excludes them from the significations of racial progress. Indeed, *Love* suggests that women's relationship to patriarchy requires them to enter into a figurative contractual agreement that places (and confirms the rightness of) men in the foreground and makes their concerns central to the workings of the political imaginary. When black male characters narrate instances when racial bias or discriminatory behaviors impact them directly, what may be hidden is the manner in which women's concerns are left untended.

For example, the question of inheritance is central to the plot of *Song of Solomon*, but at no point is the gold Milkman is sent to recover intended to further the prospects of his sisters, Lena and First Corinthians. Similarly, *Love* features a plot that involves the contestation of a will, but this time between two women. It portrays the circumstance that arises when ownership and genealogy come into proximity as if they are complementary ideas. Events in the novel, however, propose the act of simply laying claim to a set of spatial coordinates is by no means indicative of a liberatory circumstance; thus, what we witness in *Love* are the conflicts that arise when the struggle to sustain transgenerational forms of capital are equated with acts of restorative naming.[2]

Like Morrison's *Beloved*, Love presents us with "a named house (Cosey's Hotel and Resort) and … nameless women." In the case of *Love* Bill Cosey's widow, Heed, and his granddaughter, Christine, both of whom once possessed Cosey as their surname, are rendered "nameless" because each seeks to prove that Cosey's will has named one of them his "sweet Cosey child," the legitimate heir to his estate. Lacking the ability to substantiate which of them is the actual bearer of such a designation, they are trapped in a liminal status, occupying the Cosey house but unable to claim sole ownership. In ways that depart from *Song of Solomon*'s portrayal of the transformation of genealogical knowledge into a new form of cultural capital, *Love* portrays the disequilibrium created when individuals seek to equate the economics of naming with the emotional contingency of capital. If such an equation intimates an inversion of scale, a confusion of registers, it is because *Love* ruminates on the replication of complex structures and thus infers that acts of naming signify beyond the confines of family.

Though men like Bill Cosey are often viewed as the vanguard of the civil rights struggle, they incur costs because they operate at a distinct remove from the advancement of racial progress. Further, what constitutes racial progress if women's concerns are never engaged? What strategy might women adopt to redress this silence? Prior to integration, southern whites subverted black communities' acts of place-making by using violence and intimidation to enforce the importance of having blacks "know their place." The spatial and domestic geographies in which they were forced to reside were fraught with a racial pedagogy that rationalized white supremacy and insisted that the order of things decreed that blacks have less. But it also led to black communities seeking to create an alternative to the white supremacist imaginary to reiterate patriarchal and sexist assumptions that insisted that men's quest for agency would further black women's quest for liberation as well. Which, at the risk of resorting to a cliché, leads to a question: What does love have to do with the political imaginary? The novel dramatizes this question by calling our attention to the ways that power, pleasure, and desire frame characters' efforts to sustain a sense of futurity.

The most important example of doubling in Love is found in Morrison's deployment of two instantiations of the political imaginary. One is organized around principles of individual acquisition and success suggestive of *thanatos*, while the other is organized around principles of compassion and collaboration as the embodiment of *agape*. Bill Cosey's larger-than-life presence in the novel complicates matters and calls for us to conjecture about Morrison's intent. The novel pays strict attention to the black community's presumption that racial progress can occur only when someone who is part of that community replicates the hierarchy and exclusivity found in the physical geography controlled by whites. And because Cosey's Resort is read as a sign of racial possibility, the inhabitants of Silk's black community do not criticize Cosey's strict adherence to separatist discipline but are instead "proud of his finesse, his money, the example he set that goaded them into thinking that with patience and savvy, they could do it too" (40).

If this is familiar, it is likely because such thinking is reminiscent of the message trumpeted by John H. Johnson, founder of the Johnson Publishing Company and publisher of *Ebony* magazine, in whose pages he championed conspicuous consumption as a necessary handhold in the climb toward respectability (and by implication, racial equity). Hence, in creating the character of Bill Cosey, who uses his financial wherewithal to create what appears to be an orderly, well-managed business that opens doors and creates opportunity, Morrison explicates the cost of upward mobility when it becomes mired in self-interest and self-congratulation. Just as *Ebony* took the position that social inequity could be overcome by hard work and conspicuous consumption, the character of Bill Cosey represents the manner in which autonomy becomes a surrogate for collective forms of agency. In light of this conundrum, *Love* proposes that the habits of judgment that result in recurring instances of arrested mobility can only be challenged in a political imaginary that values collective leaps of faith and the establishment of spaces of resistance that see women's experiences as integral aspects of its narrative.

The novel's setting at a resort populated by guests whose pronouncements about the acquisition and exercise of political agency are informed by the locations from which they departed means that any discussions about politics they might have are transitory and contingent. In such a milieu, political momentum is impossible to sustain. "Resort" thus constitutes a double-entendre. On one hand, it is the name for the physical manifestation of the larger-than-life legacy that survives when Bill Cosey dies; on the other, it has to do with a condition in which one has little recourse to self-determination. As one of the last resorts of its kind, Bill Cosey's establishment symbolizes a marked effort to hold onto a past that is synonymous with the devaluation of black life. Viewed in political terms, then, Cosey's Resort can be either a way station for individuals engaged in struggle—a place where they can be renewed before attending to new challenges—or a null space where political aspirations are subsumed in an environment devoted to hedonism and self-congratulation, its mantra reflecting the caste distinctions of complexion, money, and status in the black community.

The recurring trope of the two-story house intimates a need to be attentive to the Resort's motto ("The best good time this side of the law") because it is both an invitation and an exclusionary practice, announcing to poor blacks living in the vicinity that they are not on the "side of the law" that would induce Cosey to welcome them as guests. Like *Song of Solomon*, *Love* intimates that Bill Cosey and Ruth Foster Dead's father are men whose political imaginaries assert a commitment to racial uplift but who, in fact, have a sense of contempt for those who happen to look like them but are less fortunate. Their affective qualities notwithstanding, these political imaginaries, then, are often sites of contention between groups whose common status should lead them to seek solidarity but whose interests diverge along lines of class, gender, or sexuality. Circumstances such as this are suggestive of how political imaginaries can reflect one group's ability to look past difference to see points of commonality that transcend boundaries and another set of individuals who insist on defining their interests so narrowly that they refuse to acknowledge difference of any sort.

The unsettled nature of political imaginaries is reflected in the history of the Cosey family. On one hand, the family is a fixture in the town of Silk; on the other, they are—and have been—caught in a tight space, a quandary of their own making. As the son of a father nicknamed Danny-Boy by whites and Dark by blacks, Bill Cosey behaves in ways that demonstrate how patriarchy creates circumstances in which sons are compelled to reprise the lives of their fathers even as they seek to establish a legacy to pass on to their own progeny. The source of the Cosey family's assets can be traced to Dark Cosey's willingness to turn what geographer Paul Adams refers to as the scanning gaze onto the black community by becoming the "one police could count on to know where a certain colored boy was hiding, who sold liquor, who had an eye on what property, what was said at church meetings, who was agitating to vote, collecting money for a school—all sorts of things Dixie law was interested in" (187, 68).[3] The conceptual doubling of Bill Cosey's father as Danny-Boy and Dark dramatizes the tenuous position he holds in both communities in Silk.

Like Ralph Ellison's Lucius Brockway, Dark Cosey is "the machine inside the machine," through whom every move the black community makes toward integration and equality is checked by white supremacist control. As the "regulating" mechanism holding black progress at bay, Dark Cosey embodies conservatism. Knowing that he cannot defeat white supremacy, Dark Cosey opts to combine the energy it generates with racial anxiety and transform it into capital, which continues to circulate in and around the town of Silk. Dark's actions are integral to the negative feedback loop that tethers the black community's fortunes to the white community in such a way that a perpetual state of inequality exists. Thought of in terms of leverage, Dark Cosey is the fulcrum the white community uses to maintain its mechanical advantage over the black community. Consider the distinction L makes between Cosey the elder from Cosey the younger:

> the son decided to enjoy his share. Not throw it away exactly, but use it on things Dark cursed: good times, good clothes, good food, good music, dancing till the sun came up in a hotel made for it all. The father was dreaded; the son was a ray of light. The cops paid off the father; the son paid off the cops. What the father corrected, the son celebrated. The father a miser? The son an easy touch. (67)

Though he appears to be a man whose "pleasure [is] in pleasing," Bill Cosey has devoted himself to redressing the sins of the father by putting Dark Cosey's 114,000 "resentful dollars" to beneficial use. When viewed from the standpoint of capital, Bill Cosey has increased his inheritance, but he has done so by exchanging one form of service for another without in any way disrupting the negative feedback loop that holds the black community in limbo.[4]

Whereas his father generated capital by transforming information about the black community into a commodity, Bill Cosey uses capital to create a fantastical image of the black community. Though it favors light skin over dark, rich over poor, and leisure over labor, the hotel is nonetheless viewed as a source of both race pride and social progress. Bill Cosey is known for his generosity of spirit, his willingness to help a neighbor in need, and Cosey's Resort is remembered by some as "more than a playground; it was a school and a haven where people debated death in the cities, murder in Mississippi, and what they planned to do about it other than grieve and stare at their children" (35). The resort's motto "The best good time," is Cosey's promise that a stay at his resort is "the best good time this side of the law." But in declaring itself "this side of the law," the motto reprises Dark Cosey's position *on the side of the law*. In the tight space of patriarchal acts of betrayal and separatism, Cosey's Hotel and Resort remains intricately linked to Dark Cosey's legacy. Though L has characterized Cosey as the antithesis of his father, it is perhaps more apt to suggest that his variation on the theme of betrayal is focused inward, enacting a brand of hurting that is aimed more precisely not at the collective, as we see with Dark, but on a personal scale, at his granddaughter, daughter-in-law, and Heed.

Though L has established that he eschews his father's dark machinations against his own community, Cosey's inheritance from his police informant father means that for all the political chatter between guests fretting over U.S. race relations, Cosey's Hotel and Resort specializes in the art of diversion. Just as the patrons begin to imagine how they might address the growing racial unrest in the South, to see themselves as the purveyors of a new racial legacy, the resort, as the tight space located between home and away from home, provides a more affable course of action. Morrison suggests as much when she writes, "Then the music started, convincing them they could manage it all and last" (35). Hence, what might have been a condition in which disillusionment occasions new habits of judgment, this is forestalled when music begins to play, inducing Cosey's guests to dance their troubles away rather than to upset the established order of things. Though it would be inaccurate to call it a den of iniquity, Cosey's Resort replicates a tight space that turns in on itself to become narcissism, which may feel better but which leaves white supremacy wholly intact. But such a condition is equally suggestive of how topophobia can be the catalyst for change when it leads people to stand up against power massed to confine them in conditions that they realize are unacceptable. But because Cosey's Resort is meant to serve as an escape from topophobic circumstances, the guests escape *into* a space whose transience creates a sense of false consciousness, whereby the ability to reside elsewhere defers the need to imagine an alternative.

Occurring as it does in a tight space created within the dominion of white supremacy by the intersection of pleasure and betrayal, the Coseys' prosperity rests on the presumption that blacks will always opt to pursue pleasure rather than to confront the realities of segregation and discrimination, a product of the white supremacist political imaginary, not the assets of the black elite. Dark's acquisition of money relies on the assumption that the place blacks hold in the racial hierarchy is a product of the dominion whites enjoy at the expense of blacks. Here, Morrison holds up for critique the propensity to misinterpret hedonism as racial progress; if the blacks able to stay at Cosey's Resort feel a sense of belonging, it has to do with how pleasure can create a false sense of topophilia. Because pleasure leads us to understand ourselves in terms of who we would like to be rather than who we are, it can thwart acts of resistance because they require habits of judgment based on the deferral of gratification, embracing hardship, and remaining optimistic about the prospects for change, irrespective of disappointment or failure. Further, because hedonism can serve as a source of leverage it cannot function as a means of engagement because it is leverage that does not seek to eliminate confinement so much as it creates the illusion of lessening the burden. When coupled with the fact that Cosey's patrons are likely, unwilling to see their interests as being in line with those they deem less fortunate, pleasure creates an impulse to escape dominion rather than confront it, with little regard for who will bear the actual cost.

What proves interesting to Morrison are the habits of judgment blacks fashion to negotiate it, which recalls Foucault's description of how power relates to pleasure, an observation that is active even in a southern town where discrimination and racial animus are part of everyday life. Morrison proposes, therefore, that it is not enough to view the misery of her characters, particularly Heed and Christine, solely through a lens of suffering or repression. Each seeks to acquire the material resources to exercise power and assume control over the legacy passed down from Bill Cosey.

But a quick survey of Morrison's fiction demonstrates her recurring interest in how people in the African diaspora pursue pleasure. She often portrays pleasure's impact on how individuals understand their place in a society contingent on hierarchies of race, gender, and class. In that sense, pleasure can function as the companion of human suffering, complicating human relations and obscuring the path to truth while masquerading as liberation. Pleasure assumes various guises in Morrison's fiction as the dynamics of power inform social relationships at multiple levels.[5]

For example, as it was noted above, *Song of Solomon*'s Guitar eschews the pleasure of sweets after his father is killed in a sawmill and the boss brings compensation in the form of a bag of candy.[6] But Guitar's disavowal of "candy, cake, [and] stuff like that" becomes transmuted into the violence he enacts as retribution as a member of the Seven Days, a group that seeks to "balance" the losses created when blacks are killed by whites. Guitar's acceptance into this society of assassins requires that he pass up the quotidian pleasures of a wife, children, or fun with his best friend, Milkman. For if pleasure can be understood as a quickening of the senses, a state in which the passage of time is intensified, accelerated, the Seven Days are characterized by their resistance to haste, which emphasizes taking "the time to last." But in opting for such a profile, they elucidate the lure of pleasure by constructing lives overdetermined by the effort to turn pleasure to violent ends. Indeed, by equating sweets with "dead people … and white people," Guitar has merely catalyzed the transience of pleasure into a sustained penchant for racial violence.[7]

The insatiability of pleasure insists that it has greatest consequence when it generates a system of comparison in which scale is distorted. In *Beloved*, the berries "that tasted *like* church" (160, emphasis added) lead the community to substitute hubris for thanksgiving. Moreover, because the thrill of pleasure relies on stimulation, it represents an alternative to the kinds of speculative circumstances that grow out of the deferral of pleasure, as if what is most palpable about pleasure is the fear that deferring it forecloses the possibility of experiencing or extending it.

Pleasure thus convinces us that our imperfections can be expunged or nullified in favor of the attributes we value most in ourselves. In *Jazz*, the narrator comments that when southerners arrive in the city, "they feel more like themselves, more like the people they believed they were," led to feel "not so much new, as themselves: their stronger, riskier selves" (35, 33). In *Sula*, Hannah Peace "ripple[s] with sex" (42) and thus functions as a constant source of pleasure for men living in the Bottom. Unlike her mother, Eva, who leaves men "feeling as though they have been in combat," Hannah "rubbed no edges, made no demands, made the man feel as though he were complete and wonderful just as he was—he didn't need fixing—and so he relaxed and swooned in the Hannah-light that shone on him simply because he was" (43). The language Morrison uses to describe Hannah's carnal attributes exposes pleasure's ability to substitute adequacy for exemplarity.

At a level that might seem counter-intuitive, then, pleasure can represent an important instrument of power, for it camouflages power relations.[8] After accompanying Bill Cosey on one of his boat parties, Sandler Gibbons promises himself "that he [will] never go again" (111) because he finds himself uncomfortable fraternizing with the town's most powerful white men and well-to-do black men. The boat party points to the ways that pleasure can temporarily suspend the workings of the social and legal disciplinary systems that provide the rationale for social inequality. So that even as Sandler finds the "laughter was easy enough" during the party, he realizes,

> It was the talk, its tone, its lie that he couldn't take. Talk as fuel to feed the main delusion: the counterfeit world invented on the boat; the real one set aside for a few hours so women could dominate, men could crawl, blacks could insult whites. Until they docked. Then the sheriff could put his badge back on and call the colored physician a boy. Then the women took their shoes off because they had to walk home alone. (111)

In the carnivalesque atmosphere of the boat party, social conventions are turned upside down; where blacks are equal with whites and women dictate men's behavior, pleasure's transience is on full display. What appears to be the abandonment of social convention in favor of *communitas* is finally a social fantasy meant to serve as a release valve for the pressures that, if allowed to mount, might lead to black demands for political and social equity. Though the black men on the boat receive temporary access to the privileges of dominance, the speed with which this access disappears leads us to understand pleasure as a way to suspend both disappointment and its inverse, purpose.[9] Morrison does not mention alcohol as the primary intoxicant—rather, it is the atmosphere pleasure creates, in which sobriety is deemed inappropriate and lack of restraint is a sign of belonging.

Besides L, whose narration occurs on an ethereal plane, Sandler Gibbons is the one person in Silk who sees through Cosey's illusion of generosity. Having been taken into Cosey's confidence as a young man, Gibbons accompanies Cosey on early morning fishing excursions and concludes, "the more [he] learned about the man, the less he knew" (45). On the one hand, Cosey traces the limitations on black progress to the fact that "every law in this country is made to keep [blacks] back" (44). But Sandler also remembers Cosey's unwillingness to sell land to local people, his polite refusals to host their celebrations, his tendency toward melancholy in the face of widespread admiration from women and men alike. Sandler is "of two minds about Cosey. Knowing him, watching him, was not so much about changing his mind; it was more like an education" (45). Sandler's experiences with Cosey are an example of conceptual doubling in which Sandler both has an "active dislike" for the man and finds that his sentimentality makes him an enigma.

Sandler's assessment needs to be understood in relation to Foucault's notion that "power is strong" because "it produces effects at the level of desire—and also at the level of knowledge" (59). Sandler's "education" represents his introduction to the ways power, irrespective of race, can be expressed through the body and its wants. He comes to understand that power rationalizes the establishment and maintenance of leverage over one's surroundings; power is an integral aspect of being considered a "race man."[10] The time spent in Cosey's company leads Sandler to conclude that "rich people could act like sharks, but what drove them was a kid's sweet tooth" (45)—that is, the illusion Cosey manages has much to do with his ability to disguise his appetites as racial purpose. What appears to be his resistance to the racism in Silk is more aptly explained by his declaration, "You can live with anything if you have what you can't live without" (112).

Sandler's "two minds" are suggestive of how the two-story house signals the danger that arises when power says "yes" rather than "no." In paralleling the behaviors of the rich and those of sharks through simile rather than metaphor, Morrison insists that what appears to be an essential need to consume everything in sight is not the product of hunger but rather a sentimentality sustained by acts of self-rationalization. Sandler knows it is inaccurate to believe, as his wife, Vida, nostalgically does, that Cosey possesses inexhaustible generosity. Rather, Bill Cosey's relation to pleasure reflects a negative feedback loop, where his equanimity is the product of forces that are held in stalemate; he is both happy and sad, angry and resigned, and the act of pleasing is consequently an instrument used to generate leverage. *Love* is distinctive in the ways its characters contend with the problem of locating themselves in a morally turbulent universe, especially since this process requires them to be located in relation to Cosey, whose charms can confuse all but the truest moral compass.

Morrison's decision to set part of *Love* at a black resort in the South has much to do with how she portrays the transient nature of topophilia: to stay at a resort might provide temporary relief from the vagaries of a racist body politic, but it ultimately means that one is substituting contingent forms of belonging for the sense of dislocation that characterizes life at home. For a variety of reasons, none of the characters seem happy with where they are. Though Heed and Christine are vying for sole ownership of Bill Cosey's assets, neither seems emotionally attached to either the resort or the house on One Monarch Street. Though they are cohabitants, their proximity is a product of one woman not wanting to cede the advantage to her rival. Though it might be more advantageous to set aside their differences and agree to share the proceeds, to opt out of the contentious politics the will represents, neither seems able to relinquish her claim as legal heir. As the novel ultimately makes clear, taken together, the resort and the house are suspended in a zone of placelessness, caught between Christine's and Heed's contrasting visions of their relationship to Cosey. It means that neither can sustain a sense of place, as is reflected through Christine's ordeal prior to returning home to Silk.

Sandler understands the life that he and Vida experience in the newly established (and integrated) neighborhood of Oceanside is predicated on all those areas in their home that are too hot or totally absent of heat. Living in a house "built as a gesture," desegregation means transience, impermanence. His house, which has been constructed using "two-inch nails instead of four, lightweight roofing guaranteed for ten years instead of thirty, single-thickness panes rattling in their molding" (39), induces a counter-intuitive whimsy in which Sandler grows "fonder of the neighborhood he and Vida had moved away from" (39). He understands that the house he and Vida occupy is an improvement over their house in segregated Up Beach, but although he cannot articulate it, he misses the sense of place that emerged from having to ascertain value as a product of what lay inside the individual (and by extension, the community). In contrast, a new house in a new neighborhood symbolizes how the exterior of a new home can approximate but never fully realize a sense of "felt value."

Here, we can see the merits of Lucille Fultz's explication of *Love* as inviting "a studied critique of the promises, successes, and failures of desegregation" that urges "those on all sides of the issue to consider the unintended, perhaps unanticipated, consequences of desegregation" (95). The novel suggests that the ability to socialize with whites and enjoy all the spoils they take as a given can lead to the conclusion that the enjoyment blacks achieve among themselves is somehow counterfeit. Bill Cosey forces us to engage the question of whether the good feelings his resort engendered were a product of a legitimate enterprise borne of blacks providing for themselves or whether those feelings were always a substitute, a reminder of all blacks could not have, a diversion from pursuing substantive concerns. As *Love* portrays it, pleasure is anathema to striving for a political imaginary based on inclusiveness because satiation has the power to nullify political assertiveness and thereby lessen the need to determine friend from foe.

Sandler's sense of dislocation from his present surroundings is duplicated in his grandson, Romen. Once again, the domestic geography of a house party provides the conceptual double for Sandler's rejection of the pleasures available on Bill Cosey's boat. Romen finds himself in a room at a house party, standing "next in line," with his "belt unbuckled, anticipation ripe" (46). Having been invited to participate, with six other boys, in the gang rape of Pretty-Fay, he feels, in a reprise of language from *Jazz*, that he is "about to become the Romen he'd always known he was: chiseled, dangerous, and loose" (46). The intensity of perception and suspension of reason lead Romen to conclude that participating in the gang rape is a necessary step to achieving a self-authenticating form of leverage. Having linked pleasure with masculine entitlement, Romen steps up to take his turn, but then he unties the girl's hands from the bedpost and carries her out of the room. In opting out of his right to "have his way" with the girl in favor of rescuing her, Romen eschews the illusion that manhood relies on acts of leveraging. Romen is caught between two conflicting notions of himself and thus acts, but he does not do so out of a deep concern for Pretty-Fay.

The sense of Romen's double self is emphasized by its juxtaposition with an earlier scene involving Romen's grandfather and Bill Cosey, in which Sandler Gibbons remembers the portrait of Bill Cosey that hung behind the registration desk of the hotel. The portrait was created from a photograph in which Cosey was looking at his lover, Celestial. Sandler knows what his wife refuses to acknowledge—that what has been captured in the painting is not Cosey's enduring charm and affability but rather his self-indulgence and unfaithfulness. The doubling of Cosey's image—first as photograph and then as portrait—indicates the people of Silk's inability to see Cosey as he is. According to the narrator, Cosey maintains a dualistic relationship with people in the town: "Cosey didn't mix with local people publicly, which is to say he employed them, joked with them, even rescued them from difficult situations, but other than at church picnics, none was truly welcome at the hotel's tables or on its dance floor" (41). Because the photograph does not capture the object of Cosey's gaze, its transmogrification into a portrait means that the place where Cosey is aiming his look—the object of his desire—becomes a mysterious instance where no one in Silk "know[s] who he [is] looking at" or *for whom* he is looking out. Because Cosey is looking at Celestial, the photograph and the portrait based on it constitute a visual act of doubling Cosey's infidelity both to his wife and to Silk's black community.

Hence, Romen's actions with Pretty-Fay are the inverse of Cosey's self-indulgence, for his act of compassion is likewise an instance of tough-mindedness. However, he wrongly believes that he has allowed sentimentality to get in the way of the camaraderie and bravado pleasure should create. But the clearheaded decision to remove Pretty-Fay, in such close proximity to his grandfather's revelations regarding Cosey's true motives, intimates that the "chiseled, dangerous, and loose" self Romen seeks to occupy is an artifice.

The act of (mis)naming that follows, where the narrator never repeats the slur (but which we can assume is either "faggot" or "punk"), renders swift judgment. As he walks away from the girl and her friends without saying a word, Romen's ears are consumed by "the trumpet blast of what Theo had called him: the worst name there was; the one word whose reverberations, once airborne, only a fired gun could end" (47). Even when he hears his "name" on the basketball court, he declines to fight because he reasons if "he fought back, he would be fighting not for himself, but for her, Pretty-Fay, proving the connection between them—the wrong connection" (48). Believing that the path to manhood is dictated by the many rather than the one, self-interest rather than concern for a stranger, Romen duplicates the habit of judgment that underlies Cosey's infidelity.

For his part, Romen interprets the sexual play he comes to have with Junior as an opportunity to discover an authentic self.[11] But what he is actually enjoying is the leverage he has achieved over his peers. Such a state indicates that the imperative of masculinity lies in its propensity to verify itself through acts of subordination. Ensorcelled in the sexual transgressions Junior occasions, Romen concludes that "all of his impulses were right, now" (113). Sex with Junior erases the episode with Pretty-Fay, and Romen concludes (in a manner suggestive of Violet's transformation into Viole[n]t) that the boy who opted against pleasure is gone: "Who was that wuss crying under a pillow," he asks himself, "because of some jive turkeys?" He has "no time for that sniveling self now" (114). He knows his "score" with Junior to be "big time," so much so that he has "new eyes" that appraise and dare and he reaches the conclusion that sex that is the product of alcohol, domination, or herd behavior is for boys who deserve the label "punk." But if the narrator offers us a framework through which to critique hegemonic masculinity in the form of herd behavior, what we realize is that Romen is enacting a form of manhood enshrined in Hollywood cinema, where the "hero" gets the girl for doing the right thing, a version of masculinity that when linked to "manifest destiny" has catastrophic consequences.

If Junior is what Romen believes to be his prize, the narrator never takes pains to pierce this delusion. The effect of this deferral of narrative judgment is that we are equally hesitant to judge Bill Cosey. Romen's "look," which recalls the one in Cosey's portrait, declares dominion over his surroundings. This sentiment extends beyond the sense of superiority he feels over the boys who rejected him for showing compassion to a girl; it also centers on the figurative acquisition of "property," which means it has spatial characteristics. Junior's access to Christine's car, which is supposed to be used for running errands and shopping, becomes a vehicle for extending what appears to be Romen's sexual dominion across the whole town. The more locations he and Junior find to have sex, the more "indelible" they become as the product of phallic inscription. Junior's plan to "make it everywhere" with Romen, to "map the county with grapple and heat," suggests that Morrison opted to give him that name because his liaisons with Junior link the permanence of writing with the establishment of empire. This explains his sense that he "owns" Café Ria and his former friend, Theo. The narrator's use of free indirect discourse implies that the spoils of heroic behavior are bestowed on him as an individual. His dismissal of boys (or men) who need "a chorus of each other to back them up," as if their sexual escapades are unreal, "doing it, not to the girl but for, maybe even to, one another" (115), intimates the role sexuality plays in the staging of the fiction of charismatic manhood. Though it is possible to ascertain the merits of Romen's position, especially since it makes him look mature beyond his years, its deeper function is to provide a window into Bill Cosey's arrogant decision to make Heed his "child-bride."

The emotional preoccupation and infatuation Junior and Romen experience in one another's company is often referred to as limerence, which is characterized by passion but rarely leads to companionate, or pair bonding, love. This proves to be an important element of *Love* because, in the words of psychologist Lisa M. Diamond, "romantic love and sexual desire are not the same thing" (116). As psychologist J. A. Lee postulates, love can be realized in a variety of ways, most often in the form of "a typology of three primary love styles": *eros* (romantic love), *ludos* (game-playing love), and *storge* (friendship love).[12] In this respect, *Love* gives us multiple examples of the limerent subject. Hence, when we look at how the novel depicts pairings between men and women, much depends on how the couple forms what Lee refers to as "secondary styles" of love, which result from compounds of the primary styles. Though Junior and Romen consider each other "prizes," what transpires between them is more aptly seen as a *mania*, combining *eros* and *ludos*. The characters who are most inept at forming healthy relations in Morrison's fiction are those who are least able to move emotionally from primary styles of love to secondary styles. In *Sula*, Nel and Sula exhibit what Lee refers to as *pragma*, a combination of *storge* and *ludos*. But what is surprising is the number of pairings that can be categorized as *mania*. For example, in *Beloved*, Sethe's love for her children could be described as *mania*, since she uses love as a way to shield them from Schoolteacher in a competition that seeks to counter the threat to her children's affection. In *Song of Solomon*, the on-again, off-again relationship between Milkman and Hagar is another example. And there is yet another example in *Jazz* in the relationship between Joe Trace and Dorcas. By contrast, Joe and Violet have rediscovered, by novel's end, *agape* love, which combines *eros* and *storge*.

In light of how Morrison sets romantic love up for a critique through the depiction of limerence, Junior Viviane is equally important to the novel's scheme of conceptual doubling, which is evident the first time she looks at Cosey's portrait: "As soon as she saw the stranger's portrait she knew she was home" (60). By naming the character "Junior," Morrison signifies on men's propensity to name their sons after them, which functions as both self-tribute and blueprint. Bestowing their names on male children places them in a straitjacket and traps them in a temporal loop where their actions are read not as their own but as a reprise of their fathers' exploits and where any charisma they might possess belongs to their fathers. Second, Morrison challenges the assumption that dominion, especially under patriarchy, is a male prerogative that depends on women's subservience. Junior's dream during her first night in the house points to a different configuration of power: "She had dreamed him the first night, had ridden his shoulders through an orchard of green Granny apples heavy and thick on the boughs" (60). The description of Junior's dream proffers how Morrison revises our conventional understanding of the Fall, in which Eve coerced Adam into sin, and replaces it with Junior's dream featuring men and women as co-conspirators staging the theft from the tree of knowledge. The dream also dramatizes the well-worn aphorism that the apple doesn't fall far from the tree, insisting that Junior's position on Cosey's shoulders ensures that the proverbial apple will not fall but will be plucked in a gesture of entitlement. The dream signals the manner in which patriarchy can deputize women as surrogates for male power where their main purpose is to further the interests of men.

For all her attention to the personal habits of Heed and Christine, Morrison's description of life in the Settlement reveals that Junior Viviane's life has been one of deprivation and abuse. It manifests in her a penchant for rough sex and an ability to discern and exploit people's motives. Understanding "Christine's generosity and Heed's stinginess as forms of dismissal," Junior's "hunger" symbolizes what happens when the quest for sustenance becomes a self-justifying practice, an end in itself. Both Junior and Cosey fetishize their original hunger; neither believes it can ever be satiated. In Cosey's case, this insatiability makes him appear larger than life: a man who sees that his lot in life is to "contradict history" and function as a counterweight to the pull of discrimination and racism. But in lieu of using his wealth as a hammer, Cosey aims to maintain control over it. As the son of a father who "worshipped paper money and coin, withheld decent shoes from his son and passable dresses from his daughters," Bill Cosey is imbued with the same hunger as Junior Viviane, which makes her—not Heed or Christine—his "rightful heir."

Thus, we can understand Cosey's production of two wills as yet another instance of conceptual doubling and as a sign of his aversion to chance, his dedication to a life organized around exigency. We see this same approach to organization in Junior:

> Unlike what people thought, in the daily grid of activities, *to plan was fatal.* Stay ready, on tippy-toe. And read fast: gestures, eyes, mouths, tones of speech, body movement—minds. Gauge the moment. Recognize the chance. *It's all you. And if you luck out, find yourself near an open wallet, window, or door, GO! It's all you. All of it. Good luck you found, but good fortune you made.* And her Good Man agreed. As she knew from the beginning, *he liked to see her win.* (118, emphasis added)

The unlikely kinship between Cosey and Junior is underscored in a scene in which she pulls on a pair of Cosey's underwear and as she does so realizes that Cosey's "happiness was unmistakable. So was his relief at having her there, handling his things and enjoying herself in front of him" (119). "Flooded" by Cosey's "company," Junior moves swiftly past the idea of being Heed's employee and formulates a plot to assume her place in a home she can call her own: "Everything was becoming clear. If she pleased both women, they could live happily together. All she had to do was study them, learn them" (119). Though it could be said that Junior's "occupation" is to serve as Heed's assistant, the mystical tie to Bill Cosey suggests that just as he has come to occupy her body, she will be his instrument for reoccupying One Monarch Street. But the "happily together" Junior imagines is not, as one might suspect, "happily ever after," which means that Morrison has provided us yet another trinity of women occupying a domicile; in this instance, however, each has an agenda that belies interdependence and mutuality. Though it would be difficult to make a case for *Love* as a ghost story on the order of *Beloved*, it is clear that Bill Cosey possesses some of the same malevolence and canniness as the spirit in the latter novel. In the trinity of Sethe, Denver, and Beloved, Sethe is the focus of both girls' attention; in the trinity of Ruth, Lena, and First Corinthians, each is dying for want of love and affection; and in the trinity of Eva, Hannah, and Sula Peace, each experience love as repellant and purely pragmatic. In this light, *Love* prompts the question, What is the cost for women seeking to love and be loved in the material world?

Nowhere is this more evident than in the character of May, whose behavior is a combination of the sensibilities of her father-in-law and his father. May's deteriorating mental state, her fall into an emotional vortex from which she will never escape, re-enacts Dark Cosey's gaze into the black community. But where his conspiratorial gaze initiated a flow of capital, May fears that Cosey's Resort will be overrun by radicalized blacks who exist in a state of perpetual *dis*pleasure and who are thus seeking to foment revolution that will deform if not altogether eliminate that capital. Recalling DeCerteau's distinction between tactical and strategic sensibilities, the difference between Dark and May is that the former enables capital expansion for reasons that are tactical, while the latter seeks to stave off the contraction of capital for reasons that are strategic. And when guests at the resort see May wearing a "stupid army hat" and carrying institutional-sized cartons filled with New Year's party favors and a stack of old menus, they fail to realize how contingency compromises her grasp on reality. This state of mind contrasts Bill Cosey's perpetual state of exigency.

May's impulsive behavior gestures toward a political imaginary whose main tenet is individual acquisition, in which the black elite in Silk see their interests as separate and distinct from the proletariat despite their common racial heritage. Rather than seeing Cosey's Resort as an asset that might be leveraged in an effort to further the ends of social change, May sees it in proprietary terms, where her interests diverge from those members of the working class who have united with the black middle-class during the Civil Rights Movement to contravene the regulatory mechanisms of Jim Crow.

Understanding Cosey's Resort as an institution leads her to believe that its resources and assets (which are dwindling as a consequence of segregation's impending demise) must be conserved. But she fails to recognize that the negative feedback loop that sustained the resort because whites were unwilling to allow blacks to enjoy the spoils of success in their midst is becoming a positive feedback loop in which the displeasure blacks feel regarding their inequitable position in the body politic begins to overwhelm pleasure's ability to mollify. Further, May's decision to wear an old army hat signals her belief that the hotel's assets are in a state of siege. The strangeness of this circumstance is perhaps best reflected in the fact that it finds an analogue in the rhetoric of the Nation of Islam. In this instance, May's desire to hold on to Cosey's dwindling assets points to black nationalism's propensity to devolve into a scramble for the spoils.

Morrison sees a profound and discernible connection between the conservatisms of Booker T. Washington and that of Malcolm X during his time as a leader in the Black Muslims. At one time, May

> had been merely another of the loud defenders of colored-owned businesses, the benefits of separate schools, hospitals with Negro wards and doctors, colored-owned banks, and the proud professions designed to service the race. Then she discovered that her convictions were no longer old-time racial uplift but separatist, "nationalistic." Not sweet Booker T., but radical Malcolm X. (80)

Under Bill Cosey's influence, May's arguments for holding the future at bay are based on her reliance upon charismatic models of leadership. Just as Junior serves as Bill Cosey's instrument for wreaking havoc in the world of the living, the charismatic scenario provides the template for May's concept of normal.

In response to the death of Emmett Till and the Montgomery Bus Boycott, May does not attempt to reconceive Cosey's Resort as a way station for radicalized blacks. Rather, she sees the increase in the amount and intensity of black political resistance as a sign that she must hold fast to methods that reflect her total adherence to a contingent mode of existence. Her response to the growing disenchantment of blacks in the late 1950s and early 1960s makes no distinction between Martin Luther King Jr.'s non-violent approach and Malcolm's calls for violence in the service of self-defense. Irrespective of how they constitute competing ideologies, May sees them as instances in which the black resistant gaze is turned *into* rather than beyond the confines of the black community. Seeing the hotel as "fortress," May's insanity takes the form of "locking away, storing up" (81). Having already hidden important legal documents, including the hotel deed, May takes to hoarding other items: "Money and silverware nestled in sacks of Uncle Ben's rice; fine table linen hid toilet paper and toothpaste; tree holes were stuffed with emergency underwear; photographs, keepsakes, mementos, junk she bagged, boxed, and squirreled away" (81). As the resort's "sole protector," May is "frantic with worry that the hotel and everybody in it are in immediate danger" and fearful that "city blacks have already invaded Up Beach, carrying lighter fluid, matches, Molotov cocktails, shouting, urging the locals to burn Cosey's Hotel and Resort to the ground and put the Uncle Toms, the sheriff's pal, the race traitor out of business" (80).

By undertaking a defense of Cosey's Resort against individuals who see Dark Cosey's tactical individualism as toxic to racial progress, May's anxiety mirrors the racial anxieties that initially led whites to coerce Dark to turn informant in the first place. What distinguishes May's actions from Dark Cosey's is the fact that Dark's activities were not a product of his fear of the black community but rather a product of his Otherness in relation to whiteness. Opting to capitalize on this seemingly immutable Otherness, Dark's accumulation of assets relies on the assumption that blacks' place in the racial hierarchy is a product of the natural order of things and thus can be regulated like any commodity.

May's effort to conserve those assets rests on a slightly different assumption: that the negative feedback loop holding white supremacy and black resistance in a state of (relative) equilibrium is deteriorating and that it is consequently only a matter of time before Cosey's Resort will be consumed in the positive feedback loop created by black rage. But here, we must understand what she is defending and why her enactment of strategic individualism is an essential aspect of the novel's inner workings. In sum, May faces a plight:

> Husband dead; her crumbling hotel ruled by a rabid beach rat, ignored by the man for whom she had slaved, abandoned by her daughter to strange ideas, a running joke to neighbors—she had *no place* and *nothing to command*. So she recognized the war declared on her and fought it alone. In bunkers of her own industry. In trenches she dug near watch fires at ocean's edge. A solitary misunderstood intelligence shaping and controlling its own environment. (99, my emphasis)

Cosey's Resort becomes a tight space for May because it foregrounds an entropic model of society that relies on racial hierarchy as a way to sustain its momentum and resist a fall into randomness. If Cosey's Resort was once a place offering goods and services that the black community could not find anywhere else, it is also the site where the hierarchy separating the dominant and subordinate classes is sanctioned and socially reproduced. And if blacks cease to believe that their subordinate place in that hierarchy is a product of nature and realize instead that it is the product of a social construction, the "work" their inferiority performs in a white supremacist political imaginary diminishes until whatever leverage the dominant culture may have held is lost.

Cosey's Resort becomes akin to a war zone, where May, in an effort to protect a place she equates with her own identity, falls into alienation. Perhaps another way to understand May is to view her sense of recalcitrant alterity as an example of what Alvin G. Burstein characterizes as ambivalent dread and desire. Having discarded her own daughter and sustained a healthy dislike of Heed, May's "solitary misunderstood intelligence" inhibits her ability to develop the mutual involvement necessary for the sustenance of community. Though the resort has been built on at least the illusion of welcome, May's ambivalence embodies Freud's overall characterization of human relationships as instances in which "unavoidable selfishness always exists in inextricable tension with the equally unavoidable need for others" (428).

However likely revolution may have seemed to May, this is also a moment when attention can turn to the character of Christine, who spends time in the midst of revolutionaries planning to overthrow the government. In coming to understand her, we likewise understand Heed, especially in light of L's comment that the true disaster of Bill Cosey's decision to marry Heed was that "he chose a girl already spoken for." By L's estimation, Heed "belonged to Christine and Christine belonged to her." In the absence of Heed, Christine can only fall back on her good breeding. She marries a G.I. and follows him to Germany but discovers his infidelity and returns to the States.

Morrison describes Christine, who has turned her search for a husband into trysts with married men with no wish to leave their wives, as living a life of "aimlessness." But in lieu of Heed's companionship, Christine moves from one man to the next, molding herself to his dictates. Indeed, one can argue that had *Jazz*'s Dorcas survived her gunshot wound and moved south, she would have become Christine. Like Dorcas, Christine has a vexed relationship with an indifferent mother. And just as Dorcas meets Acton, whose very name implies his propensity to press women into submission, Christine meets Fruit, whose clarity "was his habit and his gift." Christine opts to spend nine years with the political revolutionary, whom Morrison describes as

> a fine-boned man, intense, with large beautiful hands and a mesmerizing voice. He clarified the world for her. Her grandfather (a bourgeois traitor); her mother (a handkerchief head); Heed (a field hand wannabe); Ernie (a sellout). They were the "chumps" Malcolm X described, acid dripping from the word. Then he outlined her *own obligations*. With apology for her light skin, gray eyes, and hair threatening a lethal silkiness, Christine became a dedicated helpmate, coherent and happy to serve. (163; emphasis added)

She soon acquiesces to Fruit's insistence that she change "her clothing to 'motherland,' shar[pen] her language to activate slogans, carr[y] a knife for defense, [hide] her inauthentic hair in exquisite gelés; [hang] cowrie shells from her earlobes, and never [cross] her legs at the knees" (163). Christine's "personal vanity became racial authenticity and her flair for acting out became courage" (163).

Christine's relationship with Fruit, eight years her junior, would be just a tangential plot twist, a way for Morrison to fill in her backstory, until that relationship is situated alongside just about every other relationship between men and women in the book. Outside of Vida and Sandler, whose marriage reflects his belief "there is nothing in the world better than a good woman" (154). Morrison provides us with nothing else resembling a vital relationship. A source of confusion might be that in a novel called *Love*, we might expect to see it on display. Instead, the novel portrays with incredible nuance the malevolence directed toward black women by black men. But just as it would not be accurate to view

Morrison's portrayal of black men in her fiction as a wholesale dismissal, it would be equally misguided to ignore the constancy with which she critiques patriarchy and sexism as social constructs that induce men to think of manhood as a form of membership that puts them into a state of false consciousness that induces them to use black women as the method for substantiating their parity with white men.

Christine and Fruit have settled into a routine in which she is "the designated woman, the one everyone acknowledged as such" despite Fruit's tendency to sleep with younger women. However, Christine and Fruit are so closely equated that "their names spoken in a planning meeting sounded like a candy bar: Fruit n' Chris. Chris n' Fruit" (166). But after a "Comrade" rapes a student volunteer working in the movement, Fruit never confronts the man, because the "girl's violation carried no weight against the sturdier violation of male friendship" (166). Though she bristles at the ways that a seventeen-year-old white girl is blamed for what happened to her, Christine "shut[s] up about it," and "the good work of civil disobedience and personal obedience [goes] on" (167). Morrison's portrayal of Christine's relationship with Fruit describes how a black political imaginary seeking to challenge the dominant order replicates its most troublesome features. Men like Fruit link their charismatic outlook to the history of racial subordination as a means to ratify their place at the top of a gendered hierarchy. This is not surprising in itself, but viewed within the context of the two-story house, it is difficult to ignore the ferocity with which the men in Morrison's fiction subjugate women who need to narrate their story as much as the men do.

In the foreword to the 2005 softcover version of the book, Morrison describes a twelve-year-old girl who refuses to partake in her peers' youthful patter about boys and is separated from the other girls by a frightening secret: "When I later learned what separated her from us," Morrison writes, "I became afraid of wakefulness as well as of sleep" (ix). By relating this piece of personal history, she intimates that Heed-the-Night Cosey is based on someone from the author's past, a young girl forced to perform "acts foisted upon her by her father" (x) but whose performance of those acts is impossible to visualize.

However, Morrison proffers a disclaimer regarding her novels: "People say I am always writing about love. Always, always love. I nod, yes, but it isn't true—not exactly" (ix). Morrison's description of the young girl is so poignant because her life is bereft of emotional security.

According to Morrison, betrayal rather than love is her main theme: "Love is the weather," she writes; "betrayal is the lightning that cleaves and reveals it" (ix). In Morrison's view, love and betrayal are opposing forces that come together to create another form of turbulence. Betrayal indicates an atmospheric disturbance, so that just as one acquires the illumination necessary to understand the nature of love, it is shattered. Thus, love is a circumstance in which the very thing that can nullify it is always in its midst. Though Christine and Heed share the house on One Monarch Street, both are victimized by Bill Cosey's wrath. In view of Morrison's declaration that she is always writing about betrayal, one of the questions *Love* poses is why it is so easy to turn destructive emotions inward while electing not to share the positive.

Christine is essential to the novel's design because she figures into its structural underpinning. Adultery is one of the most destructive forms of betrayal and often one of the most public, and Morrison deploys throughout the pages of *Love* a series of what might be termed love triangles that often reflect its opposite. L's description of the transgression inherent in Cosey's decision to marry Heed is apt because in essence that marriage forms a triangle that tethers Heed, Christine, and Cosey into an awkward configuration that extends across the majority of the novel. When Junior Viviane arrives, she embodies Cosey's wishes and ultimately plays the two women against one another in hopes of laying claim to Cosey's house.

Love intimates the existence of alternatives that do not manifest the need to control or coerce. The first instance of this is one of the novel's principal narrators, L. Most easily and obviously, she is an analogue for love: she is the character who consistently rejects self-serving behaviors and enacts a reconciliatory and redistributive posture. But L is not so much an active agent as a suggestive one, since her role is to narrate the past with an eye for its underlying context. Thus, L's propensity to reminisce should not be confused with nostalgia, for she gives voice to disturbing contemporary trends that eschew discretion in favor of directness. As L makes clear, *Love* records an instance in which inheritance is de-emphasized in favor of abandonment.

Though at least one reviewer has commented on *Love*'s recapitulation of *Sula*, with Heed and Christine reprising the trajectory followed by Sula and Nel, such a conclusion neglects Morrison's increasing investment in producing narratives about black women that are compelling in themselves but that also comment on the forms such couplings assume in the political imaginary. It could be argued that *Love* is, like *Sula*, a rumination on the vagaries of sisterhood as it is reflected in the works of other African American women writers. However, such a conclusion rests on the assumption that black women write narratives that eschew the enormity of scale often attributed to the writings of black men, who are seen as the creators of works that analyze forces in the world at large.

Love is more specifically a reiteration rather than a simple revision of *Sula*, making a self-conscious effort to move beyond the limitations of the narrative of sisterhood. The novel's juxtaposition of pleasure and principle requires that we take into account the divergent forms of complementarity we find between Junior Viviane and Bill Cosey as well as Bill Cosey and Romen, which is a necessary step in piercing the illusion of principle that Bill Cosey represents. Where *Sula* ends with Nel uttering a "fine cry" that has "no bottom" and "no top, just circles and circles of sorrow," *Love* eschews circularity as a mythic construct where death and renewal can coexist, opting instead to highlight the nature of betrayal through the deployment of a series of increasingly complicated triangles. Though the circle is useful as a means to denote how the interiority of community inherently calls attention to its exterior, the fact that all points on a circle exist equidistant from the center obscures how power relations work within the circle's area. By organizing conflict in terms of triangles, Morrison is not abandoning the notion that two political imaginaries are in play; rather, she proposes that imaginaries have geometric properties that assume a variety of shapes. If Morrison's topic is betrayal, the triangle is an effective way to visualize that topic, since it involves the severing of a bond, where the two imperatives created by the severed bond are joined by its trace.

The most problematic love triangle, of course, involves Bill Cosey, Heed, and Celestial. Though Cosey's portrait hangs over Heed's bed, she never realizes that Celestial is the object of his gaze. Recalling his experience at the boat party, Sandler remembers Celestial as a constant object of male desire who "never raise[s] stakes or temperature" (112), Hence, Cosey's answer to Sandler's inquiries about Celestial's story is telling: Cosey determines that he can endure segregation and racial subordination as long as Celestial is present to fulfill his erotic needs. As a man who embodies a state of constant exigency, Cosey understands that he can't live without Celestial, who allows him to believe that his empire will remain intact if he wills his entire estate to her.

As his surrogate, Junior fashions a triangular relationship with Heed and Christine in which neither "woman was interested in her—except as she simplified or complicated their relationship with each other. Not quite a go-between, not quite a confidante, it was a murky role in which she had discovered small secrets" (119). As a girl who has "no past, no history but her own," Junior has motives that are transparent. But just as Cosey is the object of admiration and adoration, equated with accomplishment and possibility, Christine knows that Junior "will do anything" and that this quality is "precisely what [is] so appealing" (167). The clue that Junior is heir is implied by Bill Cosey's son, Billy Boy. Billy Boy represents an amalgam of his grandfather and father in that his name suggests infantilization by his father and his grandfather's compliance with white power and the ill-gotten gains that result. Junior represents the manner in which patriarchy is a system that renders power allegorical; though the passage of capital from one generation to the next seems to suggest that patriarchy's importance is manifest on a material grid, Junior's gender is immaterial in the face of her adherence to a code of exigency, which is actually what is required to hold entropy at bay.

But this triangle must be considered against the one formed by Cosey, Heed, and Christine. Though this triangle would seem most fraught with conflict, its significance lies in its ability to withstand the turbulence generated from within, in light of Cosey's whimsical decision to marry the eleven-year-old Heed. We come to understand the magnitude of betrayal experienced by Heed and Christine as the latter recalls their friendship and concludes that their struggle "was neither mindless nor wasted." Rather, Christine remembers her childhood with Heed and

> how she had fought for her, defied her mother to protect her, to give her clothes: dresses, shorts, a bathing suit, sandals, to picnic alone on the beach. They shared stomachache laughter, a secret language, and knew as they slept together that one's dreaming was the same as the other ones. (132)

Though the language invokes the girlhood bond between Sula and Nel, what is missing is that relationship's overdetermination of self-mutilation and denial. In its place exists Heed and Christine's "most private code," signaled by the phrase, "Hey Celestial" and the playhouse, Celestial Palace. In the place of the silence that inheres between Sula and Nel, Heed and Christine finally heal the breach in the space of language, leading to the mutual realization that the triangle they have imagined never existed because Celestial is positioned between them as Cosey's chosen heir. L realizes too late that "what looked like seven years of self-pity and remorse was really vengeance, and that his hatred of the women in his house had no level" (200–201). In addition, the flashback to the moment when Christine witnesses Bill Cosey's act of masturbation after he molests Heed provides the reader with a glimpse of the point to which all the contention can be traced. When Heed finds Christine and sees that she has gotten sick, she interprets both the sickness and Cosey's illicit gesture as proof that she is corrupt as a consequence of the brief moment when she wiggled her hips to the music coming from the hotel bar.

A more accurate interpretation results if we locate Heed, Christine, and Bill Cosey in a misogynist political imaginary sustained by the falsehood that women are vessels of debasement. If we return to Junior's dream of being on Cosey's shoulders to pick the apple, the dream's rewriting of Eve's role in the Fall indicates that a misogynist imaginary not only uses women to further its ends but subsequently requires women to police the boundaries between respectability and indecency, insanity and sobriety. But as with *Jazz*'s Alice and Violet, the behaviors attributed to those labels are a matter of interpretation arising out of a system of arbitrary categories that are enforced whimsically. Heed believes she has transgressed, and Christine's soiled bathing suit is akin to inscribing the transgression for all to see. Morrison's point is that the black woman—whether "crazy," "angry," "upstanding," or "trashy"—is finally subordinate, and thus the struggle between Heed and Christine sustains the Cosey legacy of self-centered dominance. This is further problematized by the fact that their focus is trained on the spoils issuing from his death as a potentially empowering circumstance. It also suggests that the endurance his patrons imagined as the bulwark against racism and discrimination is finally a sign that Cosey's corruption is inexhaustible, even after his death.

Junior leaves Christine and Heed in the old hotel, where Heed has fallen through the floor and lies mortally injured. Junior realizes that the accident represents her opportunity to be rid of both women and to assume ownership of the Cosey estate. But in truth, Cosey is *reclaiming* ownership; Junior is only the instrument. However, she underestimates the strength of the novel's final triangle, formed when Romen rescues Heed and Christine. Where the other triangles have involved manipulation and betrayal, this one, grounded in principle and concern for the Other, involves Romen's decision to eschew the pleasure of the flesh in favor of loyalty and care. He realizes that his authentic self is the one who refused to exploit the Other, not the one who acquires leverage and then revels in it. Though it would not be accurate to suggest that *Love* capitulates to calls for Morrison to create heroic male characters, Romen's trajectory in the novel is clearly meant to endorse iterative approaches to masculinity, where the discontinuities, failures of insight, and incomplete gestures are enfolded into the performance of masculinity so that it finds its rewards in adequacy rather than dominance, collaboration rather than collusion. Romen is a character who demonstrates that leverage is important to both vertical and horizontal place-making. What he helps the reader to ascertain, however, is that in the former instance the intention is to gain advantage and sustain it, in the latter, the intention is to *defeat* advantage.

L figures into a triangle formed when Cosey asks her to witness the will he writes in 1964 and has notarized by Sheriff Silk's wife. But L's decision to poison Cosey rather than allow him to leave his widow and granddaughter with nothing means that she finally refuses to participate in Cosey's vengeful act. In this, the letter L, which graphically appears to be a triangle lacking a third side, signifies her fidelity to justice, even though, by poisoning Cosey, she acts with infidelity toward the law; indeed, she goes over to "*that* side of the law." *Love* gives us a series of recursive triangles that moves from Cosey's unprincipled betrayal of Heed and Christine up through Junior's insatiable "hunger" and ends with Romen, Heed, and Christine. But our discovery at the novel's end that an ethereal L and Celestial often sit together in close proximity to Cosey's tombstone means that the triangle's missing side is reserved either for him, as Celestial sings "down- home, raunchy songs" (201) to Bill Cosey, or for the reader to witness the performance. The reader navigates these triangles to reach the end of the novel and finds that L's hum has replaced Nel's cry of despair, signaling the progression from irreparable absence to a space left open, insisting the act of disqualifying the demarcation between the living and the dead is a product of a liberated imagination.

Love reflects a sentiment that carries through Morrison's earlier works—a political imaginary in which individualism and conventional notions of death trump collectivism and the idea that "death is unnatural" is the embodiment of *thanatos*. As Romen's "rescue" of Heed and

Christine intimates, a political imaginary cannot thrive if it does not emphasize *agape* as a main signification. If sisterhood is a revolutionary posture, Morrison suggests, it is so because it is inherently based on horizontal forms of cohabitation, where stories lay next to rather than above or below. Indeed, a horizontal sense of place cannot thrive in the absence of *agape*. But *agape* results from the combination of *eros* and *storge*. So that when Morrison describes the bond that forms between Christine and Heed, we see how they move from a state of limerence to a more sophisticated secondary stage, where their sisterhood transcends socio-economic difference to take the form of *pragma* (the combination of *ludus* and *storge*), with its invented language and shared perceptions. Topophilia is difficult to sustain if it is at root a matter of erotic attachment, since pleasure is such a short-lived emotion. Meaningful attachments to place ultimately must issue from selflessness, the willingness to love the Other as we love ourselves. But it must also involve the flexibility and durability that come with the incorporation of play into the transformation of a spatial geography into a site of horizontal forms belonging.

Love is ultimately a novel about the captivating power of surfaces and the labor required to penetrate them in order to see what lies beneath. And if *Love* has dramatized the destructive power of the love triangle (Heed/Cosey/Christine or Heed/Cosey/Celestial), the ultimate responsibility for finding a resolution to the conflict falls upon the character who has opted not to pursue her own self-interest, the one in the best position to thwart Cosey's vengeful act. In this, L signifies *loyalty* or, more essentially, the power of liminality. What might be interpreted as the triangle's missing side, then, could more aptly be described as leaving one's options open. If Morrison's *Sula* was about a friendship irreparably severed by betrayal, *Love's* reiteration, portrays an instance in which we witness the repair of Heed and Christine's relationship as it reaches across the boundary between life and death. Like the thirty women who confront the ghost in *Beloved* and Pilate, who declares, "I wish I'd a knowed more people. I would of loved 'em all. If I'd a knowed more, I would loved more" (336), the joined voices of L and Celestial at the end of *Love* remind us that lasting affiliations are always cognizant of "how precious the tongue is" in the act of fashioning connections across time and space (201).

Notes

1. Within the context of physical science, leverage is the achievement of mechanical advantage through the transmission of power. As organizational expert Martin Gargiulo explains, leverage in an organizational setting is achieved when a social actor successfully builds "a cooptive relation with a player that may control [that] party's behavior" (1). In addition, it can mean that in a negotiation, one player has the ability to influence an opponent to either move closer to, if not adopt altogether, the player's position.
2. According to Elizabeth T. Hayes, naming "is an act of creation" and thus the act of naming anything (a child, an animal, an estate) "is also to claim dominion over it" (669). The conscious attention to naming, across the African Diaspora is, as Kimberly Benston puts it, "inevitably genealogical revisionism" (3). As an act of asserting cultural agency, naming seeks to counteract what Nathaniel Mackey declares is 'the normativeness, brought about by the slave trade, of Africans bearing European names throughout the Americas that has given rise to the preoccupation with (and complication of) the relationship between naming and space among African Americans' (184).
3. Adams attributes the "reduction of experience from ... multisensory intake to the scanning gaze is fundamental to the loosening of ties between people and place that have preoccupied more than one generation of human geographers" (p. 188).
4. As Pierre Bourdieu argues, phallic power structures social relations, transmuting the arbitrary into the ordered, centralizing male authority via the social construction of sexual organs—e.g. the difference between male and female organs—and creating mechanisms whereby property (mirroring the phallus) in the form of the male-dominated household (and the land surrounding it) appreciates, recurs in the form of the legal codes that nullify any claims women might make against male authority, and assumes a pattern we come to understand as history.
5. It would be an oversimplification to suggest that *Love* turns on the distinction Freud makes between the pleasure principle and the reality principle in *Beyond the Pleasure Principle.* However, it is useful to note that, according to Freud, resolving the "strong tendency toward the pleasure principle" in the tension between pleasure and reality is not a matter of nullifying pleasure. Rather, the reality principle "... demands and carries into effect the postponement of satisfaction, the abandonment of a number of possibilities of gaining satisfaction and the temporary toleration of unpleasure as a step on the long indirect road to pleasure" (7). A number of Morrison's novels have provided examples of what it means

to experience pleasure. As she presents it, pleasure is distinguished by its ability to transform noble intentions into acts characterized by debasement and excess. As purpose becomes overwrought, pleasure dispatches tranquility in favor of strife.

6. In a 1984 essay entitled, "The Sweet Life in Toni Morrison's Fiction," Elizabeth House details what she determines to be Morrison's propensity to depict two categories of dream types, one which turns on her character's aim to "live in concord with people and [remain] true to their own heritage," and another which advocates "not brotherhood but the acquisition of power or money" (184), what House describes as competitive success dreams. House looks at Morrison's first four novels and determines that Morrison "links sweets, especially commercially prepared candy and pies, with competitive success dreams; by comparing the alluring facades of sugar and outward success, she shows that neither is truly nourishing to human life" (182).
7. Hence, we can see the ways that Morrison utilizes sweets as a metaphoric vehicle to describe the relationship between pleasure and self-delusion. Though we should not conclude that this is Morrison's sole angle of critique, it is nonetheless important to recognize the role processed sugar plays in the drive to achieve ascendancy in a community, for it signals the ways that capitalism often assumes forms that are pleasing at the level of the senses. Thus, the fact that sugar can create a craving for more is easily equated with the mindset that craves an increase in material wealth; the pleasure that accompanies its acquisition diminishes until the individual must turn full attention to the necessities of acquisition.
8. The danger, Morrison intimates, is that when pleasure comes to be an end in itself, all the other aspects of life not associated with it become "dead zones," spaces in which men and women feel they have nothing to offer and are disappointed to accept anything less than the satiation pleasure affords. Though it is clear that a critique of capitalism's excesses is integral to Morrison's fiction and that she sees capitalism as an obstacle rather than an asset, her recurrent depiction of the dangers inherent in the pursuit of pleasure bespeak her investment in explicating those things that obstruct human caring and sacrifice. When pleasure becomes the measure to black people's sense of well-being, it works in concert with white supremacy to block the path to new iterations of their humanity.
9. Caught in the turbulence created by this blockage, Morrison's characters demonstrate the ways that pleasure works in the service of all those forces that threaten to tear the black community asunder. For even as it presents moments when we can feel most like ourselves, it is a point of turbulent egress, where the entry into modernity comes at a cost too great for the community to bear. Well-being, Morrison insists, is not to be found in

individual acts of self-aggrandizement or escapism; it is the product of self-acceptance and self-knowledge that often results from hardship. The apprehension Morrison feels regarding pleasure can be linked to her sense that life in Western society presents challenges to African people in the diaspora, largely because it constitutes a setting in which the individual can be seduced into believing that confrontations with modernity are best overcome through a politics of incompleteness and deferral.

10. As Hazel Carby describes the race man as a man whose racial pride reflected "the success of all." "The result of the pursuit of particular social types among which was the race man." Citing sociologist St. Clair Drake and Horace Cayton, Carby argues, "What a race man signifies for the white segments of our society is not necessarily how a race man is defined by various black constituencies." This analysis notwithstanding, Carby reveals the ways that the gendered construct of the race man is "a rarely questioned notion of masculinity as it is connected to ideas of race and nation" (Kindle vers. loc. 51 or 2436).
11. One reason for this, Morrison contends, is that intimacy depends on our ability to construct—and then maintain—an efficient means of self-appraisal. When we fail to do so, as numerous characters in the novel demonstrate, we come to rely on either materialism or escapism to do the work we have the power to undertake ourselves.
12. Qtd. in Thompson and Borello, p. 154.

CHAPTER 6

A Pox on All Your Houses: Susceptibility, Immunity, and the Dilemma of Allegory in *A Mercy*

Idealized communities of the past often disastrously excluded those who were perceived as different, or strictly regulated the lives of those within them, particularly the choices available to women. Very few feminists would invoke the ideal of community in a nostalgic sense.

—Keally D. McBride, *Collective Dreams*

Susceptibility refers to the predisposal of the host, in this case humans, to become infected.

—Michael Oldstone, *Viruses, Plagues, and History*

The white supremacist political imaginary driving social relations in the town of Silk occurred at the intersection of power and pleasure. In that respect, the black community was both a victim of and culpable in, its subordination. Though Cosey's Resort presented the illusion of black counter-public space, in fact it relied on the same kinds of misogynist forms of self-interest to be found in the dominant imaginary. One of the most salient features of the novel lies in its insistence that even as white supremacy has a deleterious impact on the lives of black folk everywhere, understanding those who benefit from sustaining a racial hierarchy (under the guise of challenging it) indicates the necessity for black communities to engage in self-assessment. Though the effects of racism are a consistent focus in Morrison's fiction, since *Tar Baby* she has proven to be just as willing to examine the black community's manufacture of tight

H. Beavers, *Geography and the Political Imaginary in the Novels of Toni Morrison*, Geocriticism and Spatial Literary Studies,
https://doi.org/10.1007/978-3-319-65999-2_6

space characterized by hierarchies that mirror and mimic existing structures of domination.

In one sense, this portrayal of intra-racial systems of confinement is made necessary because Morrison eschews narratives that look at black communities of the past with nostalgia, as if the transgressions of the previous generation could be swept under the proverbial rug. But it is just as easily a reflection of Morrison's unwillingness to portray black communities as occupying the moral high ground as a matter of course. Rather, *Love* insists that pleasure's reliance on materialism represents the black community's undoing. In this, she asserts that the global economy can be referred to as such because it includes—and thereby implicates—everyone in a tight space constituted around desire and pleasure. That Heed and Christine's animosity dissolves and is replaced at novel's end by a state of *agape* speaks to a fundamental element of Morrison's canon—that is, that the need to confront and eliminate *thanatos* is a precursor to creating vital forms of community.

Morrison's ninth novel, *A Mercy* (2008), presents a world in which the racial codes that structure social relations across lines of difference are inchoate. Set in the Seventeenth Century, *A Mercy* is certainly aware of how its plot features the effort to overcome the barriers created by difference, but it is also another opportunity for Morrison to assert once more the trope of the two-story house. The trope is reflected in the novel's narrative structure, which features both an omniscient narrator and the first-person narration of Florens, a young girl living on a farm in colonial Virginia. The farm where much of the novel takes place is the staging site for the transition from the mercantile class into landed gentry. Jacob Vaark builds a fine home whose roof, walls, and windows are acquired through his participation in the growing rum industry, which is reliant on slave labor. Among the constitutive materials of domestic space is the tight space created by the expansion of a global economy built around the commodified black body. But Vaark dies of smallpox before the house can be occupied. And though it is empty, it nonetheless stands guard over the rest of Vaark's farm, a symbol of how the emptying out of place involves acts of exploitation and subterfuge.

Where the previous chapters paid attention to how place manifests itself, this chapter concerns how what begins as place—a site characterized by a meaningful attachment to a physical setting—is transformed into space. Hence, topophilia is less relevant here, since *A Mercy* is set in a part of the New World that has yet to begin the process of becoming a nation and is therefore subject to a variety of interpretations. And because the right to occupy specific geographical spaces was often contested by opposing nations, the legal documents defining systems of belonging were subject to change. Hence, this propensity for the making and unmaking of space requires a different approach, one that emphasizes the symbolic language of credit and exchange where futurity takes on radically different contours than those articulated in the previous chapters. But the signification of individual industry will change as well, as it becomes subject to the symbolic economies springing up in the midst of the numerous religious sects vying for control of the spiritual imaginary and thus the authority to map a route to salvation.

Though the vast majority of Morrison's characters do not lack a propensity for industry, many of them engage in acts of self-making that are individualistic, at odds with the collective imagination. Morrison's decision to make Jacob Vaark's character a lender who extends credit suggests how the empty house that looms so large throughout the text signifies on the traditional image of the plantation house as the center of power relations between slaves and owners as well as on circumstances in which acts of leveraged buying redound into other forms of knowing.

The bulk of this chapter parses the conceptual underpinnings of the region that will come to be known as the South. No such entity existed at the start of *A Mercy*, but by the novel's end, the conditions that will produce such radical distinctions between the spatial geographies of North and South are well on the way to fruition. As one might suspect, the human body plays an important role in this turn of events, not only because of its commodification but also because that process is intricately linked to the rise of religious doctrine in the United States amidst the rise of a new global economy.

But I want to consider the Atlantic Slave Trade and its subsequent transformation of kidnapped Africans into property, in relation to the global event of the smallpox epidemic. As Michael Oldstone relates, smallpox "killed nearly 300 million people in the twentieth century—three times more than all the wars in this century..." Oldstone goes on to say that the "story of smallpox is interwoven with the history of human migration and wars, dramatically favoring one population over another" (27). When viewed alongside notions of susceptibility and immunity, smallpox is the very embodiment of tight space. As the first virus used in bacteriological warfare, smallpox was understood as a reflection of difference. Set long before the advent of germ theory, *A Mercy* nonetheless argues that inoculation against viral infection involves instances of transformation and deformation. In this novel, the two-story house demonstrates that just as the spread of evil relies on acts of complicity that turn a blind eye to its use of stealth, resistance to evil relies equally on the insinuation of covert gestures to corrupt it from within. Finally, the novel invites us to think seriously about how counter-publics form: Do they require physical proximity or can they cohere across space and time? In light of the fact that slavery would provide motivation for instituting oppositional thought, this chapter explores the role black bodies play in such endeavors.

When Jacob Vaark returns to his Virginia farm from his travels as an itinerant trader and lender, he begins to show signs of being sick. As Florens, the young black girl Vaark has taken in as payment of a debt, narrates, he "is different, slow and hard to please. He is short with Mistress. He sweats and wants cider all the time and no one believes the blisters are going to be Sorrow's old sickness. He vomits and curses in the day. Then he is too weak to do either."[1] Vaark dies, and according to Florens, "Still, we do not say the word aloud until we bury him next to his children and Mistress notices two in her mouth. That is the one time we whisper it. Pox. After we say it, the next morning, the two on her tongue are joined by twenty-three on her face. Twenty-five in all" (43).

While it is generally accepted that *A Mercy* is distinctive because it is set in seventeenth-century Virginia, during the complicated process of establishing and fortifying notions of racial difference in the New World,[2] it also incorporates a more fundamental level of difference between characters who have an innate immunity to smallpox and those who acquire an immunity to the virus. Of the seven inhabitants of the Vaark farm, four have a direct relationship to smallpox: Jacob Vaark dies from it; Rebekka Vaark is infected but survives; Lina's people have been wiped out by smallpox, but she is unaffected during Rebekka's illness; and Sorrow has suffered from smallpox but has been cured by the blacksmith, who utilizes a technique Michael Oldstone refers to as variolation (a precursor to vaccination), which involves the "transfer of smallpox as an inoculum into susceptible individuals" (74), a feat accomplished when the blacksmith slits open one of the lesions on her body and has Sorrow swallow the bloody contents.

Neither the omniscient narrator nor Florens provide us with the details surrounding the smallpox outbreak, but it serves nonetheless as the linchpin of the novel's plot. From an epidemiological standpoint, the Vaark farm fares pretty well, since none of the remaining inhabitants (Willard, Scully, Lina, and Florens) become ill, but we have no way of knowing how many other cases occur on neighboring farms (incidence), nor do we know how far the outbreak has spread (prevalence), making it difficult to ascertain the facts surrounding Jacob Vaark's infection. Without those facts, we cannot formulate a narrative timeline from the exact moment of Vaark's infection to the moment when Rebekka Vaark recovers from the disease and assumes her role as matriarch of the Vaark farm. What is clear is that the outbreak ushers in radical change when Rebekka decides that Willard and Scully will be paid for their labor and that Lina, Sorrow, and Florens will not. While it would not be accurate to say that the three women are slaves in a manner governed by the mechanisms that drive antebellum slavery in the next century, the fact that Rebekka is willing to put Florens up for sale means that Rebekka seeks money in exchange for human flesh. Hence, she opts to make good on the idea suggested by the Portuguese slave owner, D'Ortega, who plans to honor his debt to Jacob Vaark with a slave. Though Vaark demurs, D'Ortega presses his point, declaring, "The value of a seasoned slave is beyond adequate" to repay the debt. And when Vaark states that he has no use for a female slave, D'Ortega exclaims, "Sell her!" (28).

Though Vaark resists the impulse to become directly involved in the slave trade as a plantation owner, he spends an afternoon at the D'Ortega plantation. Looking at Jublio, with its house made of honey-colored stone, the iron fence enclosing the property, and the rows of slave quarters, Jacob experiences a mixture of revulsion and envy. Having gone through the nasty business of obtaining Florens as partial payment of D'Ortega's debt, Jacob realizes for "the first time he had not tricked, not flattered, not manipulated, but gone head to head with rich gentry" (31). The difference between him and D'Ortega is not a matter of either blood or character. Rather, it is material possessions and how they are acquired. Hence, the transaction anticipates the emergence of a managerial class that facilitates the spread of slavery and finances its growth.

Though Vaark convinces himself that he is above "trading conscience for coin," he enters a state of reverie in which he thinks,

> So mighten it be nice to have such a fence to enclose the headstones in his own meadow? And one day, not too far away, to build a house that size on his own property? On that rise in back, with a better prospect of the hills and the valley between them? Not as ornate as D'Ortega's. None of that

> pagan excess, of course, but fair. And pure, noble, even, because it would not be compromised as Jublio was. (32)

After leaving Maryland and traveling back to a Virginia tavern to eat and bed down for the night, Vaark sits with a group of men talking about rum: how it is made, the demand it generates. The man who seems to know the most about how sugar is transformed into rum is Peter Downes, who sits, "holding forth with the authority of a mayor" (34). Vaark's decision to invest in the rum trade is the direct result of contact with Downes, who persuades him that "Kill-devil, sugar—there will never be enough. A trade for lifetimes to come" (36). But along with the air of authority he exudes, what distinguishes Downes is that he is described as being "pock-faced," which means it is highly likely that he has survived a bout of smallpox.[3] By the turn of the eighteenth century, according to Oldstone, the virus "had become endemic in the major cities of Europe and the British Isles," and nearly one-tenth of the entire human population "had been killed, crippled, or disfigured by smallpox" (74).

Vaark is in a state of susceptibility, not only to the smallpox virus but also to the desire to lift himself into the privileged class. It is no surprise, then, that Vaark falls ill with the virus. The episode with Vaark, Jublio, and Downes occurs in flashback, so that when Florens resumes her role as narrator, a considerable amount of time has passed: she is sixteen, in love with the blacksmith; Sorrow has gotten ill with smallpox and been cured; and construction on Vaark's grand house is nearly complete. this chapter has shown us Vaark's acquisition of Florens, his persuasion to the benefits of trading in rum from Jamaica (which involves rationalizing the decision by telling himself that he is not directly involved in the slave trade), and his dream of the grand house rising out of the fog. Morrison's decision to collapse the distance between these events and Vaark's infection and death and Rebekka's rapid decline, creates a conceptual link between smallpox and the spread of the material desires generated by the slave trade. Morrison seeks to portray not only how swiftly the virus can spread but also how Vaark is implicated in yet another outbreak—the ideological outbreak that creates the chasm between indentured servitude and slavery, which subsequently rigidifies the boundary separating, black and white.[4]

Manifestations of tight space are legion in this instance. First, smallpox, a virus that can be spread through the air, radically alters how individuals can navigate through a particular space, whether public or private. Indeed, someone who is ill behind closed doors can still infect someone hundreds of yards away. Second, the novel is set in a moment when the maps intended to represent English colonies in the New World are in a fluid state, with boundaries established and re-established. Though the colonies lack the necessary cohesiveness to consider their experiences as a prelude to the revolution to come, the financial machinery that will dictate how black bodies are understood for the next 200 years is moving swiftly from imagination to implementation. Finally, Jacob Vaark's farm is in the midst of the transformation from being owned by an itinerant trader and lender to becoming the estate of a man situated among landed gentry. As the kissing serpents on the iron gate intimate, the house equates the U.S.'s version of Original Sin with the gateway to paradise.

Hence, *A Mercy* is equally interested in investigating the inchoate systems of meaning that will become much more firmly established in the eighteenth century—that is, the accounting methods reflecting the grammar of trust that leads to the practice of insuring owners against loss. All of the characters in the novel are seeking a way to verify their efforts, not only to conceptualize value but also to guarantee it in a world in which they recognize that they are susceptible to forces that can eradicate them as vessels of worth. Hence, both Jacob and Rebekka prove susceptible to the seductive notion of inexhaustibility. Once Jacob links the inexhaustibility of African bodies, the "fuel" for the rum industry, to profit, he never again experiences dissonance about the house he builds and the exploitative nature of capitalism. Rebekka is seduced by the notion of a heaven characterized by inexhaustibility itself; there, she will find all those things that make life pleasurable in infinite abundance.[5] What escapes notice, however, is that she will have to defer pleasure not only for herself but for all the inhabitants of "Jacob's Land" in order to ensure her safe passage and, she hopes, her children into heaven.[6]

The novel studies the personal and social impacts wrought across a landscape in which acts of speculation occur in proximity to an increasingly slippery rhetoric of materiality. In establishing itself as an outbreak narrative, *A Mercy* signals the formation of an identifiable community that grows up in response to the expanding circuit of artificial want and wealth extending across the Atlantic to create a population susceptible to the allure of slavery and its supporting mechanisms. This provides Morrison with the opportunity to ruminate on the circumstances that arise when the barter economy and its reliance on equivalence and materialism is overtaken by a world brought to heel by the tight spaces generated through the mutually imagined constructions of credit, debt, and profit.

Morrison's decision to set *A Mercy* in the seventeenth century has much to do, then, with her desire to approximate the moment when racial difference becomes a more agile means of administering the social codes underwriting notions of human value. Morrison imagines the Vaark farm—or Jacob's Land—as the metonym for ground zero of a massive viral outbreak.[7] Morrison's use of smallpox as a plot device allows her to intertwine Florens's narrative of reconciliation with the outbreak narrative she attributes to the rise and expansion of slavery in the United States.[8] To be sure, *A Mercy* ruminates deeply upon the spatial transformations wrought by capitalism as it is furthered by the demonization and commoditization of the black body. But Morrison also means for us to see smallpox as an agent whose impact is felt across the physical, emotional, and symbolic registers of all the novel's characters. In other words, smallpox and the quality of change it initiates suggest a far more menacing threat that functions on a metonymic level and indicates that its impact on the New World will be far more debilitating to the American body politic than smallpox.[9]

Jacob Vaark proves essential to this discussion not only because he falls victim to the smallpox virus but also because he has served as a lender and trader. His susceptibility both to the virus and to the rationales for the importation of African bodies to the New World, invites us to draw an analogy between the large-scale social mechanisms that emerge to support slavery and the conditions that produce the spread of communicable disease. As Priscilla Wald argues, "The experience of a communicable disease epidemic could evoke a profound sense of social interconnection: communicability configuring community" (12). In a transatlantic economy in which the numerous iterations of difference on the African continent lead, as Peter Downes puts it, to Africans being "as interested in selling slaves to the Dutch as an English planter is in buying them," the community that emerges ultimately coheres around the idea that the slave trade was, as Eric Williams relates, "the spring and parent whence the others flow" (51).[10]

At the heart of Downes's comment is his portrayal of an investment in rum as a venture that has minimal risk and maximum profit: "Each and every month five times the investment. For certain" (36). Downes's formulation occludes the uneasy balance between risk and certainty.

The "outbreak" Morrison portrays, then, expands beyond the consolidation of European identities into the more facile construct of whiteness, though it is clear by *A Mercy*'s conclusion that such a process is under way. Rather the outbreak occurs at a place where religiosity and capital intersect. *A Mercy* dramatizes a moment when the colonial subject sought to throw off the exigent consciousness of the immigrant, whose object was merely to subsist and survive, and embrace contingency as it takes the form of membership in a religious sect or the financial elite (and often, given the struggles occurring between Protestant and Anglican for dominance in the New World, a combination of them).

Jacob Vaark's "grand house" represents one way to realize this shift in consciousness; his desire to finance his rise via his own "industry" is compromised by the fact that the slave labor involved in the cultivation and processing of sugar into rum is translated into the profit he uses to make his dream real. Rebekka Vaark's sudden and apparently total conversion to Protestantism represents another realization of this shift; her turn to religion marks her turn away from the secular logic of the freethinker that holds human agency alone determines one's destiny, in favor of the belief that the accumulation of grace is the only prosperity worth pursuing, with benefits deferred until the next life.[11] But Jacob and Rebekka's trajectories, their turns of fate, indicate that the politics of scale are inherent in how they come to imagine the world: in Jacob's case, the global scale created by the competition between nations for economic dominance; in Rebekka's the imagination of an afterlife in which the adherence to religious doctrine constitutes the currency required to attain the bounty of grace.

As a lender, Jacob Vaark is involved in the commoditization of a social interaction whose main components are desire, imagination, and time. When a prospective buyer lacks sufficient capital to purchase goods and services, credit functions like a wormhole through time and space, creating a circumstance where what had been insufficient or nonexistent is now sufficient and real. Hence, the deal between Vaark and D'Ortega is the product of a mutual act of imagination that assumes the form of a legal document that creates the additional circumstance of legal redress should one of the signees abrogate the agreement. What had been a source of laughter for Vaark—the sight of Florens wearing a pair of "way-too-big women's shoes" (30) becomes a matter of great seriousness, moving from speech to writing, from oral negotiation to binding contract: "They wrote new papers. Agreeing that the girl was worth twenty pieces of eight, considering the number of years ahead of her and reducing the balance by three hogshead of tobacco or fifteen English pounds, the latter preferred" (31).

In Morrison's description, the transaction has a matter-of-fact quality, and the distance between Vaark's and D'Ortega's respective positions rapidly closes. But how did the men reach this agreement? What happened between Vaark's declaration that he would not accept the girl ("No, I said, no" [31]) and the creation of a legally binding contract? He has considered Florens as a surrogate for his daughter, Patrician, who has recently died in an accident. Looking at Florens, Vaark states his dissatisfaction with D'Ortega's offer, but he ruminates inwardly on the possibilities: "Thinking, also, perhaps Rebekka would welcome a child around the place. This one here, swimming in horrible shoes, appeared to be about the age of Patrician, and if she got kicked in the head by a mare, the loss would not rock Rebekka so" (31). Though Vaark disapproves of slavery, he nonetheless calculates a scenario in which accepting Florens as payment might produce a positive result. But he assumes that Florens's death would not be on a par with the death of his daughter. His use of the word "loss" must be read not simply as personal, in the manner of losing a loved one, but also as a financial loss when what is configured to be an asset ceases to be such. His act of speculation points to how a credit transaction plays out the entire scenario from acquisition to loss (while voicing the emotional but not the financial impact of that loss) before Florens ever sets foot on the farm.

Further, Vaark constructs the black child as an asset that is lesser in value than a white child. Hence, Florens's use value, as Vaark imagines it, is specious; he assumes that Rebekka's response to the arrival of a black child will approximate giving birth to another child to replace the one that was lost, but such is not the case. When Rebekka thinks back to Jacob's "gift," she recalls, "Jacob probably believed giving her a girl close to Patrician's age would please her. In fact, it insulted her. Nothing could replace the original and nothing should" (113). Rebekka's decision to put Florens up for sale thus means three things. First, the lapse in time between Florens's transition from child to payment to messenger does not indicate that she is no longer property. Second, the price at which she was initially valued—twenty pieces of eight—was calculated against the average life span of a slave who survived into adulthood to become a steady source of labor. Here, we find the conceptual bridge between Vaark's thinking and D'Ortega's: Florens cannot be valued simply as a little girl meant to replace Vaark's deceased child. Her value can be realized only through an act of collaborative imagination, which must take the form of the work that can be performed in the average life span of a female slave. The only template available to guide this act of imagination is D'Ortega's plantation, where female slaves perform a variety of quantifiable tasks. Hence, the third element we must understand is that the events Florens narrates happen some ten to twelve years after the origination of the "new papers," which means we must assume that her value has risen toward, if not passed, the amount originally agreed upon. For that reason, Rebekka can rationalize the prospect of selling Florens: there is a benefit to be gained that was cemented into place when the contract was signed, the unspoken notion that a mature slave is worth more than a child because she can do more work and possibly bear children.[12] Consequently, what might have been a fixed price is now open to negotiation: the twenty pieces of eight are re-imagined as a starting point rather than an end point.

But what constituted the turning point for Vaark? What intervened between "No, I said, no." and the writing of "new papers"? On the page, the only thing that happens is that Florens's mother, standing in the doorway of the cookhouse with her two children, kneels and closes her eyes. The omniscient narrator gives us nothing in the way of expository phrasing to help us interpret this act. We could read a minha mãe's act of kneeling and closing her eyes as an act of supplication. But I take her gesture as an act of speculation. That is, Florens's mother calculates the possibilities associated with giving up one of her children, an infant boy and a little girl. We do not learn her thoughts until the final chapter of the novel, where we are told that she has observed Vaark and D'Ortega's interaction and realized that an opportunity has presented itself. Knowing that her master will not agree to part with her, she trades on her small amount of leverage and offers her daughter. Having experienced the Middle Passage from Angola, worked in the sugarcane fields of Barbados, and been sold at auction, a minha mãe describes the epiphany she reaches on the auction block:

> It was there I learned how I was not a person from my country, not from my families. I was negrita. Everything. Language, dress, gods, dance, habits, decoration, song—*all of it cooked together in the color of my skin.* So it was as a black that I was purchased by Senhor, taken out of the cane and shipped north to his tobacco plants. (194; emphasis added)

A minha mãe realizes that the features that distinguished her as an individual in Angola have been collapsed into a particularized form of tight space, her skin color. By referring to her individual traits as "cooked together," then, a minha mãe voices the cultural, financial, and epistemological labor involved in transforming her from human being to property.[13]

Returning to the moment when Vaark imagines Florens's use value, we can see this process at work. At the moment when he conjectures that the girl might serve as a palliative for his wife's grief, Vaark's resistance to D'Ortega's offer begins to erode in the face of artificial want. A minha mãe's keen powers of observation lead her to conclude that the trader/lender (or "the tall man," as she refers to him) has not yet come to see Florens in terms of her exchange value. "Because I saw the tall man see you as a human child," a minha mãe relates, "not pieces of eight. I knelt before him. Hoping for a miracle. He said yes" (195).

She cannot predict whether Florens will remain a "human child" after entering the territory of the financial transaction or will come to mirror her mother's status as commodity, as property. But she speculates about whether Vaark's amusement at the sight of Florens wearing shoes will lead him to sustain his sense of her personhood. Knowing that despite her best efforts to conceal her child's female attributes, Florens has already "caught Senhor's eye," a minha mãe acts on her sense that there "is no protection but there is difference" (195): she understands that Vaark and D'Ortega possess different sensibilities and thus agendas divergent enough for her to take the gamble presented to her. How curious, then, that she concludes that Vaark's acceptance of Florens as a way to "close the debt" is not a miracle but "a mercy." This distinction illuminates the improbability generated when futurity and historicity intersect and recalls her conversation with Reverend Father, the Anglican priest. As a result of that discussion, a minha mãe realizes that the scenario he describes for her salvation is contingent on her love of God and Jesus Christ and her ability to remain "innocent in mind and deed" (195). Her entry into that space "beyond the valley of [her] woeful life into an everlasting one" hinges on her ability to honor the debt created at the moment of the Crucifixion. But the Reverend Father has failed to take into account the fact that the settlers of Maryland have located slaves outside the parameters of the Crucifixion and thus outside the possibility of salvation, a sentiment evidenced by the statute guaranteeing the rights of inhabitants of the colony: "All the Inhabitants of this Province being Christians (Slaves excepted) Shall have and enjoy all such rights liberties immunities privileges and free customs within this Province as any natural-born subject of England." This is in keeping with Winthrop Jordan's argument that these "laws make very little sense unless the term *slaves* meant Negroes and perhaps Indians" (42).[14]

Looking at Vaark's act as "a mercy" means that a minha mãe recognizes it as an instance where the certainty of punishment is suspended, creating the opportunity for an act of speculative agency. Distinguishing between an act of God and an act of humanity, a minha mãe recognizes that a debt in which the terms for repayment are unstable—volatile, even—may be preferable to one whose terms are clear and fixed. And further, she knows that she is in no position to repay her debt to Vaark, that her status as a slave carries the inherent meaning that she is always already in a state of default. But this is less important than the fact that, for the briefest of moments, a minha mãe has been extended sufficient credit to project her daughter from the present into the future.[15]

Her act of kneeling and closing her eyes is no mere act of supplication; she is not, as one might surmise, begging for her daughter's life. Rather, she is establishing a structure of feeling that seeks to meet credit's fundamental requirement.[16] Kneeling in the dust, "where [her] heart will remain each night and every day until [Florens] understand[s] what [she] know[s] and long[s] to tell [her]" a minha mãe communicates to Vaark her desire to pass something down to her daughter. What seems on its face to be an abstract desire, in which the possibility for fulfillment will likely be nullified the moment D'Ortega ships Florens to the Vaark farm, is restored to materiality by the lender's bitter realization that he has no heirs to whom he can pass his estate. Listening to the dinnertime conversation between D'Ortega's wife and sons, Vaark concludes, "Nothing that transpired in the conversation had footing in the real world" (20). The dinner, he recognizes, is a performance that has two functions: to set the stage for D'Ortega's plea for revised terms on his debt and to articulate the manner in which owning slaves is integral to doing God's work. In the face of Vaark's anti-Anglican disapproval of the vanity meant to pass as D'Ortega's devotion to Catholicism, a minha mãe's speculative act establishes credit's "grammar of trust" but does so by reversing the terms governing systems of credit by asserting the "real" expression of maternal love against the "abstract" circumstance of a financial transaction.

The Vaark farm represents the metonym for "ground zero," for an outbreak for which we must account within the space of the novel's plot. By returning to an America in its originary stages, *A Mercy* chronicles the "outbreak" of the rationale for dehumanizing and demonizing black bodies in order to enable the transition from human to property.[17] As Reiss puts it, Virginia constitutes the template "for the development of black-white relations in the rest of the South." In this view, Virginia is the staging area for the "infection" of the rest of the surrounding region, north and east to Maryland and Delaware and south into the Carolinas, that leads to the reification of racial and social categories (black and white, slave and indentured) in the cultural imaginary. Morrison utilizes the smallpox virus as the underlying symbolism for the spread of a social hermeneutic in which the moral and political authority of whiteness comes to be standardized in a way that coincides with the spread of slavery across the Americas, creating a set of distinctions that move across a plexus of signifying binaries: North and South; slave and indentured; black and white; native and colonist; Catholic and Protestant. As a feature of seventeenth-century life, smallpox sets events in *A Mercy* into motion, creating an occasion in which we learn how each of the inhabitants of Vaark's farm came to live there and chronicling the beginning of their transformation from European immigrants and racialized Others into southerners.

But the aftermath of smallpox creates a circumstance in which difference comes to be measured not only in racial or regional terms but also in terms of the distinction between acquired and innate immunity. After surviving bouts of illness, Rebekka and Sorrow achieve an acquired immunity to smallpox, the result of their bodies having experienced the insult of a foreign vector and recovered to a state of what botanist Michael Boots and mathematician Roger G. Bowers call "immunological memory" that "allows the recovered individual to remain immune to the disease" (716).[18] The bodies of Rebekka and Complete (formerly Sorrow) share the ability to "remember" the smallpox virus and thus prevent reinfection from occurring. Consequently, they no longer need live in fear of another outbreak. But with acquired immunity comes a profound transformation of their affective response to their surroundings. For Complete it means that her Twin, who has been with her since her rescue from a shipwreck, departs, "traceless and unmissed," and she sheds the impulsiveness that characterizes her behavior prior to her illness, making her relatively useless in the performance of daily chores.

At the start of the novel, Sorrow, as she is named by the sawyer's wife, has "no memory of her past life except being dragged ashore by whales" (60). As Lina observes, she lives up to her name, for Sorrow is "the daft girl who [keeps] wandering off getting lost, who [knows] nothing and work[s] less." But with her recovery, she ceases to wander and performs "routine duties, organizing them around her infant's needs, impervious to the complaints of others." And she engages in an act of self-naming: "She had looked into her daughter's eyes; saw in them the grey-green glisten of a winter sea while a ship sailed by-the-lee. 'I am your mother,' she said. 'My name is Complete'" (159).

Having been restored to health (and free of smallpox's identifying scars as a consequence of the blacksmith's treatment), Complete's life centers on her baby, and she achieves a new level of interiority in which motherhood is synonymous with selfhood. Hence, Complete's immunological memory functions as an overlay to her maternity, as if the two states exist in a mutually constitutive relationship. Complete's history begins with her acceptance of the responsibilities of motherhood because her daughter functions as both a symbol of futurity and the manifestation of her newly imagined legacy. By contrast, Rebekka's children lie buried in the family graveyard, and with the death of Jacob Vaark, she will never again bear children; for her, mothering is past tense.

To have acquired immunity, then, is to exist in a state in which the body resists viral threat because it enters a form of sustained recognition.[19] But after she is cured, Rebekka calls for a Bible and forbids entry into Jacob's grand house. With its "glittering cobras [that] kiss at the gate's crown," the house symbolizes both Edenic paradise and the subsequent fall from grace. Rebekka's refusal to pass beyond the gates, to return to paradise—which might simply mean a return to the open-minded, capable, woman who counted Lina as a companion—is prompted by her conversion to Christianity. So when Sorrow remarks that she was fortunate to be saved by the blacksmith, Rebekka answers, "Ninny, God alone cures. ... No man has such power" (157). By attributing her recovery to a mysterious and inchoate God who works through human beings rather than to Lina, Florens, or the blacksmith, Rebekka places herself outside of the realm of human relationships. This transformation can be ascertained in her face, which bears the pockmarks left by the smallpox virus, signaling her conversion from freethinker to devout Christian but also suggesting that she, too, will come to see blackness as the mark of the devil. Hence, the smallpox virus performs an act of inscription—it is the sign of her deliverance—and an act of transcription in which her conversation with a judgmental God is recorded on her face.[20] This conceptual tight space means that the Vaark farm shifts from an economy of subsistence to a spiritual economy that reads everything through a religious hermeneutic.

But it is here that we must ponder the concept of acquired immunity alongside the notion of debt. If the latter is nothing short of an obligation to the consummation of past desires, then the former represents the ability to ensure the future by keeping the past at bay. What intervenes, of course, is the extension of credit as a way to collapse the boundary between present and future but that ties the individual to a quantifiable past. For Rebekka, her recovery from the smallpox virus necessitates that she turn her attention to the future of the Vaark farm. However, her belief that God has cured her not only of the virus but also of her husband's sin of greed and pride leads her to conclude that actions falling under the category of "man's works" are specious, impelled by motivations that originate outside of the purview of religious faith. In order to understand what drives Rebekka to such a radical reimagining of human agency, we must look at the space of reflection she enters in the midst of her illness. Seeing her life as synonymous with loss (of husband, children, pleasure), Rebekka ruminates on whether happiness is merely "Satan's allure, his tantalizing deceit" and her self-sufficiency a manifestation of "outright blasphemy" (114).

Thinking about the Anabaptist doctrine that concludes that "Afterlife was more than Divine; it was thrill-soaked," Rebekka ponders its advantages:

> Not a blue and gold paradise of twenty-four hour praise song, but an *adventurous real life*, where all choices were perfect and perfectly executed. ... There would be music and feasts; picnics and hayrides. Frolicking. Dreams come true. And perhaps if one was truly committed, consistently devout, God would take pity and allow her children, though too young for a baptism of full immersion, entrance to His sphere. *But of greatest importance, there was time. All of it. Time to converse with the saved, laugh with them.* (116; emphasis added)

So Rebekka passes "her days with the joy of a clock"—she has made time synonymous with salvation. Through the acquired immunity of religious faith, she wonders if the events of her past life, from the journey across the Atlantic to her life with Jacob and the loss of her children, are "waystations marking a road to revelation" (118). The voyage in particular is a distant memory. But it represents a moment when Rebekka opts to take the gamble, having recognized that she has a limited number of futures available to her. The problem, as Morrison suggests on numerous occasions in the novel, is that women who tie their prospects to men ultimately distort their ability to author their own place in the world. But during the voyage, Rebekka and the other women below decks on the ship blot out "what they fled and what might await them," so that what begins as exile is transformed into a page that awaits their authorship, "Wretched as was the space they crouched in, it was nevertheless blank where a past did not haunt or a future beckon. Women of and for men, in those few moments they were neither" (100). For these women "unable to see the sky, time became simply the running sea, unmarked, eternal and of no matter" (100). As Paul Gilroy might suggest, the Atlantic constitutes a tight space, but with a difference since the journey forges a group of women whose radically divergent agendas and histories should leave them permanently estranged into a community that exists outside of the dictates of capitalist time and space.

But after Rebekka adopts the life of a penitent, her life becomes consumed with thoughts of time and how to quantify it on a spiritual scale. If the reliance on a credit-driven economy could manufacture forms of desire and wealth inextricably linked to the past masquerading as the stabilization of an uncertain future, Rebekka's acquired immunity mirrors this development, since the past (in the form of spiritual debt she uses as a hedge against damnation) takes on the characteristics of credit. And as the reflection on her children's prospects for the afterlife suggests, commitment and devotion to a life of penitence can create sufficient capital that both she and they will be admitted to heaven.

That such thoughts occur during Rebekka's illness suggests a substantial reduction in her resistance to ideas that she might otherwise perceive as too good to be true. Stripped of its Christian rhetoric, the Anabaptist notion of salvation as "thrill-soaked" is nothing short of the achievement of an ongoing state of pleasure, meaning that the Anabaptists conceptualize heaven as a space in which the accumulation of spiritual capital leads to an inexhaustible means for satisfying any and all desire. In the end, heaven is a space in which time itself is used on account. Such thinking represents the manner in which Rebekka has opted for a life that soon, in and of itself, will mean nothing outside the realm of religiosity. The task of accruing the necessary spiritual capital means that her entire life becomes, as Ian Baucom would suggest, a commodity she will eventually trade for entrance into heaven, which means in turn that she no longer understands her life outside of the context of allegory.[21] Her acquired immunity constitutes a hierarchy in which the symbolic is privileged over the real.

Michael Roemer opens *Telling Stories: Postmodernism and the Invalidation of Traditional Narrative*, with the poignant observation that "every story is over before it begins" (3). On its face, *A Mercy* is built around the successful containment of a smallpox outbreak on a small farm in Virginia in the seventeenth century, a time when the virus killed an estimated 400,000 people a year and was considered "the most devastating disease in the world" (63). But on closer inspection, the novel is concerned with the outbreak of new forms of knowing, or as Marc Conner describes it, *A Mercy* is "obsessed with the ethics of knowledge" (148). As such, it chronicles the process by which the colony of Virginia moves one step closer to the integration, vertically and horizontally, of what historian Kenneth Stampp famously referred to as the peculiar institution. As the virtual ground zero for the financial and speculative know-how that will allow the institution to thrive once the cash crop of cotton takes primacy over tobacco, the Vaark farm is the site of a profound transformation: from a space of possibility to a tight space in which a woman like Lina will be erased and silenced in the wake of the authorization of new forms of knowledge that are designed to articulate her inferiority and lack of grace. On the Vaark farm, two women have survived bouts with smallpox with help from a free black man and a Native American woman who witnessed the eradication of her village by the disease. One embraces the responsibilities of motherhood and finds a new level of contentment; the other takes on the role of penitent, seeking a way to accumulate sufficient grace to gain admittance into heaven for her and for her deceased children.

Two male characters, who are working-off periods of indenture, move from servitude to paid labor, further cementing the differences between black and white. One of those men, Scully, comes to embody the relationship between deferred pleasure and the accumulation of capital when he decides "to bide his time until, given the freedom fee, he [will be] able to buy a horse." Discerning difference as a reflection of mobility, Scully observes, "The carriage or cart or wagon drawn were not superior to the horse mounted. Anyone limited to walking everywhere never seemed to get anywhere" (181). At the root of this observation lies the trope of rugged individualism, manifested through the figure who will ultimately animate expansion across the North American continent in the form of first the frontiersman and later the cowboy, each of whom represents a way to overcome the ravages of tight space in urban settings. For both Scully and Willard, wages are "enough to imagine a future" (183) that will underwrite depletion and want in an American population neither can foresee. Scully's desire for a horse would seem to be innocuous, but once wage labor becomes equated with whiteness, it enables a series of oppositions that become integral to the notion of progress: white men pitted against the indigenous population in the quest to transform wilderness into civilization; the concept of civilization (e.g. city life) pitted against the frontier; and, of course, the individualism (whiteness) pitted against incapacity (blackness).

However, *A Mercy*'s depiction of an ethics of knowledge also seeks to account for the ways that human imagination becomes deeply habituated in the practice of asset accumulation, which in turn leads to a form of language use that strips all physicality from the human body and re-imagines it as an abstraction standing in for the "real" act of money changing hands. As the unlikely synthesis of capital and corporeality intimates, credit, debt, and profit constitute an unholy trinity because these constructions interpose themselves across the discursive spectrum. Hence, Rebekka Vaark goes from a belief that work is rooted in the material, physical world, a testimony to her resiliency and industry, to the religious belief that all labor is situated in an allegorical frame, where one can no longer ascertain how—or even if—the capital one amasses will be sufficient to allow passage into heaven. Lina is consigned to the liminal space between companion and servant, but she embodies the understanding that whiteness and maleness equal the impulse to "forever fence land, ship whole trees to faraway countries, take any woman for quick pleasure, ruin soil, befoul sacred places and worship a dull, unimaginative god" (63).

She has a stake in the matter of Rebekka's recovery because she understands that in Rebekka's absence, she, Florens, and Sorrow—"three unmastered women"—will become "wild game for anyone" (68):

> None of them could inherit; none was attached to a church or recorded in its books. Female and illegal, they would be interlopers, squatters, if they stayed on after Mistress died, subject to purchase, hire, assault, abduction, exile. The farm could be claimed by or auctioned off to Baptists. Lina had

> relished her place in this small, tight family, but now saw its folly. Sir and Mistress believed they could have honest free-thinking lives, yet without heirs, all their work meant less than a swallow's nest. (68)

Lina's assessment of her prospects rests on the realization that Jacob and Rebekka have not, as they believed, created a space resistant to incursion, where "like gods from nowhere beholden to nothing except their own creations" (69) their works will outlast them. Though Lina is indigenous, her association with the Vaarks has made her into an orphan twice-over: first when her village is decimated by the smallpox virus, and again when she realizes that in the wake of Jacob Vaark's death, the fiction binding the inhabitants of "Jacob's Land" is stripped away to reveal that they are yet and still, each and all, orphans, bereft of a way to sustain meaning in the absence of textualized force. Through Lina, Morrison chronicles the shift that is occurring in the New World. The myth of the self-made man, through which Jacob has come to understand himself and what he can achieve, conceals the more profound reality that "privacy," as it assumed the form of total independence from institutional and bureaucratic hegemony, is replaced by the necessity to affiliate. Selfhood comes to have meaning only through "some encircling outside thing" (68) religion, military service, kinship (especially when accompanied by property).

The chapter focused on how Lina chronicles the ways that the concept of manhood is, in the absence of physical manifestations of its authority, a speculative venture at best. Lina sees the blacksmith and Jacob working together, with "Sir behave[ing] as though the blacksmith was his brother," and watches:

> Sir slice a green apple, his left boot raised on a rock, his mouth working along with his hands; the smithy nodding, looking intently at his employer. Then Sir, as nonchalantly as you please, tipped a slice of apple on his knife and offered it to the blacksmith who, just as nonchalantly, took it and put it in his mouth. So Lina knew she was the only one alert to the breakdown stealing toward them. (71)

Though this passage conveys Lina's uneasiness in the face of impending doom, it also illustrates the beginnings of what it will take nearly three more centuries to fully understand: the ways that gendered identities can be consolidated apart from race. As she watches the two men, "their heads over lines drawn in dirt" (71) Lina witnesses the collaborative blueprint that will usher in the rise of gendered authority across racial lines. The "shattering a free black man would cause" (71) while directly referencing the blacksmith's impact on Florens, points to the disaster wrought by black men in Morrison's earlier novels—Cholly Breedlove, Macon Dead, Son Green, Joe Trace, and the men of Ruby. Ironically, this idea also gestures toward Florens's act of breaking free of the illusion created by unchecked desire.

In *A Mercy*, Morrison contemplates an America in which the protocols pertaining to white supremacy are inchoate, still in process. But the novel also depicts the destabilization of the cross-racial and cross-cultural forms of understanding that might sustain a feminist analytic capable of inventing a set of conceptual moves able to counter the structures of domination that occur at the intersection of race, gender, and class. The depiction of acquired immunity and creditworthiness function as states of being that orient the colonial subject toward the past, present, and future and offers a means through which to understand the dangers of the New World as a possibility managed through the implementation of systems of meaning, structures of feeling, which accompany the reification of racial difference.

At the Widow Ealing's house, Florens is questioned by the visitors and declared by one to be "the Black Man's minion" (133). Placing Florens under inspection, they force her to undress and go over every part of her body (teeth, tongue, scarred palm, under her arms, between her legs, her feet), at which point Florens relates, "they are looking at me my body across distances without recognition" (133). Morrison's phrasing here points to a moment when the black female body is cleaved in two: Florens is no longer simply a specimen of difference; rather, her dark complexion is invested with symbolic importance. After the Widow's daughter, Jane, helps Florens escape into the woods, Florens relates,

> I walk alone except for the eyes that join me on my journey. Eyes that do not recognize me, eyes that examine me for a tail, an extra teat, a man's whip between my legs. Wondering eyes that stare and decide if my navel is in the right place, if my knees bend backward like the forelegs of a dog. (135)

We can surmise that by "the Black Man," the visitors are referring to Satan; thus, when Florens is referred to as his minion, her difference is a product of the visitors' belief that she is not of this world. Her dark skin is not yet understood as inferiority, but it remains as a form of collateral, albeit in a different way from how it functioned on D'Ortega's plantation. Florens becomes spiritual collateral that the Widow Ealing and her fellow Baptist settlers use to guarantee whiteness as the default position of humanity and grace. It is no wonder that Florens feels as if the religious gaze that has undone her emanates from eyes that cannot place her as human or animal. In a manner that recalls Frederick Douglass's equation of writing and protection, Florens states:

> Inside I am shrinking. ... I am losing something with every step I take. I can feel the drain. Something precious is leaving me. I am a thing apart. With the letter I belong and am lawful. Without it I am a weak calf abandoned by the herd, a turtle without shell, a minion with no telltale signs but a darkness I am born with, outside, yes, but inside as well and the inside dark is small, feathered, and toothy. Is that what my mother knows? Why she chooses to live without? Not the *outside dark we share*, a minha mãe and me, *but the inside one we don't*. Is this dying mine alone? (135–136; emphasis added)

Because we are not clear that Florens is writing her story, we do not realize that we are reading her account of the process by which she comes to understand her own self-worth. The "inquisition" she has endured at the hands of the Baptist settlers has a dual function. On one hand, it stages a set of hermeneutical maneuvers in which the black body comes to be situated at the intersection of racial difference and spiritual inauthenticity. On the other, the scrutiny produces in Florens the sense that it is a product of the same criteria that led her mother to give her away to Jacob Vaark. In the first instance, blackness functions as the exterior signifier of evil, spiritual irretrievability. In the second, Florens interprets darkness as characteristic of her inherent lack of value, her irredeemable qualities as a daughter.

Florens and a minha mãe can only reconcile the act of speculation that saved Florens from a life in which "there is no protection" by Florens's act of "writing back" to a minha mãe to create a subjectivity that will prove to be her most durable asset. In undertaking to write a narrative that can explain the actions that led to the sundering of her relationship with the blacksmith, Florens brings together her ability to read and interpret signs with her desire to reconcile loss and abandonment by exercising a sense of speculative agency. Though the blacksmith can "read the world," his illiteracy forecloses on the possibility that he will benefit from Florens's narrative. Hence, when she says, "If you never read this, no one will. These careful words, closed up and wide open, will talk to themselves," she reprises her initial miscalculation at the moment when a minha mãe gave her to Vaark, that love and intimacy can be realized only through acts of human presence and touch.

Though Scully interprets the flickers of candlelight in the unoccupied house as verification of the presence of ghosts, Florens's act of writing on the walls and floor transforms the largesse of a house that has risen out of a fog meant to symbolize the shroud of slavery to tower over Vaark's farm from a tight space that symbolizes pride and materialism. However, Florens' presence converts it into a two-story house in which her story comes to exist alongside—and because it is written, ultimately supplant—the narrative of Jacob Vaark's transition from lender mediating the exchange of commodities to a member of the gentry poised to consume them. Indeed, if we return momentarily to the allegorical nature of the virus in Morrison's novel, Florens is inscribing a narrative inside of what will become Lincoln's house divided that anticipates Morrison's fictional production, her act of exploding the integrity of the divided house from within. Hence, even as the empty house monumentalizes the wealth and privilege the southern landed gentry come to see as their due, it also represents the site of an alternative political imaginary in which black women's writerly voices deform the dominant imaginary from within.

Her "one sadness," that she "cannot know what [her] mother is telling [her]," is mitigated by "what [she is] wanting to tell her" (189), but Florens does not understand that the act of writing her narrative is the allegorical bridge between her declaration, "I am become wilderness but I am also Florens," and her mother's insistence that "In the dust ... my heart will remain each night and every day until you understand what I know and long to tell you" (195). As Jamie Carlacio points out, Florens's declaration constitutes a moment when she achieves a point of contact between her physical desire for the blacksmith and her ruptured attachment to a minha mãe (143). Writing on the walls and floor of the Vaark house, this new Florens, with "feet ... hard as cypress," creates the narrative response to a minha mãe's call: "To be given dominion over another is a hard thing; to wrest dominion over another is a wrong thing; to give dominion of yourself to another is a wicked thing." The novel's final words, "Hear a tua mãe," which function both in time and out of time, are verified by all that has come before it, as inscription and the doubling of a narrative of grace.

One thinks here of the lyrics in the hymn, "Amazing Grace," which read: "Through many dangers, toils, and snares/I have already come;/'Tis Grace that brought me safe thus far/And Grace will lead me home," as they are reflected in the allegorical "connection" that Florens's narrative initiates with her mother. The final chapter of *A Mercy* narrated in a moment which is either just after, or a considerable amount time after, we cannot tell which, a minha mãe chose Florens to be saved, for reasons she did not then understand, marks Florens' passage from the realm of mercy to a state of grace. The fact that a state of complementarity exists between them that neither a minha mãe nor Florens know they have produced indicates Morrison's sense that just as love need not be communicated solely through physical touch, nor [in the case of unconditional love] does it require confirmation.

A Mercy ends with the reconciliation of Florens and her mother across time and space. Though they will never again be in one another's presence and Florens may yet be sold into chattel slavery, they nonetheless constitute a counter-public whose antiphonal link is signaled by the mother's desire to be heard and the daughter's enactment of the mother's insights regarding the tripartite nature of dominion within the space of lived experience. Just as the reconciliation between Heed and Christine will continue despite the passing of the former, the bond between mother and daughter will endure irrespective of what happens in the physical world. In this respect, the novel asks the reader to consider the possibility that the boundaries integral to the workings of one political imaginary are also the source of its undoing. In other words, Florens's act of inscribing her story on the walls and floor of the house slavery built is a metonym for the voices resonating within. Though it is writing for which, in the moment it occurs, there is no audience, Scully's belief that the house is haunted by ghosts is an accurate assessment. At a time just before the South will come into being as the home of chattel slavery, there is already a ghost in the machine. *A Mercy* can in no way be understood as a reprise of *Beloved*, but the writing on the walls of the Vaark house is testament to the archive's power to haunt the political imaginary.

There is yet one more way to characterize the significations that bring *A Mercy* to a state of closure. In light of the ways that the house of slavery will eventually become a matter of blood, Florens's narrative also anticipates the manner in which slavery's patriarchal vestments will crystallize into habits of judgment in which proponents of slavery shift away from an epidermal emphasis (the equation of slavery with skin color) to a sanguinary emphasis where the mother's blood determines the status of children born out of sexual contact between white men and their female slaves. A minha mãe's recognition that D'Ortega had plans to transform Florens from child to concubine and the tactics a minha mãe adopts to disrupt those plans occurs when she remembers how her identity was "cooked down" to racialized bondage. But once slave owners adopt the doctrine of *partus sequitor ventrem*, where the mother's condition determines whether the child is slave or free, the question of whether the child was conceived through an act of rape or consensual sex is rendered moot. Florens's writing on the walls and floors *inside* the Vaark house symbolically anticipates the manner in which the blood of a child born into slavery substantiates an alternative narrative in which the violation of black women's bodies is central. Florens' narration can be understood as a writerly form of immunological memory that is inscribed on a domestic space that stands as the embodiment of the disciplinary and ontological logics of slavery.

If *A Mercy* represents Morrison's decision to investigate the forces that will harden and crystallize into the racial entitlements that accrue to whites during antebellum slavery, then Morrison's 2012 novel, *Home*, seeks to come at things from the opposite end of the temporal continuum by situating the tight space created through acts of violation alongside the question of how freedom informs the lived experience of people in the Jim Crow South. Is healing a singular endeavor for which the individual must take responsibility? Or is healing best thought of as a communal endeavor? Are there ceremonial acts whose redemptive power can reclaim bodies desecrated by the purification ritual of lynching? In order to find answers to these queries, I now turn to Morrison's *Home*.

Notes

1. Toni Morrison, *A Mercy* (New York: Vintage Books, 2009). All subsequent quotations from the text are from this edition, p. 3.
2. Winthrop Jordan's *The Whiteman's Burden*, argues that by 1640, some twenty years after their arrival, blacks had become fully-fledged slaves. For our purposes, Jordan's account of slavery's emergence in Virginia and

Maryland is useful for his observation that slavery in the tobacco colonies *develops* which means "it is therefore possible to trace, very imperfectly, the development of the shadowy, unexamined rationale which supported it" (Jordan, 40). Jordan concludes, "The concept of Negro slavery [in Virginia] was neither borrowed from foreigners, nor extracted from books, nor invented out of whole cloth, nor extrapolated from servitude, nor generated by English reaction to Negroes as such, nor necessitated by the exigencies of the New World" (40). Rather, note Jordan's insistence that slavery in Virginia was not, as one might expect, a product of racial prejudice.

3. Oldstone reports: "The typical course of smallpox is an acute disease that produces obvious and distinct skin lesions and, after recovery, leaves its well-defined fingerprints as clearly visible, distinctive pock marks, usually numerous on the faces of survivors."
4. That this shift occurs in the colony of Virginia is significant. Historians focusing on seventeenth-century Virginia and Maryland differ in their sense of when the Africans who land at Point Comfort, Virginia in 1619 came to be collectively and resolutely understood as both different and *inferior*. Alden Vaughan's *Roots of American Racism* concludes,

   What the evidence of the decade after 1619 reveals is inconclusive but not insignificant. It shows with alarming clarity that blacks from the outset were objects of prejudice that relegated most, perhaps all, of them to the lowest rank in the colony's society, and there are strong hints that bondage for blacks did not carry the same terms as for whites. The latter served for limited times and were freed; the former, apparently in most cases, were not freed, at least in the decade after many of them arrived in Virginia. (Vaughan, 134)
5. As Ian Baucom argues in *Specters of the Atlantic*, "The genius of insurance, the secret of *its* contribution to finance capitalism, is its insistence that the real test of something's value comes not at the moment it is made or exchanged, but at the moment it is lost or destroyed" (97).
6. Contrasting this to a pure commodity-culture, Baucom asserts that the difference is that in "an insurance culture value survives its objects, and in doing so, does not just reward the individual self-interest of the insured object's owner, but retrospectively confirms the system-wide conviction that the value was *always* autonomous from its object, *always* only a matter of agreement" (97).
7. In her book *Contagious: Cultures, Carriers, and the Outbreak Narrative*, Priscilla Wald quotes virologist, Philip Mortimer, who notes, "An outbreak, like a story, should have a coherent plot" (16).
8. Though I am mindful of David Gates' insistence that Morrison's novel stands as proof that she is "a conscious inheritor of America's pastoral tradition," I would argue against seeing the novel's plot as being solely

about how to reckon with man's expulsion from paradise and insist additionally that Morrison's novel captures the volatility that results when futurity and the historicity of trauma seek to occupy the same space.

9. According to Oldstone, smallpox is "interwoven with the history of human migrations and wars, dramatically favoring one population or army over another." During the 20th Century alone, 300 million people infected with the virus died. Only after vaccination became standard practice was the disease eradicated, which did not occur until 1978. Oldstone cites smallpox as the likely cause for the decimation of the native Indian population, both in Hispaniola and the Americas. And he notes further that during the war of 1763 between England and France, Sir Geoffrey Amherst ordered Colonel Henry Bouquet to provide hostile Indians with blankets infected with smallpox, making it the first agent to be used in bacteriological warfare (33).
10. Marcus Rediker asserts as much in his book *Slave Ship*, which chronicles the process by which English sailing ships are employed in the Triangle Trade; how they are crewed, financed, and managed as well as the geographical points on the West African coast where the trade flourishes.
11. As Max Weber makes clear in *Protestantism and the Spirit of Capitalism*, the deferral of pleasure coincided with the impulse to plow profits back into the enterprise and thus extend and increase the sphere of financial influence. And as Eric Williams makes clear in *Capitalism and Slavery*, "The triangular trade thereby gave a triple stimulus to British industry. The Negroes purchased with British manufactures; transported to plantations, they produced sugar, cotton, indigo, molasses, and other tropical products, the processing of which created new industries in England; while the maintenance of the Negroes and their owners on the plantations provided another market for British industry, New England agriculture and the Newfoundland fisheries. By 1750 there was hardly a trading or a manufacturing town in England which was not in some way connected with the triangular or direct colonial trade" (Williams, p. 52).
12. One thinks here of the description in the narratives of both Frederick Douglass and Harriet Jacobs, of their respective childhoods. In both instances, the childhood of a slave exists in a liminal space, between a life characterized by play and one in which that life is measured in an accounting ledger as an asset that has the potential to increase in value as the child becomes able to perform labor. And, in the case of a female slave, we must consider as well her ability to give birth to children, which means that her value is two-fold: as "implement" and as breeder. Hence, D'Ortega's declaration that, "The value of a seasoned slave is beyond adequate" takes into account (once again, in ways that are not voiced) the right of a slave master to interpret "seasoned slave" in a variety of ways: as commodity, as sexual partner or reproductive tool, and as labor.

It is this flexibility that Vaark and D'Ortega bring into being once their contract is finalized.

13. However, as Ian Baucom suggests, this is a much more complicated process than we might assume at first glance. As a circuit in a system Baucom refers to as the Anglo-Atlantic cycle of accumulation, the slave trade was tied into a transnational set of financial terrains (83). This cycle of accumulation was characterized by its progression from the simple trade in goods and services to something much more pervasive: the transition from a barter economy—where the transaction turned on the exchange of items of equivalent value—to a credit-driven economy.
14. What is striking about the manner in which the language is rendered is that its lack of punctuation anticipates Morrison's deconstruction of the school primer in which she removes all punctuation in the paragraphing the activities of Dick and Jane, subsequently removing the space between the words till they run together into an indecipherability that underscores the commonsensical nature of white supremacy.
15. Again, Baucom is instructive in articulating the implications when he notes that trust

    > was, indeed, the system-wide currency upon which the system depended and which it had learned to trade, trust expressed both in the literal monetary credit parties requested from or extended to one another and through the abstract confidence everyone had to have in the system itself, the belief they were required to invest in the credibility of its forms of value and the value of its guarantees. (89)

16. As Baucom observes:

    > For the system to work most profitably and most efficiently it needed not only a standard set of exchange mechanisms with which to translate the value of pounds, textiles, slaves, "coast money," dollars, sugar, and tobacco into one another, but a standard imaginary, a standard grammar of trust, a standard "habit" of crediting the "real" existence of abstract values. (89)

17. In light of the assessments by Deal, Jordan, Vaughan, Smith, Wright, and Reiss, it is clear that Morrison's decision to set the novel in and around the Chesapeake is meant to suggest that at the root of the Protestant and Anglican colonial projects in the region was the desire to generate profit and configure a rhetorical posture that translated the profits generated by African laborers as paeans to God.
18. One of the most fascinating (and troubling) aspects of HIV-infection was the manner in which, by suppressing the victim's immune system, the virus robbed the body of the ability to fight off common infections, as

if it had lost the capacity to recognize ostensibly harmless pathogens and eradicate them. If acquired immunity is based on the body's ability to sustain immunological memory, HIV constitutes an instance where death occurs because the body loses the ability to remember.

19. But, as Boots and Bowers point out, acquired immunity is distinguished by the fact that it possesses "two distinct processes that may have differing cost structures." While Boots and Bowers are referring to the mechanisms that fight off disease and how there are "costs associated with the maintenance of immunity to the parasite" (716), I would submit that *A Mercy* works out its own notion of "differing cost structures," which is evidenced by Rebekka's affect in the days after her illness. With a face forever marked by the scars left by the departed virus, Florens observes that "Mistress has cure but she is not well. Her heart is infidel. All smiles are gone. Each time she returns from the meetinghouse her eyes are nowhere and have no inside" (186).
20. Florens' use of the word "infidel," is most intriguing, in that it reflects the social anxieties created by the act of variolation. As David Shuttleton describes in his book *Smallpox and the Literary Imagination, 1660–1820*, variolation was personified by Restoration elegists as a "predatory barbarian attacking an angelic, female Christian beauty" (161). Given that the technique is thought to have originated in China, moving on to India, and from there to Turkey and Persia, it evoked xenophobic fears regarding the influence of the racial Other. Shuttleton states "inoculation was associated in the European imagination with the mercenary protection of an economic investment in the commodified beauty of trafficable girls" (162). Hence, the technique was rejected by the Catholic Church, which characterized it as the product of infidels. In English society, the practice was viewed as vulgar since it involved disrupting the body's integrity through the insertion of foreign matter into the body. As Shuttleton relates,

> The seemingly perverse act of grafting contagious matter into a healthy body not only went against intuitive attitudes towards physical integrity and disease, but posed a practical challenge to traditional relations of trust between the patient and their physician and/or surgeon; an ethical dilemma for any practitioner who, as a licensed member of the established medical faculties, had sworn allegiance to a Hippocratic oath which expressly required him to do nothing to harm the patient.

It is not until Lady Mary Montagu, the wife of the British ambassador to Turkey, brings the technique back to England, that it becomes an accepted practice among the British elite. In the description of Rebekka Vaark's pockmarked face at the end of *A Mercy*, we find traces of the Montagu narrative since she is said to have possessed legendary beauty, which was lost when she contracted smallpox. Inoculation was represented, Shuttleton argues, not as a medical technique, but rather a cosmetic one, since its "primary purpose is presented as the preservation of female beauty, not human *lives*" (165).

21. As Baucom explains, Walter Benjamin's "understanding of the nineteenth century's continuation or repetition of the seventeenth lies in his reading of the centrality, to both periods, of allegory and in his conception of the essentially allegorical nature of that process by which capital produces exchange values and, hence, commodities. Baucom goes on to cite a passage from Benjamin that allegorization and commodification share a link based on their mutual ability to debase "the 'thingliness' of the things on which they go to work. Whether allegorically construed or circulated as a commodity, things, in both systems, signify not themselves but some superordinate "value"—whether that value is understood as meaning or an exchange value. What I am suggesting is that Rebecca Vaark's decision to view everything in her life through a religious lens means that her experience is sheathed in a symbolic gloss that can be assessed in the same way one would assess a commodity.

CHAPTER 7

The Most Absurd Garments Space-Time Can Imagine: *Home's* Precarious Counter-Topography

In mapping, as in the conception of individuality, objectivity comes to the fore as the sole arbiter of truth and reality. Logic and reason increasingly dominate the scheme of the mind, acting as the orienting principle of personhood. In both realms, idiosyncrasy and emotionality, physicality and specificity, are increasingly marginalized.

—Kathleen Kirby, "Lost in Space: Re-establishing the Limits of Identity"

As an already—and always—raced writer, I knew from the very beginning that I could not, would not, reproduce the master's voice and its assumptions of the all-knowing law of the white father. Nor would I substitute his voice with that of his fawning mistress or his worthy opponent, for both of these positions (mistress or opponent) seemed to confine me to his terrain, in his arena, accepting the house rules in the dominance game. If I had to live in a racial house, it was important, at the least, to rebuild it so that it was not a windowless prison into which I was forced, a thick-walled, impenetrable container from which no cry could be heard, but rather an open house, grounded, yet generous in its supply of windows and doors. Or, at the most, it became imperative for me to transform this house completely. Counterracism was never an option.

—Toni Morrison, "Home"

A Mercy's final words: "Florens. My love. Hear a tua mãe," remind us that acts of voice can sometimes traverse incalculable distances. Though Florens' mother will never hear her speak in the voice of a grown woman or learn of her decision to "last," by opting to give *a minha mãe* the final word, Morrison proposes that acts of communication issuing from the

H. Beavers, *Geography and the Political Imaginary in the Novels of Toni Morrison*, Geocriticism and Spatial Literary Studies,
https://doi.org/10.1007/978-3-319-65999-2_7

imagination toward an intended destination always hit their mark. The plea *a minha mãe* directs toward her daughter insists that she wishes to be understood and, if not forgiven, then not forgotten. In this instance, the last words of the novel insinuate that an act of desperation deserves to be ascertained as an indication of love's bountiful possibilities, not its nullification; a gesture affirmed by the novel's opening words, "Don't be afraid." Of course, part of the problem lies in the fact that we have no way to determine when *a minha mãe* has given utterance to her words, but what interests me here is the manner in which novelistic closure invites us to return to the gesture of reassurance that opened the narrative.

Morrison's thematic looping needs once more to be contextualized within this study's overriding concern with geography, specifically, notions of place and place-making. In this respect, I'm intrigued by Andrew Hock Soon Ng's insistence that the physical manifestation of a house comes alive because it "embodies its dwellers' desires," with that "aliveness" ultimately serving "as a critical juncture where the trauma of memory and identity converge" (232). Though Ng's remarks are aimed at Morrison's *Beloved*, they are nonetheless applicable here, since *A Mercy*, too, features a house beset by the weight of historical trauma. According to Ng, trauma… "is not something ensconced within, and which perpetually disturbs, the psyche, but can become *transcribed on the very walls of a lived environment*" (232, my italics). Hence, trauma can be "spatially captured and conceptualized in Morrison's novel [as] 'rememory,'" or, as Florens puts it, "my telling." Since we do not ascertain the location where Florens' is inscribing her trauma till near the end of *A Mercy*, when she insists that "My telling can't hurt you…" at the start of the novel, it seems she is less interested in haunting's often presumed agenda of reprisal and more invested in the durability of words and what one might do to ensure their persistence. Realizing that the blacksmith's illiteracy constitutes an obstacle to deciphering the writing scrawled across the walls and floor of a single room in an abandoned house, Florens nonetheless recognizes that her words may yet have purchase out in the world. She imagines Lina leaping at the opportunity to help her burn the house to the ground, when her words can "fly up then fall, fall like ash over acres of primrose and mallow. Over a turquoise lake, beyond the eternal hemlocks, through clouds cut by rainbow and flavor the soil of the earth" (188). Though *A Mercy* is set in the seventeenth century, before soil is transformed into a signification of

American national sovereignty, by postulating how the topography surrounding the Vaark farm might serve as an archive, Florens professes that language and soil can become indistinguishable, a site of continuity and regeneration.

As I noted in the previous chapter, *A Mercy* occurs at a time prior to that moment when racial categories in the American colonies become rigidly fixed. However, Morrison's decision to inhabit the novels with a range of subjectivities, none of whom shares a point of origin, all of whom occupy varying forms of intersectional identity, raises questions about how something as inchoate as a political imaginary can achieve geographical substance. Recalling Guitar's declaration that his "whole life is geography," this chapter proceeds by acknowledging a conceptual reality that needs to be factored into a consideration of Morrison's works. It is well-documented that her novels are unique in their ability to dramatize whiteness and the acts of erasure, exclusion, and silence it occasions without making white characters central to the plot. Indeed, one can interpret the absence of white characters in her books to mean that whites need not even be present for white supremacist mechanisms to function, as if they represent a kind of incessant automaticity, machinations that seem to require little in the way of maintenance. But she is equally interested in portraying characters who possess the ability to first recognize and then minimize white supremacy's effects. Such an assessment notwithstanding, I want to push beyond it to get at a more fundamental point, namely that Morrison's investment in the act of place-making has to be situated alongside her refusal to privilege what she calls the "white gaze" in her work. In a 1998 interview with Charlie Rose, she stated:

> I have spent my entire writing life trying to make sure that the white gaze was not the dominant one in any of my books...I didn't have to be consumed by or be concerned by the white gaze. That was liberation for me... The problem of being free, to write the way you wish to without this other racialized gaze, is a serious one for an African American writer.

Such a declaration lends new meaning to Morrison's observation that "the language must not sweat," as an indication of how she devotes no energy to the task of making her characters legible to white readers through the conventional means of marking them racially,[1] refusing to participate in the sociological project that would require her to explain the details of black life for non-black readers.[2] Morrison elaborates on her refusal of the white gaze in *Playing in the Dark*, where she states, "My work requires me to think about how free I can be as an African American women writer in my genderized, sexualized, wholly racialized world" (4).[3] In her essay, "Home," which began as a keynote address at the "Race Matters" conference at Princeton in 1994, she elaborates:

> Yet in that freedom, as in all freedoms (especially stolen ones), lies danger. Could I redecorate, redesign, even reconceive the racial house without forfeiting a home of my own? Would life in this renovated house mean eternal homelessness? Would it condemn me to intense bouts of nostalgia for the race-free home I have never had and would never know? Or would it require intolerable circumspection, a self-censoring bond to the locus of racial architecture? In short, wasn't I (wouldn't I always be) tethered to a death-dealing ideology even (and especially) when I honed all my intelligence toward subverting it?[4]

And she continues:

> These questions, which have engaged so many, have troubled all of my work. How to be both free and situated; how to convert a racist house into a race-specific yet nonracist home. How to enunciate race while depriving it of its lethal cling? They are questions of concept, of language, of trajectory, of habitation, of occupation, and, although my engagement with them has been fierce, fitful, and constantly (I think) evolving, they remain in my thoughts as aesthetically and politically unresolved.[5]

Upon encountering Morrison's insistence that she has no investment in reproducing the white gaze in her novels, I was forced to think about the detailed depictions of place to be found in her work from a very different standpoint. If her novels are concerned with portraying an alternative political imaginary in which the white gaze is immaterial, Morrison's representation of neighborhoods and towns represents a sustained commitment to place-making legitimated by *human* concerns not simply racial ones.[6] An appropriate question might be, then, whether Morrison has an interest in depicting moments where the definitive last word is uttered, or whether she aims to bring her readers to a new level of appreciation for that moment that precedes utterance? If this is the case, what are we to make of the last few sentences of *Jazz*, "If I were able to say it. Say make me, remake me. You are free to do it and I am free to let you because look, look. Look where your hands are. Now" (229). Or, *Song of Solomon*, "For now he knew what Shalimar knew: if he surrendered to the air, he could ride it" (337). And what of Nel's realization that "circles and circles of sorrow," signal the frayed edges of a life whose main signification is absence? In each of these instances, Morrison places the reader in the midst of highly active spaces of inquiry. It is the book in our hands speaking to us, announcing that we are implicated in the act of story-making, not mere observers. Nel's "second-hand lonely" evokes what Kathleen Kirby calls "social" space, in which a variety of spatial registers come together to generate the subject. According to Kirby, "Such instantiations of the subject take place in real space, in the network of paths and buildings and parks and sidewalks and hallways we traverse daily" (15). Hence, subjectivity requires us "to take into account topological, geopolitical, corporeal, psychic, discursive, and social spaces," while understanding "that divisions between these registers of space will not hold" (15). In light of how "each space offers its own degree of freedom and imposes its own kind of confinement," we might conclude that Morrison's ultimate aim is to insist that the act of defining "space for the purposes of discussing the subject might instead tend to demonstrate just how flexible space can be" (16).

In this final chapter, I want to think about the ways Toni Morrison situates place-making in proximity to what Doreen Massey describes as the inter-relatedness of space and time, where space's "relational and constitutive" properties can be found (29). Numerous critics have argued that Morrison's fiction is a product of the complex workings of postmodernity. One way to recognize this, according to Brenda K. Marshall, is to accept that when we "acknowledge that within the postmodern moment local 'truths' used for specific purposes have replaced an acceptance of Absolute Truths which struggle for dominance, we [also] need to remember that those local truths also skirmish for dominance" (188). Or, consider Mahdu Dubey's assertion that Morrison's *Song of Solomon* offers an exemplary instance "of a postmodern literary-practice taking the folk turn in order to secure its claims to representing racial community" through a juxtaposition of Northern cities and rural spaces in the South (158). And finally there is Kimberly Chabot Davis's assertion that "Morrison's fiction has much to contribute to a postmodern theoretical-debate about history and representation," and that if her career "reveals both a desire for 'authentic' history-as-life-lived and the postmodern realization that history is a fictional construct, [then] the plot of *Beloved* is marked by a parallel dialectic—the mind's struggle between remembering and forgetting the past" (83).[7]

Hence, it is worthwhile to consider whether Morrison's work constitutes a bulwark against what David Harvey has called postmodernity's replacement of "a space of places with a space of flows" (28). It is equally efficacious to consider Linda McDowell's assessment of space which asserts, "The almost instantaneous transfer of information across the globe and the vastly speeded up possibilities of physical movement of people and goods has reduced the 'friction' of space, the transactional costs of overcoming distance" (29). Thinking about the imagined exchange between Florens and her mother, McDowell's comments prove to be an interrogative pivot of sorts. For, if, as McDowell proposes, "we seem now to be fast approaching a depthless world of surface in which all experience might soon be simultaneous: a postmodern world of hyperreality, characterized by the speeding up of time and blurring of boundaries," then an apt question might be: does Morrison's fiction seek to circumvent the foreclosures intimated in such a characterization by insisting that place [still] matters? Or, could it be that Morrison's abandonment of the conventional narrative techniques of realism is a different approach to space and time? These observations gain purchase in Michelle Wright's *The Physics of Blackness* in which she argues that blackness needs to be disentangled from narratives that privilege linear progress in order for greater attention to be directed at "identities [that are manifest] through intersecting spacetimes [which] can produce a diverse but coherent narrative" (Kindle edit. loc. 120).[8] According to Wright, "The only way to produce a definition of Blackness that is wholly inclusive and nonhierarchical is to understand Blackness as the *intersection* of constructs that locate the Black collective in *history* and in the *specific moment* in which Blackness is being imagined—the 'now' through which all imaginings of Blackness will be mediated" (Kindle vers. loc. 285 of 4640).

I want to place Wright's theorizing of space-time into conversation with McDowell's notion that "people are differentially located in space," with differential abilities and opportunities to overcome what geographers refer to as the "frictional effects of distance" (31). If, as McDowell contends, geography's "focus is on connections, looking at the links between processes and people at a range of spatial scales from the local to the global," the political imagination in Morrison's work seeks not only to illuminate, but subsequently problematize, the ways her characters negotiate the question of interconnectedness in relation to both spatial and temporal scales. If the white supremacist political imaginary sanctions the creation of ideological, bureaucratic, and protectionist networks designed to ensure whiteness as the dominant signification of belonging in the form of a linear narrative of progress, Morrison's fiction can be said to represent a praxis that seeks to delegitimize the influence of racial categories on everyday life by insisting that moving through time and space cannot be fully accounted for via linear approaches to time. Indeed, the entire plot of *Beloved* can be thought of as a depiction of an iteration of space and time afflicted by the resulting chaos arising out of the incompatibility (and the incomprehensibility) of conflicting systems of scale. On the one hand, Sethe's belief that the spirit inhabiting her house is the reincarnation of the daughter she murdered to "save" from enslavement cannot be reconciled with the spirit's declaration that:

> Sethe is the face I found and lost in the water under the bridge. When I went in, I saw her face coming to join me and it was my face too. I wanted to join. I tried to join, but she went up into the pieces of light at the top of the water. I lost her again, but I found the house she whispered to me and there she was, smiling at last (252).

The disparate explication of events past and present ultimately proves to be an inadequate method for sealing the gap created by the traumatic encounter between European and African bodies in what Morrison has called "the largest forced transfer of human bodies in the history of the world: slavery." When considered simply as a matter of spatial scale, Schoolteacher's ability to reinstate Sethe and her children into bondage originates in Kentucky and Sweet Home and extends across the Ohio River to Cincinnati, and ends at 124 Bluestone Road. However, Sethe's radical autonomy is out of sync with Beloved, whose search for "the woman with my face is in the sea" (211) is meant to evoke "several generations of daughters cut off from their mothers by the Middle Passage and slavery" (10).

The plot that emerges in *Beloved* indicates the difficulty that accompanies efforts to fashion "differential abilities and opportunities" into a viable network in which the inhabitants of a local space can understand place as a signification able to accommodate both the physicality of flesh *and* the abstraction of narrative. Once more, Morrison's two-story house proves to be instructive. In her Nobel Lecture, Morrison juxtaposed an old blind woman arguing that "word work is sublime" against a group of youths who chastise the old woman for "keeping her good opinion of herself" by playing it safe and avoiding the ruptures affecting the lives of black children whose experiences reflect the black community's failure to protect them. Though the old woman's narrative imagines a house of language in which liberatory practice ensures that there are no null spots to be accounted for, the young people's resistance to her narrative, their insistence that the absence of their voices be considered integral to subsequent efforts to portray black life in the United States, declares that there is a narrative that must be viewed as the necessary supplement to the old woman's sublime task. Morrison's call for a collaborative narrative posture is at once pragmatic in its logistics and decisive in its preference for the negotiated over the totalized as it functions in the service of bringing divergent narrative schemes into a state of localization. Localization proves to be an important element for understanding the two-story house as a potential site of resistance and recovery and it helps us to see spaces like the Clearing or a group of thirty women whose voices "br[eak] the back of words," as instances where recombinant forces are at work at a specific moment in time and space.[9]

In light of this, I would like to introduce a new term into the discussion that I hope will provide the catalyst for further thinking about Morrison's novels and the political landscape they seek to map. In their edited volume, *Precarious Worlds: Contested Geographies of Social Reproduction*, geographers Katie Meehan and Kendra Strauss introduce the concept of *precariousness* as a way to frame women's lives and subsequently problematize the work/life binary. By their reckoning, precariousness (and its analogue, precarity) "are multivalent concepts grounded in different intellectual and political genealogies" (1), from feminist political economy, where it "describes the feminization of labor markets," and in political philosophy, where Judith Butler develops "a social ontology of precarity to articulate a more generalized concept of mutual dependency as a condition of human life."

Meehan and Strauss declare that the intention they seek to realize in their volume is "to bring into conversation different approaches to conceptualizing and resisting inequality and exploitation, and to consider whether new alliances of theory and justice might be forged through a feminist materialist politics grounded in the concept of social reproduction."[10] As feminist geographers, they employ the term social reproduction (originally conceptualized by Karl Marx and Frederick Engels to mean "the labor necessary to ensure that workers arrive the next day at the factory gate,") as a "critical lens onto the entwined spheres of paid labor and unpaid work of daily life" (3). They find that social reproduction is "also a lens for focusing on the unequal distribution of flourishing that render some bodies, some workforces, and some communities far more precarious than others" (2).[11]

Given this study's emphasis on the political imaginary and its' influence on the various forms of place-making we find in Morrison's novels, introducing terms like precariousness and social reproduction has the potential to obfuscate my insistence that place-making involves agential forms of consciousness. In the interest of proceeding with care, an apt approach might lie in recognizing how the woman-centered analytic at work in Toni Morrison's political imagination is integral to the creation of female characters whose lives are fraught with precariousness, but whose agency is contingent on their ability to transcend conventional formulations of space-time. Hence, place-making and precariousness are in evidence in *Love*'s Christine and Heed, whose mutual love and friendship is destroyed by Bill Cosey's sexual indiscretion that serves to pit them against one another in a decades-long struggle over the mundane spoils of inheritance. However, the reader realizes that their reconciliation prompts the resumption of their mutuality across the barrier separating the living from the dead. And Florens and her mother in *A Mercy* embody precariousness through their shared status as unpaid laborers. While *a minha mãe* is firmly entrapped in slavery, her individuality "cooked" into what Charles Johnson would term, "epidermalized being," Florens is not yet a slave, but the fact that Rebekka Vaark elects to pay white laborers Willard and Scully, sets in motion a key distinction between slavery and wage labor. Rebekka's reactivation of Florens' status as a financial asset cannot disrupt the connection she and her mother forge across time and space.

Thinking back to Chaps. 2 and 3, which consider Morrison's Southern men and their relationship to tight space, I want to propose that as a matter of consequence, the women who find themselves in close proximity to those characters are, almost to a person, in precarious circumstances. One of the most salient examples is *Song of Solomon*'s First Corinthians. Though she has been well-educated, her "success" rides on being selected as a suitable mate for an upwardly mobile black man, she is little more than another of Macon Dead's assets. Her life begins to change for the better when she goes to work as a maid for a local poet, who puts Corinthians in charge of handling her correspondence. She meets Henry Porter and they begin a relationship that represents her best chance at a life not controlled by her father. Her precarious status is in evidence when Macon makes her quit her job and forbids her to see Porter. Though we get the impression that Corinthians will not obey her father's demands, the time Morrison devotes to Corinthians' story drives home the sense that middle-class black women's lives are likely to be as precarious as their working-class counterparts. Further, it is also clear that Milkman's quest for gold will have little to no impact on her life; what is equally clear is that the Dead family's patriarchal narrative is one which situates the needs and desires of Ruth, Pilate, First Corinthians, Magdalene, and Hagar adjacent to the "main" narrative.

However, as Michael Awkward has suggested, what appear to be digressions in Morrison's fiction are actually meant to suggest that black women are integral actors in a political imaginary seeking to contest vertical forms of place-making. Political imaginaries that embody individualism as the principal avenue to belonging are subverted by the materialism, violence, and disaffection of black men confined in the tight space of past trauma. Confronting misogyny, patriarchy, and sexism is fundamental to furthering a truly libratory political agenda. Hence, the two-story house might begin as the site of narrative contestation, but it might also be productively imagined as a crucible in which the impurities of tight space are stripped away till what results is the topophilia horizontal forms of place-making occasion.

I have no objections to Jean Wyatt's characterization of Morrison's trilogy of novels—*Beloved*, *Jazz*, and *Paradise*—as an instance in which she seeks to draw "the reader into 'co-creating' the text, not only through ambiguous discourse…but also by conundrums that are solved only late in the novel, or not at all" (11). However, as early as "Recitatif," (published 1983) we find evidence that Morrison had begun thinking about how to induce readers to see the shortcomings of realist discourse. I would assert further that the story in which Morrison attempts to reinvent how the reader traverses what she calls "the race house," is a precarious endeavor because by stripping the characters of conventional racial designations, she leaves the reader without the signposts she may have deemed "necessary" to gleaning the plot. In so doing, the precariousness to be found in "Recitatif" destabilizes the authority we accord maps, in which location in time and space gets reduced to coordinates on a grid, is called into question along with the credence we lend to notions of forward and back, up and down as iterations of progress.[12]

I find myself haunted by Morrison's juxtaposition of "how free [she] can be" against the impulse to map identity onto race, class, and gender as the only coordinates available to locate the black female subject on a social grid. One way to ruminate on Morrison's need to qualify her freedom is by clarifying its underlying motives via Susan Stanford Friedman's book *Mappings* in which she states, "geographic discourse often emphasizes not the ordered movement of linear growth but the lack of solid ground, the ceaseless change of fluidity, the nomadic wandering of transnational diaspora, the interactive syncretisms of the 'global ethnoscape,' or the interminable circuitry of cyberspace. Its mobile figurations adapt the landscapes of accelerating change, the technologies of information highways, and the globalization of migratory cultures" (19). Noting that "identity is constructed relationally through difference from the other," Friedman's insistence that "the geographics of identity moves between boundaries of difference and borderlands of liminality," is an apt way to frame the argument I present below.

It is with Friedman's "geographics of identity" in mind that I turn to Morrison's 2012 novel, *Home*. The opening chapter's arresting image of horses who "stood like men", recalls the meaning Yi-Fu-Tuan attaches to the upright human body. As the image is meant to suggest, standing upright constitutes a metaphor for manhood situated in a spatio-temporal framework in which geography and history are manifest. Further, that it is horses standing "like men," and not black men, who elect to resist the power of a white mob, suggests life in the Southern political imaginary locates black manhood on a scale somewhere beneath beasts of burden. *Where* bodies are located in space, Tuan suggests, can be understood physically and conceptually,[13] hence, habits of judgment associated with freedom can only be found in a "future [that] is ahead and 'up'" (36). Morrison's Frank Money occupies a liminal space in which the future is much in doubt because he occupies tight space that renders him symbolically prone.[14] The "prone position" in *Home* is characterized by historical events whose tenacity situates past and present in coterminous space. The novel gives us characters caught in tight spaces in which they find their bodies are "drawn into history," therefore robbing them of the ability *to be* in one place because no matter where they are, a site they associate with trauma accompanies them, rendering topophilia an impossibility.

The thought of remaining symbolically prone invites us to situate the political imaginary, with its cogitations on possibility and boundaries, alongside Tuan's insistence that social relations are played out on vertical and horizontal planes. If verticality is how we spatialize agency, equating it with self-powered ascent and, by turns quantifying it till it can only be conceived relationally, we would do well to recall Erica Edwards's critique of charismatic leadership, in which verticality can just as easily be understood as a space of delusion, where the desire to escape the prone position is pursued at the expense of social equity and inclusion. *Home* proposes that the only way to determine the *what* sourcing our disjointedness, requires that we prioritize the question of *where*.

This question is central to Frank's mistaken belief that Lotus, Georgia is a tight space where he does not belong. Because he is ill-equipped to believe that his hometown is a real *place* and that his life there involved acts of place-making, caring for Cee represents the only way he can rationalize his life there. When Frank thinks about his sister, Ycidra, his "only family" and relates to his interlocutor, "When you write this down, know this: she was a shadow for most of my life, a presence marking its own absence, or maybe mine" (103). More importantly, Frank asks the question, "Who am I without her—that underfed girl with the sad, waiting eyes?" (103). After Mike dies and Frank is forced to shoo birds away from the dead body, he realizes

> What died in his arms gave a grotesque life to his childhood. *They were Lotus boys who had known each other before they were toilet-trained, fled Texas the same way, disbelieving the unbelievable malignance of strangers.* As children they had chased after straying cows, made themselves a ballpark in the woods, shared Lucky Strikes, fumbled and giggled their way into sex. … *They argued, fought, laughed, mocked, and loved one another without ever having to say so.* (98, my emphasis)

Recalling the assertion of horizontal place-making by *Beloved*'s 30 women, Morrison proposes that *place* can reside in the imagination, becoming concrete through personal relationships that need not ever be framed in the space of language. But with the death, first of Mike and later of Stuff, Frank becomes "brave," feeling that there "were not enough dead gooks or Chinks in the world to satisfy him. The copper smell of blood no longer sickened him, it gave him appetite" (98). Just as Guitar Bains adopted the behavior of the warrior gone berserk as a member of the Seven

Days, Korea offers the occasion for Frank to embrace violence that serves the U.S. military's objectives. However, back in Lotus, Cee's "presence as absence" calls for him to understand how the self can be simultaneously impacted by local and global systems of scale. He believes he must sustain the "free-floating rage [and] the self-loathing disguised as somebody else's fault" he brought home from Korea in order to confront the situation Sarah describes in her letter to Frank.

Frank believes this state of mind is necessary if he is to rescue Cee from a maniacal white physician who has performed eugenic experiments on her reproductive organs. With no place else to go, he returns to Lotus where he leaves her in the care of his neighbor, Miss Ethel, and the cadre of women who live in the vicinity. Without consciously recognizing it, Frank looks at Lotus and sees that far from being a space of total and complete disempowerment, Lotus is brighter than he remembered.

> The sun, having sucked away the blue from the sky, loitered there in a white heaven, menacing Lotus but failing, failing, constantly failing to silence it: its children still laughed, ran, shouted their games; women sang in their backyards while pinning white sheets on clotheslines; occasionally a soprano was joined by a neighboring alto or a tenor just passing by. (117)

The language Morrison deploys suggests the way black life in the South can flourish despite the threat of white supremacist violence. As a symbol of a white authority that refuses to brook any resistance, the sun's "punishing heat" is constructed as the negation of color. While Lotus is by no means the site of prosperity, it thrives in spite of the figurative punishment administered by a menacing sun. In an odd configuration of place, Frank listens to an old man and his nephew playing mouth organ and guitar and feels "color, silence, and music [envelop] him" (118), a reversal of the trauma that robbed him of the ability to see color.

The true power in Lotus is to be found in the womenfolk who reside there. As they nurse Cee back to health, they take an assertive posture that, upon first reading, seems to take the form of blaming Cee for her plight. In the midst of woman-centered place-making, Frank's heroic masculinity is superfluous, with the potential to "worsen [Cee's] condition" (119). Morrison writes that "the women took turns nursing Cee and each had a different recipe for her cure" (119). Two months later, however, Frank notices that Cee is "different":

> Two months surrounded by country women who loved mean had changed her. The woman handled sickness as though it were an affront, an illegal, invading braggart who needed whipping. They didn't waste their time or the patient's with sympathy and they met the tears of the suffering with resigned contempt. (122)

What is the difference between this posture and that assumed by Morrison's Southern Men? Why do Pilate, Baby Suggs, the thirty women outside 124, Lena, and the "woman in yellow" find a way to resist adversity in spaces dominated by whites?[15] It is not that Morrison's women from the South are "tougher" or more resilient than their male counterparts. The kind of intersectional violence black women experience, in which black men are just as likely to inflict injury as white men, requires them to temper investments in futurity with a sensibility that acknowledges precariousness without succumbing to its effects.

Hence, Miss Ethel remembers Cee's hard upbringing and her "big pretty eyes." Unlike Cee and Frank's maternal grandmother, Lenore, who considers Cee's birth "on the road" to be "a very bad sign for Cee's future," Miss Ethel insists that Cee is the source of her own salvation, insisting that "Nothing and nobody is obliged to save you" (126). Hence, when she states, "*Somewhere inside you is that free person I'm talking about.* Locate her and do some good in the world" (126; emphasis added), Miss Ethel is equating slavery with allowing others to define us. What Miss Ethel describes is quite markedly in opposition to thinking that insists freedom is measured solely by physical acts, for example, Milkman's grandfather, Solomon, flying back to Africa. Rather *Home* interrogates what it means when personhood is rooted in self-reliance. Morrison is not simply recapitulating Emerson here; Miss Ethel equates selfhood with accountability, which means that "freedom" as she conceptualizes it is primarily *local*, so doing "good in the world" has little to do with long intervals of body travel coupled intermittent acts of charity. Paying heed to her immediate circumstances offers Cee a way to place equal priority upon saving her own life and being of service to her community.

The intersection of place and the political imaginary in Morrison's fiction illustrates that what we can and cannot do are not absolutes. She uses the Lotus women to demonstrate how in the midst of an oppressive racial climate they nonetheless retain an unimpeded sense of who they are and what they can control because precariousness is factored into all that they do. Baby Suggs anticipates such thinking through her sense that though precariousness is a factor in the lives of black women, hence she insists that Denver "know it and go on out the yard." Women in Lotus function with the knowledge that those who consider them indistinguishable from one another (and therefore disposable) are external to what they believe about themselves.

To be sure, the Jim Crow South in 1955 is far from a site of social mobility or political influence, but Morrison's point is that we have to determine *how* blackness means in the white Southerner's symbolic economy. She insists, further, that what it means to be black is determined through an individual's *local* experience. Women in Lotus take "responsibility for their lives and whatever, whoever else needed them. The absence of common sense irritated them but did not surprise them. Laziness was more than intolerable to them; it was inhuman. Whether you were in the field, the house, your own backyard, you had to be busy" (123). In the midst of the "can't be done" inflicted on them by racist whites or ill-tempered black men, these women embrace what needs to be done and thereby assert that what might distinguish a productive life from a wasteful one is not necessarily a matter of increase but rather, upkeep. Morrison proposes that the transformation of space into place is less a matter of place-making as an avenue to surplus and more to do with making the fullest *use* of the places we occupy, expenditure that refuses to be hindered by the threat of exhaustion.

Morrison is not rejecting the notion that dangerous circumstances have the power to overwhelm. But the Cee who emerges from the healing powers of a group of women who are "markedly different from the others in looks, dress, manner of speech, food and medicinal preferences" (123), comes to equate belonging in Lotus with a life whose demands continue despite the grief she feels at the loss of her ability to have children. Precariousness is not a reason for black women to embrace sameness (and thus invisibility) and fade into the crowd, nor is Morrison insisting that black women need magic to enchant their way out of trouble. If their "similarities are glaring" it is because, despite difference, all have embraced accountability. Hence, they know that adulthood involves the belief that mourning notwithstanding, "God [is] better and they did not want to meet their Maker and have to explain a wasteful life. They knew He would ask each of them one question: 'what have you done?'" Knowing that Miss Ethel had a son murdered in Detroit, that Maylene Stones was blinded in one eye in a sawmill accident, and that Hanna Rayburn and Clover Reid work beside their brothers and husbands despite suffering from polio, Cee comes to understand that life's difficulties do not countermand the necessity of doing—both for others and herself.

This is an altogether different mindset from those characters in Morrison's fiction that liken motion, overcoming the friction of socially produced space, with the nullification of past injury via compensatory force. Hence, when Frank returns to their parents' house to find Cee cooking, he realizes that this version of Cee "was not the girl who trembled at the slightest touch of the real and vicious world. Nor was she the not- even-fifteen-year-old who would run off with the first boy who asked her. And she was not the household help who believed whatever happened to her while drugged was a good idea, good because a white coat said so" (128–129). Without fully understanding the process, Frank sees that the self-sustaining accountability of the Lotus women has "delivered unto him a Cee who would never again need his hand over her eyes or his arms to stop her murmuring bones" (129). Both Cee and Frank have missed the kind of mothering that would have insisted on providing boundless affection (129). But the "new" Cee discovers the capacity for rescue within her own body.

In the past, Frank "alone valued [Cee]," however he comes to understand that his devotion "shielded her" but "did not strengthen her." Realizing only she can perform this job for herself, Cee informs Frank that she can never have children and starts to sob. But when Frank seeks to soften the blow and asks her not to cry, she declares, "Why not? I can be miserable if I want to. You don't need to try and make it go away. It shouldn't go away. It's just as sad as it ought to be and I'm not going to hide from what's true just because it hurts" (131). Cee no longer requires Frank's protection, which is evidenced by her realization that "she neither missed nor wanted his fingers at the nape of her neck telling her not to cry, that everything would be all right" (131).

Since it is the 1950s, Frank's post-traumatic stress disorder is simply designated as shell shock, even as trauma erases parts of his memory, so that he has no recollection of how he ended up in a hospital bed under restraint. When Reverend Locke's wife asks why Frank was arrested, her husband can only shrug, but Frank knows:

> Other than that B-29 roar, exactly what he was doing to attract police attention was long gone. He couldn't explain it to himself, let alone to a gentle couple offering help. If he wasn't in a fight was he peeing on the

> sidewalk? Hollering curses at some passerby, some schoolchildren? Was he banging his head on a wall or hiding behind bushes in somebody's backyard? (14–15)

One of the most prominent symptoms is Frank's inability to discern color. During the bus ride out of Portland, for example, he sits next to a woman wearing a "loud red" blouse and a flowered skirt. Soon, however, he watches "the flowers at the hem of her skirt blackening and her red blouse draining of color until it [is] white as milk" (23). Subsequently, "everybody, everything. Outside the window—trees, sky, boy on a scooter, grass, hedges. All color disappeared and the world became a black-and-white movie screen" (23). When "a smattering of color" returns, he feels confident enough to get on a train to Chicago.

During the ride, Frank awakes from a Scotch-induced nap to find a man sitting next to him, who is described as "a small man wearing a wide-brimmed hat. His pale blue suit sported a long jacket and balloon trousers. His shoes were white with unnaturally pointed toes" (27). When Frank settles back down to resume his nap, the "zoot suited man [gets] up and disappear[s] down the aisle" without leaving an indentation in the train car's leather seat. But, here, we need to attend to the incident that precedes the zoot-suited man's presence. Right before he notices the man in the seat next to him, Frank hears the sobs of a young woman injured by a rock thrown in her face when she tried to come to the aid of her husband who was being kicked and beaten by racist whites. As he listens to the couple whispering to each other, Frank thinks:

> He will beat her when they get home...And who wouldn't? It's one thing to be publicly humiliated. A man could move on from that. What was intolerable was the witness of a woman, a wife, who not only saw it, but had dared to rescue—rescue!—him. He couldn't protect himself and he couldn't protect her either, as the rock in her face proved. She would have to pay for that broken nose. Over and over again. (28)

We need to discern the underlying assumptions motivating this flash forward in time where Frank essentially scripts the angry husband's response to his wife's failed rescue attempt. His foreknowledge of what will happen should be familiar to us: lacking the ability to punish those who render them prone, black men "stand up" by punishing those in closest proximity.[16]

At another stop on the train ride, Frank encounters two women fighting, sees them "[r]olling around, punching, kicking the air…beat[ing] each other in the dirt" (101). He is surprised to see a man standing nearby, watching the fight with indifference and boredom. Confronted by the two women's pimp, Frank beats him unconscious. Notably, the two women stop fighting each other to pull Frank off by his collar and save their pimp. Thinking about "the excitement, the wild joy" he feels during the fight, when he is unable "to stop and unwilling to," he cannot pinpoint the source. Though it is counter-intuitive to see Frank's violence as being of a piece with that of the two women, Morrison's aim is to highlight the relationship between violence and coercion. The prostitutes coming to the aid of their pimp underscores how coercion's underlying logic involves the use of force to create overlapping states of efficacy and obedience. How do we determine the forces acting on Frank when he "leaps on the prone body" of the pimp? Unlike the "mindless, anonymous" killing he perpetrated in Korea, beating the pimp feels "personal" (102). As we will discover, Frank has resorted to personal violence once before and just as the joy he derives from the fight with the pimp signifies the distinction to be made between standing and lying prone, the phrasing the omniscient narrator employs to contextualize is noteworthy: "Good, he thought. He might need that thrill to claim his sister."

A moment like this, when it seems that the novel's omniscient narrator gives voice to Frank's innermost feelings, needs to be understood, once again, in relation to the interplay of coercion and violence. Riding the train, first to Chicago, and then back to Georgia, are occasions for Frank to speak in the first person to someone "set on telling [his] story" (5). Unlike Florens who is writing her own story, Frank is relating his to someone (Morrison herself perhaps?) whose job it is to write down what he says. It could be that Morrison simply intends for us to interpret these moments as the one instance when her omniscient narrator yields the floor to Frank. Perhaps Franks' voice is meant to function contrapuntally to the novel's omniscient narration. But to what end? It is tempting to approach this novel as Morrison's return to the conventions of realism; however a moment comes when she disabuses us of this notion. Recall that the story of the couple victimized by the white mob is related in the third-person. But later in the novel, she introduces a wrinkle into the narrative by suggesting the omniscient narrator is unreliable, inclined to propose her own interpretation of events as the definitive version of reality.

While he is narrating the story of how he came to meet his former lover, Lily, who Frank describes as "the woman who changed everything," he pushes back on what he perceives to be the writer's assumptions about his motives, "*You are dead wrong if you think I was just scouting for a home with a bowl of sex in it. I wasn't. Something about her floored me, made me want to be good enough for her. Is that too hard for you to understand*" (69)? Frank's flashback to meeting Lily disrupts what has heretofore been the novel's unimpeachable reliability as a record of what happened during his return to Lotus. Hence, asking the writer if it's "too hard for [her] to understand" the importance of being "good enough" for Lily intimates that whatever faith we may have about Toni Morrison's reliability as a novelist is falsely placed. Moreover, we are reminded of the way narrative's most insistent imperative lies in its propensity for coercion.

In thoughts aimed at interpreting Morrison's *Paradise*, Jean Wyatt makes an observation that proves to be useful to my argument regarding *Home*'s wavering commitment to reliable narration, in which we find the veracity of Morrison's novel suddenly displaced. "Displacement—both geographic and psychic—is the force," Wyatt writes, "that moves both plot and character" (17). And she continues:

> Narrative form echoes the thematics of displacement, sometimes by transporting the reader into an unknown fictive world lacking all signposts of time, place, and character, sometimes by baffling, through an overabundance of enigma and paradox, a reader's search for meaning. (17)

One might argue, then, that one source of confusion in *Home* is its use of the signposts of realism: the incessant movement of linear time (albeit with intermittent flashbacks), dialogue between characters, each of whom possesses a minimal backstory, omniscient narration that locates us geographically and spatially, and a traumatic circumstance that is the catalyst for the narrative's motion.[17]

If Frank is speaking to Morrison herself, where he declares, "You can't come up with words that catch it," or challenges her to describe heat able to cook a turtle in its shell ("Describe that if you know how."), it could be a sign indicating that Morrison is equally engaged in a dialogue with herself, as if to lay bare the self-doubt all novelists confront with varying degrees of success and which they come to understand as part of the process. What is distinctive about Morrison's decision to incorporate Frank's skepticism about her writerly talents into the narrative, however, is that it is also proposes that *Home* needs to be understood as a metafiction that seeks to locate the difficulties of writing a novel alongside a rumination on fiction's coercive power. When Frank's thoughts returns to the couple on the train, he sets about correcting an assumption projected onto him by the writer:

> *Earlier you wrote about how sure I was that the beat-up man on the train to Chicago would turn around when they got home and whip the wife who tried to help him. Not true. I didn't think any such thing.* (69, italics in original)

Quite the contrary, Frank insists, "What I thought was that he was proud of her but didn't want to show how proud he was to the other men on the train" (69). And then he makes the startling observation, "I don't think you know much about love…Or me" (69). Here is a moment when the gap between novelistic license and a character's independence from the novelist becomes apparent. Viewed apart from their creators, characters possessing sufficient self-awareness to take the writer to task for imposing her assumptions become arguments for the fictional world as both artifice *and artifact*. Which is to say that if novelists utilize techniques that function to deceive the reader, inducing her to reach substantive conclusions about what it means to be human, the novel is also a form of cultural technology that seeks to become an instrument readers can use to map their own emotional topography. *Jazz*'s declaration for us to "Look. Look where your hands are now" is evidence that reading a novel is also an occasion for the novel to read us.

If Morrison uses Frank as a way to call her own abilities into question, it also works reflexively to highlight Frank's struggles with himself. It could be that she means to suggest, that in addition to being "radical," as she proposed in her Nobel Lecture, narrative (both telling and recording) is precarious business. Complicating our relationship to the omniscient narrator mirrors Frank's struggle to relate the circumstances that lead to the young Korean girl's death. He narrates the moment when he becomes aware of the girl's presence as she scavenges for food in the soldiers' garbage and he realizes the girl is not a threat. "I saw her face only once," he states, "Mostly I just watched her head moving between the stalks to paw garbage. Each time she came it was as welcome as watching a bird feed her young or a hen scratching dirt for the worm she knew for sure was buried there" (94–95). However, Frank's original version is omniscient, and so he narrates the moment he observed as another soldier arrives to relieve him from guard duty:

> I've watched raccoons more choosy raiding trash cans. She wasn't picky. Anything not metal, glass, or paper was food to her. She relied not on her eyes, but on her fingertips alone to find nourishment. K-ration refuse, scraps from packages sent with love from Mom full of crumbling brownies, cookies, fruit. An orange, soft now and blackened with rot, lies just beyond her fingers. She fumbles for it. My relief guard comes over, sees her hand and shakes his head smiling. (95)

Hearing the girl say something in her own language that sounds like "Yum-yum," Frank's eyes go from the hand she puts near the soldier's crotch to her face, sees her two missing teeth and her "eager eyes." Just then, the guard kills her by shooting her in the face. Remembering the corruption that reduced adults to "marketing children," Frank's story ends with conjecture, "I think the guard felt more than disgust. I think he felt tempted and that is what he had to kill" (96).

Frank's act of trying to parse the guilt that follows murdering a child happens in the midst of Miss. Ethel's insistence that "somewhere inside [us] is [a] free person" tasked with doing "some good in the world." In a South filled with whites who lynch black men with impunity irrespective of their innocence, Miss Ethel insists that fixating on the danger is akin to bondage. Hence, *Home* insists that we do not look back on blacks in the Jim Crow South with pity because white supremacy made their lives miserable or with scorn because expediency demanded they accept the abuse. Morrison's unwillingness to instantiate the white gaze assumes a willingness to embrace the free person inside us. As Frank's struggle to narrate what really happened in Korea is meant to suggest, locating the free persons inside us should not be reduced to an enterprise whose sole objective is either absolution or racial liberation. While the importance of overcoming white supremacy in order to achieve coherent subjectivity cannot be gainsaid, race is but one way difference affects us. In the absence of the white gaze, Morrison's *Home* opts against entertaining the notion that Frank's willingness to take full responsibility for killing the Korean girl symbolizes a form of accountability whites fail to attribute to black communities. Adopting such a posture, Morrison proposes, is to capitulate to what she critiqued in the Rose interview, mainly that her life as a fiction writer is wholly devoted to confirming the existence of a discrete form of racial identity and that it is a responsibility African American writers bear solely. Narrating our transgressions is, as both Ralph Ellison and Sherley Anne Williams have insisted, not a gesture whose sole intent is to transcend them, but rather to enfold them as necessary chapters of our story.[18] Her decision to dramatize the negotiation between writer and character, where the latter has leave to hold the former accountable for what gets written, seeks to bring into the foreground the belief that black letters on the white page are the very embodiment of precariousness and should be approached with caution.

But here, the zoot-suited man helps us interrogate the question of whether living in a state of precariousness empowers or dehumanizes. What are we to make of a character who does not utter a single line of dialogue and whose style of dress evokes the 1930s or 1940s? Considering the outrageous image he presents, the initial impulse is to interpret the zoot-suited man as a symbol of racial conservatism wearing apparel meant to recall minstrelsy. Indeed, having never seen a zoot suit, and mainly on the basis of hearsay, Frank decides "he would have preferred a loincloth and some white paint artfully smeared on his forehead and cheeks. Holding a spear, of course" (34). Though he opts for the Hollywood stereotype of the black savage, a more definitive reading of the zoot suit is to be found in *The Great Black Way* R. J. Smith's history of black Los Angeles during the World War II period. According to Smith, for young black Angelenos living in a community dominated by "methodical elders who chose their words carefully" and who regarded "those who raised their voices" with scorn, the zoot suit

> symbolized a generation filling the streets, taking up more than the space allotted them by the Golden State Mutual Insurance Company. It was bountiful, but first of all it was big. The zoot contravened wisdom and challenged physics. The jacket had more padding than a cell at Camarillo State Hospital, the sleeves overachieved all the way to the fingertips. The slacks hoisted almost to the armpits, and the seat was super loose, as were the legs—all the way down to the ankles. (36)

Frank is aware that the zoot suit is "enough of a fashion statement to interest riot cops on each coast" (34), but in his current state, he has no way to understand the zoot-suited man as anything more than a hallucination confirming his dysfunction. When compared to the image of birds eating his friend's entrails in Korea, however, a man in a zoot suit represents a dream of comic proportions. Though Frank wonders if the odd little man is "a sign trying to tell him something" (34), he spends little time trying to determine what that might be.

But recalling Smith's description of zoot suit wearers as "taking up more than the space allotted them" by dominants, we see that it represents an act of signifying, its' outrageousness and excessiveness physically embody a transgressive posture. Viewed in the context of its original historical moment, the zoot suit's utility lay in its unabashed absurdity. However, in her study of the historical and cultural significance of the zoot suit, Kathy Peiss takes care to emphasize the necessity of not jumping to the conclusion that wearing a zoot suit was, in and of itself, a political statement. Looking at the "proliferation of meanings and values attached" to the zoot suit, Peiss cautions the reader to resist "the mode of cultural understanding that reflexively reads the aesthetic as politics by other means," (4). Peiss's aim is to look at the zoot suit as a way to determine "the circumstances in which a cultural style may or may not be in fact political," seeking instead to "put the political in its place—not outside culture but occupying less of the cultural domain than contemporary scholarship bestows" (4). Acknowledging that the zoot suit did, in fact, become "an overt public issue in Los Angeles in 1942 and 1943," Peiss asserts "the political overtones of the style are difficult to perceive" (62). Echoing R. J. Smith, Peiss states:

> To be sure, the style scorned standards of respectability, violated wartime conservation measures, and offended elders. But should it be understood as a gesture of refusal to white supremacy and "hegemonic" culture? The evidence points in a different direction. Rather than wearing the zoot suit as an inchoate symbol of resistance to discriminatory treatment and racial prejudice, it was more often the case that men found in the style a compelling aesthetic that embodied a new sense of themselves at a moment of possibility and transformation. (62)

In light of the fact that Morrison opts to set *Home* in 1955, what are we to make of the apparition of a man wearing a zoot suit? Returning to the moment of the apparition's first appearance, just after the melee that has resulted in the physical abuse suffered by the husband and wife, what might be at issue is the tonality of Frank's assessment of what is to come. Compared to the declarative tone of Frank's prediction, his certainty of *what will happen* when the injured husband and wife get home, the zoot-suited man's arrival intimates that the antidote to tight space is thinking disproportionally about *what can happen*. In the midst of systems of domination whose conservative pronouncements translate into restrictive enforcements of scale, the best way to nullify their effects is to embrace volatilities of scale that provide access to a mindset ready to eschew normative thinking "inside the box" in favor of the outlandish and the absurd.[19] In short, the zoot suit signals habits of judgment oriented toward *space-taking* that plays fast and loose with limits. Further, the apparition's presence, always in proximity to Frank, but never in an engaging fashion, is suggestive of the need to embrace a posture that privileges self-fashioning that eschews *voicing dissidence* in favor of embodying dissensus. The zoot suit's fluid lines, its rejection of the minimalist styles that resulted from World War II's fabric shortages, may have more to do, then, with the adoption of a personal aesthetic whose most salient characteristic is playfulness in the face of Jim Crow's foreclosures on spatialized (and racialized) identities.

Hence, Frank's act of pushing back on the omniscient narrator's imposition of what he felt seeing the couple is important because it emphasizes stock forms of interpretation over one whose novelty issues from our propensity to conceptualize manhood so narrowly that we are skeptical when men adopt the tenets of an alternative political imaginary, whose most salient feature is an emphasis on the centrality of women's voices and actions to communal progress. His belief that the husband's true feelings toward his wife have to do with pride and an unwillingness to engage in emotional displays in front of other passengers, places both Frank and the husband outside of conventional forms of manhood, which insists upon independence predicated on a myth of the male body as an impenetrable surface. Seen in this way, the apparition of the zoot-suited man intimates that an act of self-fashioning whose most essential quality is radical autonomy is ultimately of little utility in the Jim Crow South.[20] Peiss's characterization of the zoot suit as iterative, the embodiment of a *local* aesthetic sensibility, points to Morrison's predication that the logics informing transformative gestures are not, as we might assume, the product of globalized encounters in which black life everywhere responds to white supremacy in the same way, at the same time.

Just as Baby Suggs' endeavor to recombine flesh and emotion occurs in a local context, Cee's recovery is local and needs to be understood as such before moving to a consideration of collective progress. When she tells her brother that the prospect of not having children makes her sad and that *it ought to*, she opts to *live with* the tragic rather than seeking to avoid or escape it. She begins to describe a baby's toothless smile as it appears in everyday objects like a green pepper or the curvature of a cloud, but doesn't "finish the list" and sits sorting quilt pieces while "[e]very now and then [wiping] her cheeks with the heel of her hand" (132). Such thinking speaks to the power inherent in making our shortcomings and our disappointments an intrinsic part of who we are—not to claim them as excuses for failing but rather to see them as constituting a quality of insight that, like the blues, calls less for solace than for self-acceptance. *Home* argues that before we strike out against those we deem to be the enemy; we must take stock of our inner resources. Morrison's novel ultimately returns to the idea that for those seeking "some kind of tomorrow" (322), this turning inward to understand one's deficits and assets as equally important is a necessary step.[21]

Cee's recovery is also the occasion for Frank's own epiphany. Recognizing the Lotus he has returned to is *a new place*, he muses on how "he could not believe how much he had once hated this place. Now it seemed both fresh and ancient, safe and demanding" (132). As if for the first time, he understands that an attachment to place involves acts of both making and unmaking. The sweet gum he sees, which "look[s] so strong … So beautiful" but is nevertheless wounded, "hurt right down the middle," illustrates that home need not be such a safe place that it shields us from injury. Morrison suggests that black life in the South needs to be understood as being capacious enough that acts of place-making embrace the idea of conflicting iterations of space-time.[22]

Chapter 14 in *Home*, which follows Frank's realization that Lotus is home, proves to be that moment when Frank elects to hold himself accountable for murdering the Korean girl. Because tight space proves to be at its most persistent when Morrison's characters cede responsibility—and therefore accountability—for the task of adapting as the situation requires, we must contend with the substance of Frank's admission of guilt. Whether it is because he has spent time in the midst of Lotus' womenfolk whose expectations accept life as a struggle or seeing a restored Cee embracing the prospect of childlessness, taking an improvisatory posture toward precariousness, he arrives at an important truth. When Cee tells him about "seeing a baby smile all through the house, in the air, the clouds," he states, "It hit me. Maybe that little girl wasn't waiting around to be born to her. Maybe it was already dead, waiting for me to step up and say how" (133). What follows is Frank's admission:

I shot the Korean girl in her face.
I am the one she touched.
I am the one who saw her smile
I am the one she said "Yum-yum" to.
I am the one she aroused.

I'm less interested, here, in the substance of Frank's admission and more engaged by the form it assumes, which, of course, is a product of Morrison's authorial intent. Here, we find Frank returning to the declarative, but on the following page, we find that his declaration of guilt seeks to modulate the instinctive quality of his act. I noted above that Frank's beating of the pimp had much to do with the relationship between coercion and violence. But the assertion only makes sense if we situate Frank alongside Guitar Baines, in Jonathan Shay's lexicon of the berserk state. Morrison's decision, essentially, to pile Frank's sins one atop another, using "I am" as agential prefix points to the declarative mode's roots in Biblical discourse. In the Book of Exodus, Moses requests that God provide him with a name so that his task is authorized in the eyes of the Israelites. God's response, *I AM THAT I AM* (Exodus 3:13) is both declaratively and definitively, a symbol of God's ubiquity. But Frank's use of the phrase "I am," refers to the qualities of the berserk state: the belief that one is godlike, indiscriminate, cold, and indifferent. When he concludes that it is "better" that the little Korean girl should die, he does so because the distance separating the moment's symbolic implications and its moral consequences has thoroughly collapsed, he shoots her because of the girl's gesture. Note, then, how Frank's declarative tone shifts to the interrogative, where his questions culminate with "What type of man is that? And what type of man thinks he can ever in life pay the price of that orange" (132)?

It is fitting, then, that the chapter in which Frank confronts his culpability for the girl's death and the strategy he has adopted to rationalize it, is also the one in which he hears the story about the father and son tethered together and forced by white men to fight to the death with switchblades. After a sleepless night, "churning and entangled in thoughts relentless and troubling," Frank thinks about how

> he had covered his guilt and shame with big-time mourning for his dead buddies. Day and night he had held on to that suffering because it let him off the hook, kept the Korean child hidden. Now the hook was deep inside his chest and nothing would dislodge it. The best he could hope for was time to work it loose. (133)

Frank sees his sister's "newly steady self," whose most prominent characteristics are no longer fear, grief, or self-recrimination, but a manifestation of selfhood that is "confident, cheerful, and occupied." Taking to heart the Lotus women's admonition that "you had to be busy," Cee is ready to occupy space and place in a wholly different way, a way perhaps that will lead her to collaborate with Frank in completing the "worthwhile things that needed doing" (133). Recalling the place where he and Cee had encountered the horses that "stood like men," he asks what happened to the stud farm. Sitting at a table that includes veterans from World Wars I and II, along with his grandfather, Salem Money, Frank learns the story of how the farm provided a location for what Fish Eye calls "men-treated-like-dog-fights." It is significant that all Cee knows is that dogfights were held on the farm because it demonstrates how the black community was as interested, albeit for very different reasons, in erasing these atrocities from public memory as the white men who enabled them. It takes a group of war veterans who "ranked battles and wars according to the loss numbers," to relate how the white men responsible had "graduated from dogfights. Turned men into dogs" (139). As they narrate an atrocity beyond their control, Frank can only listen. The men's military experience leads them to identify with warriors to the extent that they classify combat's importance on the basis of who has made the ultimate sacrifice, not the incompetence of the commanding officers. Thus, the act of narrating a story of two men, father and son, brought to Lotus from Alabama, roped together with orders to fight to the death has the effect of nullifying the mythic scale of military conflicts, reinforcing the notion that a battle with a single casualty is far more ominous, because the battle culminates with the father's demand that his son stab him dead, saying, "Obey me, son, this one last time. Do it" (139) so that he will be allowed to walk free.

The pacing of the dialogue gathers momentum till there is little in the way of expository phrasing. At the penultimate moment of the tale, just before relating how this tragedy comes to pass, Morrison writes, "The men became a chorus, inserting what they knew and felt between and over one another's observations" (139). If we set this moment alongside Miss. Ethel's declaration regarding the free person we carry inside us, we are in a position to conjecture as to how political imaginaries come into existence. For black communities shrouded in the grief, rage, and uncertainty that accompany white men's acts of violating black humanity with such incessant impunity, a most important next step is stripping away the false belief that the words of some matter more than those of others.

In such a circumstance, even those in which dissensus is the end result, every voice comes to be valued for what it can contribute, no matter how small such a contribution might be. More important than being *in* or *at*, Morrison insists, horizontal place-making is a product of assuming stewardship over those stories set in close proximity to our own without thoughts of how to reconcile them into a coherent, smoothly flowing narrative. Situated *after* Frank's admission of guilt and Cee's internalization of her barrenness, a story of patricide narrated by an ensemble of male voices who, because the majority of them (save for Salem Money, who is not a vet) have performed military service, share an intimate understanding of what it means to kill with purpose, where local violence functions in the service of a global objective that lies well beyond their understanding.

Home ends with Frank and Cee journeying five miles from their home to recover the bones of the man whose lynching and murder they witnessed at the start of the novel. In the meadow in which the "horses stood like men," brother and sister bury the bones under the sweet gum tree that stands "beheaded and undead" (144) beside the stream called Wretched on the edge of Lotus. Here, the moment when Frank and Cee shroud the dead man's bones in Cee's first quilt recalls *topography*'s relationship to topophilia, as their act reverses white supremacy's tendency to ascribe black bodies as surfaces lacking depth. Burying the bones is akin to a tree extending its roots into the soil to substantiate its right to be. But Morrison is far too canny to equate topophilia with the act of laying claim to a physical location. Just as Frank's journey from Lotus to Korea to Seattle to Atlanta and finally back to Lotus suggests that where we are (and subsequently, who we are) is, as James Clifford would insist, not a matter of roots, but routes, Frank and Cee's burial ritual constitutes a metaphor for visual acuity able to breach surfaces and delve beneath them in search of more substantive truth-claims.

While the irony of the wooden marker's declaration that "Here Stands a Man" is noteworthy, it also harkens back to Frank's initial encounter with Billy's son, Thomas, a boy "good at everything." When Frank asks what he wants to be when he grows up thinking he can use some humility, the boy replies, "A man." The boy's response to Frank's half-hearted observation that he will "go far," is "And I'll go deep" (32), which resonates since burying the bones allows Frank to actualize this aspiration. Even though Thomas's right arm has been rendered useless after being shot by a policeman, his plan to be a man is, in fact, a goal whose profundity lies in using what he is good at (Civics, geography,

English) as foundational elements of place-making. In the 1950s South, where the best Frank can hope for in an encounter with a white man is to be called "Boy," Thomas's example declares that self-acceptance rejects fetishizing injury as a necessary aspect of our personhood. He teaches Frank that our injuries should be a source of tactical inventiveness, a reason for adaptation rather than resignation. In this sense, then, Thomas symbolizes what it means to stand like a man. His injury means his success will not be a product of overpowering the opposition, emulating white supremacy's impulse to dominate. Rather, his aspiration to be a man refutes the claim that manhood is quantified on the basis of bureaucratic forms of scale; going far and going deep asserts the necessity of balancing vertical and horizontal concerns in an effort to annul the limits imposed by hostile systems of scale.

Like *Love* and *A Mercy*, Home's plot centers on the South, with Frank's journey from Seattle to Atlanta functioning like a journey on the Underground Railroad in reverse to rescue his sister.[23] As such, the novel invites us to ruminate on what it means to stand up in a circumstance in which black lives trapped in the prone position is assumed to be the norm. Lotus's womenfolk embody a commitment to living that insists upon accountability and utility and thus provide examples of social reproduction on a local scale. However, the healing both Frank and Cee experience calls for us to explore the link between his experiences in Korea and her ordeal in Atlanta. What is distinctive about both is that they manifest both local and global (ubiquitous) characteristics that combine to create an imaginary in which neither Frank nor Cee can productively engage in acts of social reproduction. In the case of the latter, Cee's inability to have children requires her to "know the truth, accept it, and keep on quilting." For Frank, burying the bones of the dead man, means returning to the place where the horses symbolized power refusing to be harnessed in proximity to a white supremacist power whose main aim is to enforce restraint and codify difference. If social reproduction involves the creation of practices meant to guide how we set about undertaking the "practices of life work," the South Frank Money returns to is trapped in a feedback loop in which the life-work white supremacy occasions ensures that black labor is the gauge for ascertaining whites' superiority. Though *Home* is set in the south of the 1950s, the fact that it was written in the second decade of the twenty-first century means that Morrison understands that the south of the earlier period is already entering a state of transformation, where urban settings like Atlanta, Nashville, New Orleans, Mobile, and

Birmingham are being connected by a growing interstate road system and identified as locations that within a generation will signal the rise of information, transportation, legal, and medical systems that emerge in ways that will make these locations more amenable and accountable.[24]

According to Cindi Katz, the "ubiquity and necessity of social reproduction means that these practices are well positioned to transform all of the social and material relations and spaces they touch, including capitalist relations of production" (83). Morrison's invention of a woman-centered space like Lotus "embraces not only a politics of ubiquity (its global manifestation) but a politics of place (its localization in places created, strengthened, defended, or transformed)" (83). Katz introduces the concept of counter-topography, which brings "together a politics of ubiquity and a politics of place" in order to connect "local struggles over social reproduction taking place in different parts of the world" (83). Counter-topographies, Katz insists:

> help us to imagine a politics that maintains the distinctiveness of a place while recognizing that it is connected analytically to other places along contour lines that represent not elevation but particular relations to a social process (e.g. globalized capitalist relations of production) (83).[25]

As Frank is busy burying the bones of the dead man in Cee's first quilt, she looks across the stream and sees the zoot-suited man. "It looked to her," Morrison writes, "like a small man in a funny suit swinging a watch chain. And grinning." The return of the zoot-suited man is suggestive of Frank's and Cee's collaborative act of self-fashioning that resonates across space-time. I find evidence for this assertion in the fact that he is grinning and swinging the watch chain. Unlike on the train when he simply stared ahead and did not acknowledge Frank's presence, or at Billy's house where he stands silently and disappears before Frank can reach him, the zoot-suited man's departure signals that Frank and Cee's burial ritual, placing the marker over the grave, symbolizes their abandonment of the prone position through an act of standing up in the face of difficult odds. Further, the inscription, "Here Stands a Man," is suggestive counter-topography in which the boundaries separating past, present, and future collapse, since the wooden marker commemorates past courage, resists present insinuations that the best position for black people is prone, and has the prospective function of reminding Lotus inhabitants of the future that they are not outside space-time, rather, the marker asserts a complicated relationship to spatial and temporal "reality."

I want to revisit, once again, Toni Morrison's rumination on the question of how free she can be in a society that places so much emphasis on various iterations of difference (e.g. race, gender, or class). Linda McDowell's observation that, "people are differentially located in space, with differential abilities," prompts us to read *Home* as a work that cautions against the conclusion that tight space possesses a single set of characteristics through which to ascertain its effects. Indeed, if tight space is constituted solely as a question of *where*, could it be that pursuing the question of *how to get free* is misguided, since such thinking emphasizes finding the right map, discerning its scale, and then following the prescribed path? To be sure, Frank and Cee's journey back to Lotus from Seattle and Atlanta, respectively, certainly involves physically traversing geographical terrain to arrive at a destination. But the zoot-suited man insists that what ultimately proves to be most liberating factor for Frank and Cee Money is not that they find a route out of tight space, but rather that they embrace an alternative blueprint in order to propose that tight space can be *fashioned* into a bridge that connects the local and the ubiquitous. Recall Kathy Peiss's insistence that the zoot suit has more to do with a commitment to self-fashioning than politics, with creating a personal aesthetic whose main signification is eschewing fixed and immutable boundaries. Contextualizing Peiss's argument in relation to *Home* it is possible to argue that the zoot suit argues for a more fluid relationship to space-time. As an alternative blueprint whose most salient feature is privileging the absurd and the outrageous, the zoot suit invites us to eschew the thought of how our actions might fit into an established social matrix in favor of thinking, that sees greater value in the excessive and the incommensurate. Though figuratively speaking the bones Frank and Cee have recovered and interned lie prone beneath the sweet gum tree, placing a placard that says, "Here Stands a Man," insists, as Wright would have it, marks what she refers to as epiphenomenal time "that takes into account all the multifarious dimensions of Blackness that exist in any one moment, or 'now'—not 'just' class, gender, and sexuality, but all collective combinations imagined in that moment" (loc. 411 of 4630).

In her book *Precarious Life: The Powers of Mourning and Violence*, philosopher Judith Butler reflects on the tragedy of 9/11 and specifically upon the impact that event had on public discourse. Butler states that "it is one matter to suffer violence and quite another to use that fact to ground a framework in which one's injury authorizes limitless aggression against targets that may or may not be related to the sources of one's own suffering" (4). Calling for us to "shore up the first-person point of view," she argues that one of the side effects of 9/11 lay in "a decentering of the narrative 'I' within the international political domain." She argues that a "narrative form emerges to compensate for the enormous narcissistic wound opened up by the public display of our physical vulnerability" (7).

Butler makes an observation that illuminates with almost crystal clarity Morrison's decision to dramatize the gap between Frank's first-person narration and the errors and assumptions that result from trying to record it. Citing Levinas, Butler states, "the human is not *represented by* the face. Rather, the human is indirectly affirmed in that very disjunction that makes representation impossible, and this disjunction is conveyed in the impossible representation" (144). She concludes:

> For representation to convey the human, then, representation must not only fail but it must *show* its failure. There is something unrepresentable that we nevertheless seek to represent, and that paradox must be retained in the representation we give... In this sense, the human is not identified with what is represented but neither is identified with the unrepresentable; it is, rather, that which limits the success of representable practice. The face is not "effaced" in this failure of representation, but is constituted in that very possibility. (144, italics in original)

Thinking about Frank's instinctive act of shooting the Korean girl in the face, then, requires us to accept that we cannot ascertain what led to the shooting if we isolate the act as mere atrocity divorced from mourning. His "big-time mourning" for Mike and Stuff indicates that what has unfolded over the course of the novel is the nagging question of how to re-establish a workable model of humanity.[26] Just as Butler declares that a necessary preoccupation for her is "the question of the human," so too does *Home* seek to engage her question of "Who counts as human" (20)? The novel interpolates Butler's concomitant questions, "Whose lives count as lives?" and "What *makes for a grievable life*" (20, italics in original)?

Though Lotus can be said to represent Frank's and Cee's "location" on a map, what is perhaps more important is that by coming to terms with loss they have adopted a different posture toward mourning (in Frank's case for lost friends, in Cee's the children she cannot bear). "Perhaps mourning has to do," Butler writes, "with agreeing to undergo a transformation (perhaps one should say *submitting* to a transformation) the full result of which we cannot know in advance. There is losing, as we know, but there is also the transformative effect of loss, and this latter cannot be charted or planned" (21). Such a declaration proposes that the salience of the counter-topographical space *Home* seeks to depict cannot be conceptualized as an act of mapping. The zoot-suited man who appears throughout the novel is not, as Frank surmised, a symbol, the interpretation of which will lead him to the destination of enlightened thought. Alternatively, he is illustrative of the political imaginary as blueprint. Just as the zoot suit proved to be a local gesture intended to take up more than one's allotted space, the interpretive volatility it occasioned points to a fundamental lesson about loss. As Butler puts it, in the face of loss, "Something is larger than one's own deliberate plan, one's own project, one's own knowing and choosing" (21). Hence, just as circumstances dictate that blueprints undergo massive revision before achieving a "final" form, *Home* uses the zoot-suited man as a way to insist that the monumental task of donning the vestments of our humanity must begin at the point of absurdity and proceed toward possibilities that, at their most uncertain, are safe in the knowledge that the word "stand" functions as both noun and verb.

Notes

1. Historically, it has been easy for mainstream critics to dismiss the work of African American writers as "parochial" because it was perceived as being preoccupied with writing about race, as opposed to producing more universalist formulations of humanity. But as Morrison observed in a 1998 interview with Charlie Rose, a number of writers considered to be among the "greatest" in Western letters—Tolstoy, Zola, and Joyce were her examples—"write about race all the time." Her point there was that whiteness is so invisible, so backgrounded in their work, that critics have assumed that they were writing about the human experience, sans any mention of race. But Morrison's reference to a question posed several years earlier by journalist, Bill Moyers, as to whether she could write a book that featured white characters, that was not "about race," was her way of suggesting that African American writers labor under the assumption that because their characters are black, their burden, their most important duty, is "writing about race." Cf. Interview with Charlie Rose at https://youtu.be/F4vIGvKpT1c (Digital source).

2. In that same interview, Morrison states, "Yes I can write about white people. White people can write about black people. Anything can happen in art, there are no boundaries there. Having to do it or having to prove I can do it is what was embarrassing or insulting" (Ibid).
3. Morrison continues: For some time now I have been thinking about the validity or vulnerability of a certain set of assumptions conventionally accepted among literary historians and critics circulated as "knowledge." This knowledge holds that traditional, canonical American literature is free of, uninformed, and unshaped by the four-hundred-year-old presence of, first, Africans and the African Americans in the United States. It assumes that this presence—which shaped the body politic, the Constitution, and the entire history of the culture—has had no significant place or consequence in the origin and development of that culture's literature. Moreover, such knowledge assumes that the characteristics of our national literature emanate from a particular "Americanness" that is separate and unaccountable to this presence (Dark, pp. 4–5).
4. Toni Morrison, "Home," in *The House that Race Built.* ed. Wahneema Lubiano (New York: Pantheon Books, 1997).
5. Ibid.
6. Morrison's *Playing in the Dark*, read in concert with several of her interviews, forces us to consider the manner in which black writing continues to labor under the obligation to provide a window into black life that is categorized as otherness. However, by calling our attention to the white gaze, she identifies a racial project in which black life is transformed into a spectacle viewed from the safety and superiority of whiteness. But the protocols underwriting our understanding of American literature proffers writing by writers who think of themselves as white as a constant and consistent portrayal of non-racialized humanity. Her refusal to explain the details of black life for non-black readers is meant to reflect her assumption that black writing is always already about what it means to be human.
7. Cf. Brenda K. Marshall, *Teaching the Postmodern: Fiction and Theory* (New York and London: Routledge, 1992); Mahdu Dubey, *Signs and Cities: Black Literary Postmodernism* (Chicago: University of Chicago Press, 2003); Kimberly Chabot Davis, "Postmodern Blackness: Toni Morrison's *Beloved* and the End of History," in *Productive Postmodernism: Consuming Histories and Cultural Studies*, ed. John N. Duvall (Albany, NY: SUNY Press, 2002).

8. Wright states that her book "shows how Black discourses can endlessly expand the dimensions of our analyses and intersect with a wider range of identities by deploying Epiphenomenal concept of space-time that takes into account all the multifarious dimensions of Blackness that exist in any one moment, or 'now'—not 'just' class, gender, and sexuality, but all collectives combinations imagined in that moment" (loc. 410 of 4640). Cf. Michelle Wright, *The Physics of Blackness*: Beyond *Middle Passage Epistemologies*. Minneapolis: University of Minnesota Press, 2016.
9. And I mean convergence to signify their willingness to bring their respective talents, perspectives, and insights together in a manner that allows them to be individuals in a collective even as their skills enhance the collective's overall possibilities. One thinks, for example, of *Tar Baby* and its' depiction of the woman in yellow. Though she and Jadine could not be more different in their modes of presentation and agendas, Jadine's desire to be independent and live a life of self-determination converges with the image of the woman in yellow to create a new kind of personhood.
10. Katie Meehan and Kendra Strauss, eds *Precarious Lives: Contested Geographies of Social Reproduction* (Athens, GA: University of Georgia Press, 2015).
11. Meehan and Strauss invite us to think about African American women's writing as a creative praxis whose central aim is dramatizing precariousness in the lives of black women. An incomplete list of authors and works might include: Linda Brent in Harriet Jacobs' *Incidents in the Life of a Slave Girl* (1865), Nella Larsen's Helga Crane in *Quicksand* (1928), Zora Neale Hurston's *Jonah's Gourd Vine* and *Their Eyes Were Watching God* (1934, 1937, respectively), Ann Petry's Lutie Johnson in *The Street* (1945), Morrison's Polly Breedlove in *The Bluest Eye* (1970); the young Eva Peace in *Sula* (1973); First Corinthians Dead in *Song of Solomon* (1978), Ursa Corregidora in Gayl Jones' Corregidora (1975), Velma Henry in Toni Cade Bambara's *The Salt Eaters* (1980), Celie in Alice Walker's *The Color Purple* (1982), and more recently Hattie Shepherd in Ayana Mathis' 2012 novel *The Twelve Tribes of Hattie*, and the two sisters growing up in 1940s and 50s Chicago described in Margo Jefferson's 2015 memoir, *Negroland*. Obviously, this is not an exhaustive list, especially since the list focuses on African American women writing prose. One could certainly add Lorraine Hansberry,

Gwendolyn Brooks, Audre Lorde, and Alice Childress, among others, to this list.

12. Geographer, Yi-Fu Tuan's *Space and Place* asserts that "Space is an abstract term for a complex set of ideas." Tuan goes on to suggest, "Ways of dividing up space vary enormously in intricacy and sophistication, as do techniques of judging size and distance" (34). And he continues:

> [I]f we look for fundamental principles of spatial organizations we find them in two kinds of facts: the posture and structure of the human body, and the relations (whether close or distant) between human beings. Man, out of his intimate experience with his body and with other people, organizes space so that it conforms with and caters to his biological needs and social relations. (34)

13. In the figure below, consider Tuan's conceptualization of how the human body functions in space and time:

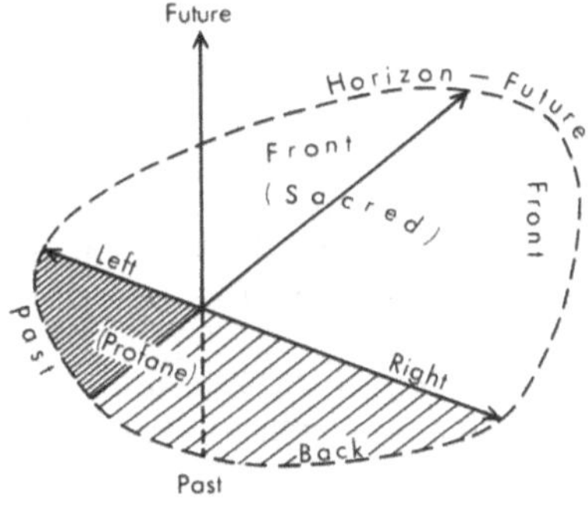

Figure 2. Upright human body, space and time. Space projected from the body is biased toward the front and right. The future is ahead and "up." The past is behind and "below."

Note how Tuan locates the horizon and the future as an imperative, with the frontal plane representing the sacred, as space "opens out before [us]." Note also how the past, located behind the upright body is also the realm of the profane. Looking at this representation of how human relations can be represented on a conceptual grid, an intriguing set of critical possibilities emerge in relation to Morrison's fiction. For it seems clear that the line separating front and back, past, present, and future, is by no means fixed. Indeed, it could be argued that much of Morrison's fiction explores the implications of a highly unstable line, where the capaciousness of the future is impinged upon by the past in such a way as to eradicate the ability to conceive of anything beyond mere subsistence in the present moment.

14. Tuan argues that the "prone position is submissive, signifying the acceptance of our biological condition," which means that to be upright is to assume one's full human stature. Tuan identifies the importance of standing upright is signified by the cluster of words in our language that use "stand" as their root concept: e.g. "status," "stature," "statute," "estate," and "institute," each of which implies "achievement and order" (37).
15. I am imagining each of these characters as Southerners, Pilate and Eva are both from Virginia, with Mary Threrese in *Tar Baby* originating in the "south" of the Caribbean and the character known only as the Woman in yellow likely coming to France from somewhere on the African continent. And certainly, looking at Violet in *Jazz*, we see that this is by no means a constant; Violet is unhinged despite her southern upbringing, a result of the traumatic loss of her mother.
16. Frank imagines the man is operating within the same tight space we find Cholly Breedlove and Sethe, both of whom are denied the right to direct anger at those who committed crimes against their personhood. Their rage and self-loathing comes to be directed at someone in close proximity. Here, I want to draw the relationship between a state of precariousness and the irrational individualism of the sort that lead to Sethe's filicide and Cholly's hatred of Darlene, and subsequently, the "freedom" that sanctions his decision to rape his own daughter.
17. Morrison's use of an "as-told-to" technique is not new. Readers familiar with her first novel *The Bluest Eye* will remember that we are introduced to the character of Pauline Breedlove through first-person narration that functions in stark contrast to the limited omniscience of Claudia MacTeer. It is Pauline who narrates how she has been so seduced by Hollywood romantic narratives that they lead her to see her husband differently. And while it is significant that Pauline describes the sensation of sex with her husband, a useful detail since it allows us to understand the love-hate nature of her relationship with Cholly,

the other characters are reliant on Claudia to narrate their innermost feelings.

18. Cf. Ralph Ellison, "Richard Wright's Blues," and Sherley Anne Williams, "The Blues Roots of Black Poetry."
19. The assymetrical nature of the zoot suit corresponds to other iterations of outlandishness in African American expressive culture. For example, the progression from spirituals and hymns to gospel music or from swing to bebop music can be viewed as iterations of "excessive behaviors," whether it is through the fusion of sacred music and the blues or overloading a bar of music with chord progressions consisting of sixteen notes played very fast. Though the initial response to these innovations are often negative, leading to calls from cultural or political conservatives for tighter controls to inhibit outlandish behaviors, both of these instances—and one might also think of the Afro hairstyle and the all-black attire (e.g. beret, sunglasses, leather jackets, and pants) of the Black Panthers, the syntactical and rhythmic outrageousness to be found in hip-hop, along with the sagging jeans and oversized t-shirts as other examples—as harbingers of what Smith refers to as "the new belligerence." Cf. Smith, *The Great Black Way*, p. 57.
20. In her book *Southscapes: Geographies of Race, Region, and Literature*, Thadious Davis recounts an interview with writer Randall Kenan, who claims Morrison and Gabriel Garcia Marquez as twinned influences on his creative outlook. Kenan's work, she insists, is grounded in his belief that "[c]ulturally speaking blackness is both a chimera and an angel of change." According to Davis, Kenan "correctly invokes the changes that new modes of communication and new practices of citizenship have brought about. In this way, he can remark how in terms of postmodern culture, blackness is not merely a binary opposite of whiteness but is itself a product of the imagination and a model of change" (313). Morrison's deployment of the illusion of a man wearing a zoot suit, then, might well be her nod back in Kenan's direction, her declaration that she, too, embraces the notion that Blackness is both chimeric and transformative. Setting *Home* in the 1950s, a time when new material and cultural technologies like television, interstates, and non-violent protest were coming online, is Morrison's rejection of Faulkner's notion that blackness is a symbol of endurance, in favor of her sense that it is the site of constant invention and innovation.

21. And as Sethe's attempt to attack Mr. Bodwin with an ice pick suggests, rage, sadness, and bewilderment at our circumstance need to be directed outward toward its point of origin, not at ourselves. That the thirty black women outside 124 Bluestone Road stop Sethe before she can harm the old man is essential, because Morrison insists that such gestures need not take physical shape, they can be symbolic.
22. Wright, loc. 285 of 4640.
23. In my first book, I discussed those characters in Ernest J. Gaines' fiction who opted not to leave the South because they could only find a sense of purpose, a sense of place there. I referred to them as *articulate witnesses*, a term I used to convey the quality of purpose required to remain in the South, not to "endure," as Faulkner might insist, but rather to discover and assert acts of voice that might testify to the ordeals intrinsic to a civil rights struggle that was only partially successful in achieving its goals. Allan Tullos observes that politics in his home state of Alabama is characterized by what he calls "debilitating habits of judgment and feeling" that "pile stones in its path." According to Tullos, habits of judgment constitute local and historicized practices, "take hold with the formation of subjectivity, through a mutual structuring of cultural values and strong emotions," that "cluster around reflexive fundamentalisms of religion, race, gender, economics, and sexuality."
24. One of the most significant instances of this comes when a court rules in favor of the survivors and descendants of the group of black men who participated in the Tuskegee Syphilis Study. In 1972, after Jean Heller of the Associated Press broke the story of 399 black men who were denied treatment for syphilis in order to study the resulting effects. The survivors and their families were represented by attorney Fred Gray, who filed a lawsuit for $1.8 billion (which settled out of court for $10 million, with none of the researchers who conducted the study ever admitting guilt). My point is not that the settlement should be interpreted as contrition but that it occurs in the years just prior to the election of Maynard Jackson as Atlanta Mayor, which ushers in a period of tremendous growth in the city, culminating in the construction of the Hartfield (now Hartfield-Jackson) International Airport, now the largest, busiest airport in the U.S. When seen in relation to the arrest and conviction of Byron De La Beckwith, the man who masterminded the bombing of 16th Street Baptist Church in Birmingham, AL, we can see the rise of political influence and the accruing of the

necessary capital to transform the nature of black social reproduction. Cf. *Tuskegee Truths: Rethinking the Syphilis Study*, ed. Susan M. Reverby (Chapel Hill, NC: UNC Press, 2000).

25. Katz, cited in Morrow and Dombroski, p. 83.
26. In the second chapter of *Precarious Life*, Butler asserts that in the years following 9/11, we have to find a way to equate the "dimension of political life that has to do with our exposure to violence and our complicity in it, with our vulnerability to loss and the task of mourning that follows," we use as a basis for community (19). "Perhaps, then, it should come as no surprise," she writes, "that I propose to start and end with the question of the human."

Bibliography

Adams, Paul, Steven Hoelscher, and Karen E. Till, eds. *Textures of Place: Exploring Humanist Geographies.* Minneapolis, MN: University of Minnesota Press, 2001.

Adero, Malaika, ed. *Up South: Stories Studies and Letters of This Century's African American Migration.* New York: The New Press, 1994.

Alexander, Elizabeth. *The Black Interior.* Minneapolis, MN: Greywolf Press, 2004.

Alfieri, Anthony V. "Faith in Community: Representing 'Colored Town.'" *California Law Review* 95, no. 5 (October 2007): 1829–78.

Amin, Ash. "Regions Unbound: Towards a New Politics of Place." *Geografiska Annaler: Series B. Human Geography* 86, no. 1 (2004): 33–44.

Antonsich, Marco. "Meanings of Place and Aspects of the Self: An Interdisciplinary and Empircal Account." *GeoJournal* 75, no. 10 (2010): 119–32.

Arendt, Hannah. *The Human Condition.* Chicago: University of Chicago Press, 1958.

———. *Responsibility and Judgment.* New York: Schocken Books, 2003.

Armstrong, Nancy. *How Novels Think: The Limits of Individualism from 1719–1900.* New York: Columbia University Press, 2005.

Awkward, Michael. "'Unruly and Let Loose': Myth, Ideology, and Gender in *Song of Solomon.*" *Callaloo* 13, no. 3 (Summer 1990): 482–98.

Bachelard, Gaston. *The Poetics of Space.* Boston: Beacon Press, 1958, rpt. 1969.

Baucom, Ian. *Specters of the Atlantic: Finance Capital, Slavery, and the Philosophy of History.* Durham, NC: Duke University Press, 2005.

H. Beavers, *Geography and the Political Imaginary in the Novels of Toni Morrison*, Geocriticism and Spatial Literary Studies,
https://doi.org/10.1007/978-3-319-65999-2

Bauder, Harald. "Citizenship as Capital: The Distinction of Migrant Labor." *Alternatives: Global, Local, and Political* 33, no. 3 (July–September 2008): 315–53.

Beavers, Herman, Wrestling Angels into Song: The Fictions of Ernest J. Gaines and James A. McPherson. Philadelphia: University of Pennsylvania Press, 1995.

Benston, Kimberly. 'I Yam What I Yam: Naming and Unnaming in Afro-American Literature.' *Black American Literature Forum* 16, no. 1 (Spring 1982): 3–11.

Bhreithiun, Bharain Mac an, and Anne Burke. "Language, Typography, and Place-Making: Walking the Irish and Ulster-Scots Linguistic Landscape." *The Canadian Journal of Irish Studies.* Special Issue, *Text and Beyond Text: New Visual, Material, and Spatial Perspectives in Irish Studies* 38, no. 1 (2014), 84–125.

Blake, Susan. "Folklore and Community in *Song of Solomon.*" *MELUS* 7, no. 3 (August 1980): 77–82.

Blunt, Allison, and Gillian Rose. *Writing Women and Space: Colonial and Postcolonial Geographies.* New York: Guilford Press, 1994.

Boots, Michael, and Roger G. Bowers. "The Evolution of Resistance Through Costly Acquired Immunity." *Proceedings: Biological Sciences* 271, no. 1540 (April 7, 2004): 715–23.

Bowlby, Sophia. "Feminist Geography and the Changing Curriculum." *Geography* 77, no. 4 (October 1992): 349–60.

Brenkman, John. "Politics and Form in *Song of Solomon.*" *Social Text*, no. 39 (Summer 1994): 57–82.

Brenner, Neil. "The Urban Question as a Scale Question: Reflections on Henri Lefebvre, Urban Theory and the Politics of Scale." *International Journal of Urban and Regional Research* 24, Vol. no. 2 (June 2000): 361–78.

Butler, Judith. *Precarious Life: The Powers of Mourning and Violence.* New York: Verso, 2004.

Butler, Judith, and Athena Athanasiou. *Dispossession: The Performative in the Political.* London: Polity Press, 2013.

Butler, Robert James. "Open Movement and Selfhood in Toni Morrison's *Song of Solomon.*" *The Centennial Review* 28/29, no. 4/1 (Fall 1984–Winter 1985): 58–75.

Castoriadis, Cornelius. *The Imaginary Institution of Society.* Cambridge, MA: MIT Press, 1998.

———. *The Castoriadis Reader.* Edited and Translated by David Ames Curtis. London: Blackwell, 1997.

———. *Political and Social Writings*, Vol. 3, *1961–1979: Recommencing the Revolution: From Socialism to the Autonomous Society.* Minneapolis: University of Minnesota Press, 1993.

Carby, Hazel. *Race Men*. Cambridge, MA: Harvard University Press, 1998.

Carlacio, Jamie. "Narrative Epistemology: Storytelling as Agency in *A Mercy*." In *Toni Morrison: Paradise, Love, and A Mercy*, edited by Lucille P. Fultz. London: Bloomsbury, 2012.

Cashan, Sheryl. *Place Not Race: A New Vision of Opportunity in America*. Boston: Beacon Press, 2014.

Chambers, Ross. *Room for Maneuver: Reading Oppositional Narrative*. Chicago: University of Chicago Press, 1991.

Christianse, Yvette. *Toni Morrison: An Ethical Poetics*. New York: Fordham University Press, 2013.

Cidell, Julie. "The Place of Individuals in the Politics of Scale." *Area* 38, no. 2 (January 2006): 196–203.

Clark, Andrew, ed. *Riffs and Choruses: A New Jazz Anthology*. London: Continuum, 2001.

Clifford, James. *Routes: Travel and Translation in the Late Twentieth Century*. Cambridge: Harvard University Press, 1997.

Cohen, Harvey G. *Duke Ellington's America*. Chicago: University of Chicago Press, 2010.

Connell, R. W. *Masculinities*. Berkeley: University of California Press, 1995.

Connolly, James. "Bringing the City Back in: Space and Place in the Urban History of the Gilded Age and Progressive Era." *The Journal of the Gilded Age and Progressive Era* 1, no. 3 (July 2002): 258–78.

Connor, Marc C. "What Lay Beneath the Names: The Language and Landscapes of *A Mercy*." In *Toni Morrison: Paradise, Love, and A Mercy*, edited by Lucille Fultz. London: Bloomsbury, 2013. pp. 147–65.

Coombe, Rosemary J. "An Anthropology of Social Orders: Time, Space, and the Body." *Political and Legal Anthropology Review* 15, no. 3 (1993): 61–8.

Cox, Kevin R. "Spaces of Dependence, Spaces of Engagement and the Politics of Scale: Looking for Local Politics." *Political Geography* 17, no. 1: 1998. pp. 1–23.

Crary, Jonathan. *Suspensions of Perception: Attention, Spectacle, and Modern Culture*. Boston, MA: MIT Press, 1999.

Cuba, Lee, and David M. Hummon. "A Place to Call Home: Identification with Dwelling, Community, and Region." *The Sociological Quarterly* 34, no. 1 (Spring 1993): 111–31.

Davidson, Rob. "Racial Stock and 8-Rocks: Communal Historiography in Toni Morrison's *Paradise*." *Twentieth Century Literature* 47, no. 3 (Fall 2001): 355–73.

Davis, Thadious. *Southscapes: Geographies of Race, Region, and Literature*. Chapel Hill, NC: University of North Carolina Press, 2011.

Deal, J. Douglas. *Race and Class in Colonial Virginia: Indians, Englishmen, and Africans on the Eastern Shore During the Seventeenth Century*. New York: Garland Publishing, 1993.

deCerteau, Michel. *The Practice of Everyday Life.* Berkeley: University of California Press, 1984, rpt. 1988.

Demetrakopoulos, Stephanie A. "Maternal Bonds as Devourers of Women's Individuation in Toni Morrison's *Beloved.*" *African American Review* 26, no. 1. *Women Writers Issue* (Spring 1992): 51–9.

Domosh, Mona, and Joni Seager. *Putting Women in Place: Feminist Geographers Make Sense of the World.* New York: Guilford Press, 2001.

Douglas, Ann. *Terrible Honesty: Mongrel Manhattan in the 1920s.* New York: Farrar, Strauss, Giroux, 1995.

Douglas, Mary. *Purity and Danger: An Analysis of Concepts of Pollution and Taboo.* London: Routledge, 1966, rpt. 2003.

———. *Risk and Blame: Essays in Cultural Theory.* London: Taylor & Francis, 2002.

Dubey, Mahdu. *Signs and Cities: Black Literary Postmodernism.* Chicago: University of Chicago Press, 2003.

Dufour, Pascale, and Isabelle Giraud. "Globalization and Political Change in the Women's Movement: The Politics of Scale and Political Empowerment in the World March of Women." *Social Science Quarterly* 88, no. 5 (December 2007): 1152–73.

Duncan, James G., and Nancy G. Duncan. "Sense of Place as a Positional Good." In *Textures of Place: Exploring Humanistic Geography*, edited by Paul C. Adams, Steven Hoelscher, and Karen Till. Minneapolis: University of Minnesota Press, 2001.

Duncan, Nancy G. *BodySpace: Destabilizing Geographies of Gender and Sexuality.* New York: Routledge, 1996.

Duvall, John. "Descent in the "House of Chloe": Race, Rape, and Identity in Toni Morrison's "Tar Baby"." *Contemporary Literature* 38, no. 2 (Summer 1997): 325–49.

———, ed. *Productive Postmodernism: Consuming Histories and Cultural Studies.* Albany, NY: SUNY Press, 2002.

Edwards, Erica. *Charisma and the Fictions of Black Leadership.* Minneapolis: University of Minnesota Press, 2012.

Edwards, Paul. "Citizenship, Inc.: Negotiating Civic Spaces in Post-Urban America." *Critical Survey* 18, no. 3, *Subject and Citizens* (2006): 19–36.

Ellison, Ralph. *Invisible Man.* New York: Vintage Books, rpt. 1988.

Ewen, Stuart. *All Consuming Images: The Politics of Style in Contemporary Culture* (revised edition). New York: Basic Books, 1988, rpt. 1999.

Faulkner, Anne Shaw. "Does Jazz Put the Sin in Syncopation." Republished in *Keeping Time: Readings in Jazz History*, edited by Robert Walser, 32–6. London: Oxford University Press, 1999.

Fisher, Philip. "American Literary and Cultural Studies Since the Civil War." In *Redrawing the Boundaries: The Transformation of English and American*

Literary Studies, edited by Giles Gunn and Stephen Greenblatt, 232–50. New York: Modern Language Association, 1992.

Fisher, Rudolph. "The Caucasian Storms Harlem." *Keeping Time: Readings in Jazz History*, 60–4. New York: Oxford UP, 1999.

Foucault, Michel. *Power/Knowledge: Selected Interviews & Other Writings, 1972–1977*, edited by Colin Gordon. New York: Pantheon Books, 1980.

Friedman, Susan Stanford. *Mappings: Feminist and the Cultural Geographies of Encounter*. Princeton, NJ: Princeton University Press, 1998.

Freud, Sigmund. *Beyond the Pleasure Principle*. New York: W.W. Norton, 1920, rpt. 1961.

Frug, Jerry. "The Geography of Community." *Stanford Law Review* 48, no. 5 (May 1996): 1047–108.

Fultz, Lucille F. *Toni Morrison: Playing with Difference*. Urbana-Champaign, IL: University of Illinois Press, 2003.

Gabbert, Lisa, and Paul Jordan-Smith. "Introduction: Space, Place, and Emergence." *Western Folklore* 66, no. 3/4 (Summer–Fall 2007): 217–32.

Gates, David. "Original Sins." Review of *A Mercy*. *New York Times Sunday Book Review*. November 28, 2008.

Gieryn, Thomas. "A Space for Sociology." *Annual Review of Sociology* 26, no. 1 (2000): 463–96.

Gilmore, Matthew B. "Metro Washington Studies: Recent Scholarship on the Washington, D.C. Area." *Washington History* 24, no. 1 (2012): 63–9.

Goldberg, Jesse. "(Re)Memory and Modernity: Toni Morrison's *A Mercy* and the 2008 Housing Crisis." Unpublished Conference Paper, NEMLA Conference, 2011.

Goodwin, Doris Kearns. *A Team of Rivals*. New York: Simon & Schuster Paperbacks, 2005.

Griffin, Farah Jasmine. *"Who Set You Flowin?": The African American Migration Narrative*. New York: Oxford University Press, 1995.

Grosz, Elizabeth. "Bodies-Cities." In *Sexuality and Space*, edited by Beatriz Colomina, 241–53. New York: Princeton Architectural Press, 1992.

———. *Volatile Bodies: Toward a Corporeal Feminism*. Bloomington, IN: Indiana University Press, 1994.

Harris, A. Leslie. "Myth as Structure in Toni Morrison's *Song of Solomon*." *MELUS* 7, no. 3 (Autumn 1980): 69–76.

Haug, W. F. *Critique of Commodity Aesthetics*. Minneapolis: University of Minnesota Press, 1971, rpt. 1986.

Hayden, Delores. "Placemaking, Preservation, and Urban History." *Journal of Architectural Education (1984–)* 41, no. 3, *Urban History in the 1980's* (Spring 1988): 45–51.

Herod, Andrew. "The Production of Scale in United States Labour Relations." *Area* 23, no. 1 (March 1991): 82–8.

Highmore, Ben. *Everyday Life and Cultural Theory*. London: Routledge, 2002.

Hill-Collins, Patricia. "Gender, Black Feminism, and Black Political Economy." *The Annals of the American Academy of Political and Social Science* 568, no. 1 (March 2000): 41–53.

Hilfer, Anthony C. "Critical Indeterminacies in Toni Morrison's Fiction: An Introduction." *Texas Studies in Literature and Language* 33, no. 1, 1991. pp. 91–5.

Hopkins, Donald R. *The Greatest Killer: Smallpox in History*. Chicago: University of Chicago Press, 1983, rpt. 2002.

Hou, Jeffrey. "Border-Crossing and Placemaking: Negotiating and Reimagining Traditions in the Transcultural City." *Traditional Dwellings and Settlements Review* 26, no. 1, *Whose Tradition? Biennial Conference of the International Association for the Study of Traditional Environments December 14–17, 2014 Kuala Lumpur, Malaysia* (Fall 2014): 18.

Hughes, Langston. The Collected Poems of Langston Hughes. New York: Vintage Books, 1994.

Imbrie, Ann E. "'What Shalimar Knew': Toni Morrison's *Song of Solomon* as a Pastoral Novel." *College English* 55, no. 5 (September 1993): 473–90.

Jacobsen, Kristina. "Rita(hhh): Placemaking and Country Music on the Navajo Nation." *Ethnomusicology* 53, no. 3 (Fall 2009): 449–77.

Jarrett, Michael. *Drifting on a Read: Jazz as a Model for Writing*. Albany: SUNY UP, 1999.

Jefferson, Margo. *Negroland: A Memoir*. New York: Pantheon Books, 2015.

Jimenez, Alberto Corsin. "On Space as a Capacity." *The Journal of the Royal Anthropological Institute* 9, no. 1 (March 2003): 137–53.

Jordan, Winthrop D. *The White Man's Burden: Historical Origins of Racism in the United States*. New York: Oxford University Press, 1974.

———. *White over Black: American Attitudes Toward the Negro, 1550–1812*. Baltimore, MD: Penguin Books, 1969.

Kakutani, Michiko. Book Review of *Love*. *The International Herald Tribune*, reprinted from *The New York Times* (November 6, 2003): 20.

Kim, Yeonman. "Involuntary Vulnerability and the Felix Culpa in Toni Morrison's "Jazz"." *The Southern Literary Journal* 33, no. 2 (Spring 2001): 124–33.

Kinloch, Valerie. "Literacy, Community, and Youth Acts of Place-Making." *English Education* 41, no. 4. Critical Literacy Research with Urban Youth: Implications for Teaching and Teacher Education (July 2009): 316–36.

Kirby, Kathleen M. *Indifferent Boundaries: Spatial Concepts of Human Subjectivity*. New York: Guilford Press, 1996.

Kurson, Ken. "Credit-Default Swaps: A Complicated Way to Say Ten-Bagger." *Esquire*, Volume, 146, issue no. 3. (September 2006): 54–6.

Lefebvre, Henri. *The Production of Space*. Translated by Donald Nicholson-Smith. London: Blackwell, 1974, rpt. 1998.

Leitner, Helga, Eric Sheppard, and Kristin M. Sziarto. "The Spatialities of Contentious Politics." *Transactions of the Institute of British Geographers*, New Series 33, no. 2 (April 2008): 157–72.

Leonard, Neil. *Jazz: Myth and Religion.* New York: Oxford University Press, 1987.

Lewis, Jimmie Franklin. "Black Southerners, a Shared Experience, and Place: A Reflection." In *The South: An American Problem*, edited by Larry J .Griffin and Don H. Doyle, 210–33. Athens: University of Georgia Press, 1995.

Lipsitz, George. *How Race Takes Place.* Philadelphia: Temple University Press, 2011.

Looker, Benjamin. "Microcosms of Democracy: Imagining the City Neighborhood in World War II-Era America." *Journal of Social History* 44, no. 2. *The Arts in Place* (Winter 2010): 351–78.

Lopes, Paul. *The Rise of a Jazz World.* Cambridge: Cambridge UP, 2002.

Lupton, Deborah. *Risk.* London: Routledge, 1999.

Mackey, Nathaniel. *Discrepant Engagement: Dissonance, Cross-Culturality, and Experimental Writing.* Cambridge: Cambridge University Press, 1993.

Marshall, Brenda K. *Teaching the Postmodern: Fiction and Theory.* London: Routledge, 1991.

Marxsen, Patti M. "The Map Within: Place, Displacement, and the Long Shadow of History in the Work of Edwidge Danticat." *Journal of Haitian Studies* 11, no. 1 (Spring 2005): 140–55.

Mathis, Ayana. *The Twelve Tribes of Hattie.* New York: Alfred A. Knopf, 2013.

Mayberry, Susan Neal. *Can't I Love What I Criticize: The Masculine and Morrison.* Athens: University of Georgia Press, 2007.

McBride, Keally D. *Collective Dreams: Political Imagination and Community.* University Park: Pennsylvania State University Press, 2006.

McDowell, Linda. *Gender, Identity, & Place: Understanding Feminist Geographies.* London: Polity Press, 1999.

McDowell, Linda, and Joanne P. Sharp. *Space, Gender, Knowledge: Feminist Readings.* New York: Wiley, 1997.

McEvoy-Levy, Siobhan. "Youth Spaces in Haunted Places: Placemaking for Peacebuilding in Theory and Practice." *International Journal of Peace Studies* 17, no. 2 (Winter 2012): 1–32.

Meehan, Katie, and Kendra Strauss. *Precarious Worlds: Contested Geographies of Social Reproduction.* Athens, GA: University of Georgia Press, 2015.

Meltzer, David, ed. *Reading Jazz.* San Francisco, CA: Mercury House, 1993.

Merelman, Richard. *Representing Black Culture: Racial Conflict and Cultural Politics in the United States.* London: Routledge, 1995.

Moglen, Helene. "Redeeming History: Toni Morrison's 'Beloved.'" *Cultural Critique*, Volume no. 24 (Spring 1993): pp. 17–40.

Monmonier, Mark. *How to Lie with Maps.* Chicago: University of Chicago Press, 1991.

Moon-Kie, Jung. *Beneath the Surface of White Supremacy.* Palo Alto: Stanford University Press, 2015.

Morrison, Toni. *The Bluest Eye.* 1970. New York: Pocket Books, 1972.

———. *Sula.* 1973. New York: Bantam Books, 1980.

———. *Song of Solomon.* 1977. New York: Plume Books, 1987.

———. *Tar Baby.* 1981. New York: Plume Books, 1982.

———. *Beloved.* 1987. New York: Plume Books, 1988.

———. *Jazz.* 1992. New York: Plume Books, 1993.

———. *Paradise.* 1997: New York: Plume Books; 1999.

———. *Love.* 2003. New York: Vintage Books, 2005.

———. *A Mercy.* 2008. New York: Vintage Books, 2008.

———. *Home.* 2012. New York: Vintage Books, 2012.

———. *Playing in the Dark.* Cambridge, MA: Harvard University Press, 1992.

———. *Nobel Lecture in Literature, 1993.* New York: Knopf, 2000.

———. *What Moves at the Margins: Selected Nonfiction*, with an Introduction and edited by Carolyn C. Denard. Jackson: University Press of Mississippi, 2008.

Munton, Alan. "Misreading Morrison, Mishearing Jazz: A Response to Toni Morrison's Jazz Critics." *Journal of American Studies* 31, no. 2 (August 1997): 235–51.

Myers, Fred R. "Ways of Place-Making." *La Ricerca Folklorica*, no. 45, *Antropologia delle sensazioni* (April 2002): 101–19.

Niranjana, Seemanthini. *Gernder and Space: Femininity, Sexualization, and the Female Body.* Thousand Oaks, CA: Sage, 2001.

Oldstone, Michael B. *Viruses, Plagues, and History.* New York: Oxford University Press, 1998.

Page, Philip. "Traces of Derrida in Toni Morrison's *Jazz.*" *African American Review* 28, no 1. (Spring 1995): 55–66.

Pal, Sunanda. "From Periphery to Centre: Toni Morrison's Self Affirming Fiction." *Economic and Political Weekly* 29, no. 37 (September 1994): 2439–43.

Paquet-Deyris, Anne-Marie. "Toni Morrison's Jazz and the City." *African American Review* 35, no. 2 (Summer 2001): 219–31.

Pavlic, Edward. *Crossroads Modernism: Descent and Emergence in African American Literary Culture.* Minneapolis: University of Minnesota Press, 2002.

Peebles, Gustav. "The Anthropology of Credit and Debt." *Annual Review of Anthropology* 39 (2010): 225–40.

Perez-Gomez, Alberto. *Built Upon Love: Architectural Longing After Ethics and Aesthetics.* Cambridge, MA: MIT Press, 2008.

Perry, Melissa Harris (nee Melissa Harris-Lacewell). *Barbershops, Bibles, and BET: Everyday Talk and Black Political Thought.* Princeton, NJ: Princeton University Press, 2004.

Peteet, Julie. "Chapter Four: "Producing Place, Spatializing Identity, 1948–68"." In *Landscape of Hope and Despair: Palestinian Refugee Camps.* Julie Peteet, ed. Philadelphia: University of Pennsylvania Press, 2005.

Peyton, Dave. "A Black Journalist Criticizes Jazz." Reprinted in *Keeping Time: Readings in Jazz History*, 57–9. New York: Oxford UP, 1999.

Phelps, Nicholas A., and Mark Tewdwr-Jones. "If Geography Is Anything, Maybe It's Planning's Alter Ego? Reflections on Policy Relevance in Two Disciplines Concerned with Place and Space." *Transactions of the Institute of British Geographers*, New Series 33, no. 4 (October 2008): 566–84.

Pilsworth, Elizabeth G., and Martie G. Haselton. "The Evolution of Coupling." *Psychological Inquiry* 16, no. 2/3 (2005): 98–104.

Polanco, Mieka Brand. *Imagining Black Community in a Black Historic District.* New York: New York University Press, 2014.

Ranger, Terence, and Paul Slack. *Epidemics and Ideas: Essays on the Historical Perception of Pestilence.* Cambridge: Cambridge University Press, 1992.

Rediker, Marcus. *The Slave Ship: A Human History.* New York: Viking, 2007.

Reed, Harry. "*Song of Solomon* and Black Cultural Nationalism." *The Centennial Review* 32, no. 1, 1988. pp. 50–64.

Reiss, Oscar. *Blacks in Colonial America.* Jefferson, NC: McFarland & Company, 1997.

Rhodes, Chip. *Structures of the Jazz Age.* London: Verso, 1998.

Rice, Alan. "Jazzing It Up a Storm: The Execution and Meaning of Toni Morrison's Jazzy Prose Style." *Journal of American Studies* 28, no. 3 (December 1994): 423–32.

Rosenberg, Charles E. *Explaining Epidemics and Other Studies in the History of Medicine.* Cambridge: Cambridge University Press, 1992.

Scott, Emmett J. "Letters of Negro Migrants of 1916–1918." *The Journal of Negro History* Volume 4, Issue no. 3 (July 1919): 290–348.

———. "Additional Letters of Negro Migrants." *The Journal of Negro History* 4, no. 4 (October 1919): 412–65.

Scott, William B., and Peter Rutkoff. *New York Modern: The Arts and the City.* Baltimore: Johns Hopkins University Press, 1999.

Seward, Adrienne, and Justine Tally, eds. *Toni Morrison: Memory and Meaning.* Jackson, MS: University Press of Mississippi, 2014.

Shay, Jonathan. *Achilles in Vietnam: Combat Trauma and the Undoing of Character.* New York: Touchstone Books, 1994.

Shelby, Tommie. *We Who Are Dark: The Philosophical Foundations of Black Solidarity.* Cambridge: Belknap/Harvard University Press, 2005.

Shibley, Robert G. "The Complete New Urbanism and the Partial Practices of Placemaking." *Utopian Studies* 9, no. 1 (1998): 80–102.

Shuttleton, David A. *Smallpox and the Literary Imagination, 1660–1820.* Cambridge: Cambridge University Press, 2007.

Sies, Mary Corbin. "North American Urban History: The Everyday Politics and Spatial Logics of Metropolitan Life." *Urban History Review/Revue d'histoire urbaine* 32, no. 1, Micbele Dagenais, redactrice inuitee (Fall 2003 automne): 28–42.

Slotkin, Richard. *Regeneration Through Violence: The Mythology of the American Frontier, 1600–1860.* Norman: University of Oklahoma Press, 1973, rpt. 2000.

Smith, Mark M. *How Race Is Made: Segregation and the Senses.* Chapel Hill: UNC Press, 2006.

Spain, Daphne. *Constructive Feminisms: Women's Spaces and Women's Rights in the American City.* Ithaca: Cornell University Press, 2016.

Spohrer, Erika. "Colonizing Consciousness: "Race," Pictorial Epistemology, and Toni Morrison's "Jazz"." *Amerikastudien / American Studies* 54, no. 1, 2009. pp. 79–98.

Story, Ralph. "An Excursion into the Black World: The 'Seven Days' in Toni Morrison's *Song of Solomon*." *Black American Literature Forum* 23, no. 1, 1989. pp. 149–58.

Straume, Ingerid S. "The Political Imaginary of Global Capitalism." In *Depoliticization: The Political Imaginary of Global Capitalism*, edited by J. F. Humphery and Ingerid S. Straume. Sweden: NSU Press and Aarhus University Press, 2011.

Swyngedouw, Eric, and Nikolas C. Heynan, eds. "Urban Political Ecology, Justice, and the Politics of Scale." In *Antipode*, 898–919. Oxford: Blackwell Publishing, 2003.

Tally, Justine, ed. *The Cambridge Companion to Toni Morrison.* Cambridge: Cambridge University Press, 2007.

Tauber, Alfred I. "The Immune System and its Ecology." *Philosophy of Science* 75, no. 2 (April 2008): 224–45.

Taylor, Paul C. "Post-Black, Old Black." *African American Review* 41, no. 4, *Post-Soul Aesthetic* (Winter 2007): 625–40.

Thompson, Bruce, and Gloria M. Bordello. "Different Views of Love: Deductive and Inductive Lines of Inquiry." *Current Directions in Psychological Science* 1, no. 5, 1990. pp. 154–6.

Tuan, Yi-Fu. *Space and Place.* Minneapolis: University of Minnesota Press. 1975.

———. *Landscapes of Fear.* Minneapolis, MN: University of Minnesota Press, 1979.

Tucker, Jonathan B. *Scourge: The Once and Future Threat of Smallpox.* New York: Atlantic Monthly Press, 2001.

Tullos, Allen. *Alabama Getaway: The Political Imaginary and the Heart of Dixie*. Athens: University of Georgia Press, 2011.

Vaughan, Alden T. *Roots of American Racism: Essays on the Colonial Experience*. New York: Oxford University Press, 1995.

Wald, Priscilla. *Contagion: Culture, Carriers, and the Outbreak Narrative*. Durham, NC: Duke University Press, 2008.

Wardi, Anisssa Janine. "A Laying on of Hands: Toni Morrison and the Materiality of *Love*." *MELUS* 30, no. 3 (Fall 2005): 201–18.

Warren, Kenneth W. *What Was African American Literature*. Cambridge, MA: Harvard University Press, 2011.

Weber, Max. *The Protestant Ethic and Spirit of Capitalism*. New York: Acheron Press, 2012.

Wilkerson, Isabel. *The Warmth of Other Sons: The Epic Story of the Great Migration*. New York: Random House, 2010.

Williams, Eric. *Capitalism and Slavery*. Chapel Hill, NC: University of North Carolina Press, 1944, rpt. 1994.

Williams, Robert W. "Environmental Injustice in America and Its Politics of Scale." *Political Geography* 18, no. 1 (1999): 49–73.

Wilson, August. *Ma Rainey's Black Bottom*. New York: Vintage Books, 1985.

Wilson, Harriet. *Our Nig: Or Sketches From the Life of a Free Black*. New York: Vintage Books, 1859, rpt. 2011.

Wortham-Galvin, B. D. "The Fabrication of Place in America: The Fictions and Traditions of the New England Village." *Traditional Dwellings and Settlements Review* 21, no. 2 (Spring 2010): 21–34.

Wyatt, Jean. "Love's Time and the Reader: Ethical Effects of 'Nachtraglichkeit' in Toni Morrison's *Love*." *Narrative* 16, no. 2. (May 2008): 193–221.

———. *Love and Narrative Form in the Late Novels of Toni Morrison*. Athens, GA: University of Georgia Press, 2017.

Author Index

H. Beavers, *Geography and the Political Imaginary in the Novels of Toni Morrison*, Geocriticism and Spatial Literary Studies,
https://doi.org/10.1007/978-3-319-65999-2

Subject Index

H. Beavers, *Geography and the Political Imaginary in the Novels of Toni Morrison*, Geocriticism and Spatial Literary Studies,
https://doi.org/10.1007/978-3-319-65999-2